A COMPANION TO
MIDDLE ENGLISH HAGIOGRAPHY

A COMPANION TO MIDDLE ENGLISH HAGIOGRAPHY

Edited by Sarah Salih

D. S. BREWER

© Editor and Contributors 2006

All Rights Reserved. Except as permitted under current legislation no part of this work may be photocopied, stored in a retrieval system, published, performed in public, adapted, broadcast, transmitted, recorded or reproduced in any form or by any means, without the prior permission of the copyright owner

First published 2006
D. S. Brewer, Cambridge
Paperback edition 2010

Transferred to digital printing

ISBN 978-1-84384-072-5 hardback
ISBN 978-1-84384-246-0 paperback

D. S. Brewer is an imprint of Boydell & Brewer Ltd
PO Box 9, Woodbridge, Suffolk IP12 3DF, UK
and of Boydell & Brewer Inc.
668 Mt Hope Avenue, Rochester, NY 14620, USA
website: www.boydellandbrewer.com

A CIP catalogue record for this book is available
from the British Library

This publication is printed on acid-free paper

Contents

List of Illustrations	vi
Acknowledgements	vii
Notes on Contributors	viii
Abbreviations	x
Introduction: Saints, Cults and *Lives* in Late Medieval England SARAH SALIH	1
1. Hagiography in Context: Images, Miracles, Shrines and Festivals SAMANTHA RICHES	25
2. Corpora and Manuscripts, Authors and Audiences MARY BETH LONG	47
3. Power and Authority CLAIRE M. WATERS	70
4. Violence, Community and the Materialisation of Belief ROBERT MILLS	87
5. Gender and Sexuality ANKE BERNAU	104
6. History, Historiography and Rewriting the Past KATHERINE J. LEWIS	122
7. Crossovers and Afterlife MATTHEW WOODCOCK	141
Bibliography	157
Index	177

Illustrations

Figure 1. Pilgrim badge of St Edmund, fifteenth century, pewter. 29
Museum of London, MoL 78.13. Photograph: Museum of London

Figure 2. St George and the Dragon, late-fifteenth-century polychromed 31
wooden sculpture. Herbert Museum and Art Gallery, Coventry.
Photograph: Dr Jenny Alexander

Figure 3. The Martyrdom of St Edmund, fourteenth-century wall painting. 38
Stoke Dry (Northamptonshire). Photograph: Anne Marshall,
www.paintedchurch.org

Figure 4. The Martyrdom of St Edmund, early-twelfth-century manuscript 39
illumination attributed to the Alexis Master. New York, Pierpont Morgan
Library MS M. 736, fol. 14. Photograph: Pierpont Morgan Library

Figure 5. The Relics of St Edmund on a Narrow Bridge, early- 40
twelfth-century manuscript illumination attributed to the Alexis Master.
New York, Pierpont Morgan Library MS M. 736, fol. 20v.
Photograph: Pierpont Morgan Library

Acknowledgements

My contributions to this book were researched in the library of the University of East Anglia and in the British Library. I am grateful to everyone who helped me to obtain the time and materials needed to complete this project.

Thanks too to all at Boydell and Brewer, especially Caroline Palmer who first suggested it, and Ellie Ferguson for dealing with last-minute queries and panics; thanks to everyone who has made helpful suggestions and sympathetic remarks, especially but not only: John Arnold, Tom Betteridge, Ruth Evans, Sandy Heslop, Clare Lees, Diane Negra, Carol O'Sullivan and Cath Sharrock. Thanks too to all the UEA students who have asked interesting questions about the saints. Special thanks to Kenneth Dean for making space in London for me and the book.

Primarily, however, I would like to thank the contributors for their scholarship and enthusiasm: it has been a pleasure and an education to work with them.

Notes on Contributors

ANKE BERNAU is a lecturer in medieval literature and culture at Manchester University. She has written on hagiography, as well as on the trope of virginity in a range of medieval and contemporary genres and is the co-editor of *Medieval Virginities* (University of Wales Press, 2003). She is currently working on two projects: a history of virginity from the twelfth to the twenty-first century, and a study of medieval British foundation myths.

KATHERINE J. LEWIS is a senior lecturer in history at the University of Huddersfield. She is author of *The Cult of St Katherine of Alexandria in Late Medieval England* (Boydell, 2000) and co-editor of *Holiness and Masculinity in the Middle Ages* (University of Wales Press, 2004) and *A Companion to Margery Kempe* (Brewer, 2004). She is currently writing a book on ideas of gender in later medieval England.

MARY BETH LONG recently completed a Ph.D. in English at the University of Massachusetts, Amherst. She has published on Ralph Buckland, the beguines and Milton, and is currently working on a book-length project about English legendaries of women. She lives and works in Arkadelphia, Arkansas.

ROBERT MILLS is a lecturer in English at King's College London. His research is interdisciplinary, spanning literary studies, art history, religious history and cultural studies. He is author of *Suspended Animation: Pain, Pleasure and Punishment in Medieval Culture* (Reaktion, 2005), and co-editor of *The Monstrous Middle Ages* (University of Wales Press, 2003) and *Troubled Vision: Gender, Sexuality, and Sight in Medieval Text and Image* (Palgrave Macmillan, 2004). He is currently working on a study of erotic responses to the art and literature of medieval Christian devotion.

SAMANTHA RICHES is a late medieval cultural historian with a special interest in pseudo-historical saints' cults, gender and monstrosity. She has taught both medieval history and art history at a number of UK universities, and now holds the position of Director of Studies for History and Archaeology in Continuing Education at Lancaster University. She is the author of *St George: Hero, Martyr and Myth* (Stroud: Sutton 2000 and 2005) and co-editor of *Gender and Holiness: Men, Women and Saints in Late Medieval Europe* (Routledge, 2002). She is currently researching a monograph on the narratives of saints who encounter monsters.

SARAH SALIH is a senior lecturer in literature at the University of East Anglia. She is the author of *Versions of Virginity in Late Medieval England* (Brewer, 2001) and co-editor of *Gender and Holiness: Men, Women and Saints in Late Medieval Europe* (Routledge, 2002) and *Medieval Virginities* (University of Wales Press, 2003). She is currently researching the representation of paganity in late medieval East Anglian writing and art.

CLAIRE M. WATERS is associate professor of English at the University of California, Davis, where she teaches courses on medieval literature, including Chaucer, hagiography and the Arthurian legend. She recently published *Angels and Earthly Creatures: Preaching, Performance, and Gender in the Later Middle Ages* (University of Pennsylvania Press, 2004) and is completing an edition of four Middle English saints' lives.

MATTHEW WOODCOCK is a lecturer in English at the University of East Anglia, Norwich, and has teaching and research interests in medieval and Renaissance literature. He is the author of *Fairy in The Faerie Queene: Renaissance Elf-Fashioning and Elizabethan Myth-Making* (Ashgate, 2004), the editor of an essay collection on Fulke Greville (*The Sidney Journal* 19.1–2 2002) and has published work on Spenser, Shakespeare and entertainments for Elizabeth I. He is currently working on a student guide to Sir Philip Sidney and the Sidney Circle.

Abbreviations

Bible	*The Holy Bible: Translated from the Latin Vulgate and Diligently Compared with Other Editions in Divers Languages (Douay, AD 1609; Rheims AD 1582)* (London: Burns Oates and Washbourne, 1914)
BL	British Library
Bokenham, *Legendys*	Osbern Bokenham, *Legendys of Hooly Wummen*, ed. Mary J. Serjeantson, EETS os 206 (London: Oxford University Press, 1938)
D'Evelyn and Foster, 'Saints' Legends'	Charlotte D'Evelyn and Frances A. Foster, 'Saints' Legends'. *A Manual of the Writings in Middle English 1050–1500*, vol. 2, ed. J. Burke Severs (New Haven: Connecticut Academy of Arts and Sciences, 1970), pp. 410–39, 553–635
EETS	Early English Text Society
es	extra series
os	original series
ss	supplementary series
Golden Legend, trans. Caxton	[Jacobus de Voragine] *The Golden Legend or Lives of Saints as Englished by William Caxton*, ed. F. S. Ellis, 7 vols (London: Dent, 1900)
Golden Legend, trans. Ryan	Jacobus de Voragine, *The Golden Legend: Readings on the Saints*, trans. William Granger Ryan, 2 vols (Princeton: Princeton University Press, 1993)
Kalendre	*Kalendre of the Newe Legende of Englande, edited from Pynson's Printed Edition, 1516*, ed. Manfred Görlach (Heidelberg: Universitätsverlag C. Winter, 1994)
Lydgate, *St Edmund Facsimile*	*The Life of St Edmund, King and Martyr: John Lydgate's Illustrated Verse Life Presented to Henry VI: A Facsimile of BL MS Harley 2278*, intr. A. S. G. Edwards (London: British Library, 2004)
SEL	*The South English Legendary, edited from Corpus Christi College Cambridge MS 145 and British Museum MS Harley 2277, with variants from Bodley MS Ashmole 43 and British Museum MS Cotton Julius D.ix*, ed. Charlotte D'Evelyn and Anna J. Mill, 3 vols, EETS os 235, 236, 244 (London: Oxford University Press, 1956–9)
Supplementary Lives	*Supplementary Lives in Some Manuscripts of the* Gilte Legende, ed. Richard Hamer and Vida Russell, EETS os 315 (Oxford: Oxford University Press, 2000)

Introduction:
Saints, Cults and Lives *in* Late Medieval England

SARAH SALIH

Saints and Cults

The saints were at once the superheroes and the celebrities of medieval England. They pervaded the landscape: their names, images and narratives were attached to buildings, geographical features, parishes, guilds and towns. Saint-cult was multimedia and interactive. Every church displayed paintings and sculptures of the saints; their feast days were celebrated with liturgies, readings, plays, processions and feasts. They were represented in images ranging from great public objects, such as the 350cm-high stone carving of St Christopher from Norton Priory, Cheshire, to personal clothing and jewellery such as 'þe reyng wyth þe emage of Seynt Margrete' which the pregnant Margaret Paston sent her absent husband 'for a rememravnse'.[1] If the body of Christ, simultaneously absent and present, was the centre point of late medieval culture, then it was regularly imagined and depicted within a frame formed of the bodies of his imitators, the saints.[2] They were both in heaven and ever-present; utterly and concretely present in their relics, but also, more complexly, present in their images and embodied in dramatic representation. Saints were locations of paradox, who could establish their sanctity by conformity to societal values or in opposition to them. They were both role models and intercessors, alien and distanced; their bodies stretched across the spaces between life and death, heaven and earth.

The company of saints was a multicultural assembly, bringing together various textual traditions and seamlessly mingling history and fiction.[3] Saints from all the times and places of Christendom rub shoulders in the calendar. The

---

[1] The St Christopher is no. 8 in Richard Deacon and Phillip Lindley, *Image and Idol: Medieval Sculpture* (London: Tate Publishing, 2002); *Paston Letters and Papers of the Fifteenth Century*, ed. Norman Davis, 2 vols (Oxford: Clarendon Press, 1971–76), vol. 1, letter 125.

[2] On Christ's body, see Sarah Beckwith, *Christ's Body: Identity, Culture, and Society in Late Medieval Writings* (London: Routledge, 1993) and Miri Rubin, *Corpus Christi: The Eucharist in Late Medieval Culture* (Cambridge: Cambridge University Press, 1991).

[3] This collection is concerned with the Catholic Christian tradition of sanctity, but other faiths have similar concepts; for some comparative studies, see *Sainthood: Its Manifestations in World Religions*, ed. Richard Kieckhefer and George D. Bond (Berkeley: University of California Press, 1988).

Bible and its apocrypha are the original sources for several important saints from the earliest days of Christianity, in particular the apostles and Christ's presumed earthly relatives such as St Anne and her family, whose legends were much elaborated in later medieval narratives. From a modern perspective, the former were historical figures and the latter pious fictions, but this distinction was not obvious to most medieval writers and devotees. Some native British saints may be Christianisations of pre-Christian deities or spirits of place. It is frequently argued that Bridget or Brigid of Ireland, for example, was such a figure, but it is possible that there are many more, disguised more or less convincingly as historical persons.[4] John Bale, the sixteenth-century reformer, certainly thought so when he contemptuously identified Walstan of Bawburgh, a putatively Anglo-Saxon saint who patronised agricultural labour and livestock, as 'Priapus the God of theyr fieldes in Northfolke'.[5] Folkloric motifs appear in the legends of many early British saints with no apparent harm done to their credibility or intercessionary powers: to take just one example, Finan of Kinnity was the son of a salmon.[6] Other British and English saints, of course, were historical persons – the monk Cuthbert, the king Edmund, the abbess Mildred – whose lives were then reshaped to varying extents by hagiographic conventions. Some versions of the legend of the indisputably historical Thomas Becket acquired a thoroughly romantic supplement in which his mother was said to be a Saracen princess who had fallen in love with a London merchant.[7] The category of universal or Latin saints included historical persons such as the martyrs Perpetua and Felicitas, the theologians Ambrose and Augustine and the monastic founder Benedict. Medieval writers, however, expanded the category of early martyrs with the inclusion of many, such as George or Katherine of Alexandria, who were essentially fictive. Even if persons of these names once lived and died as Christians, their surviving legends consist in their entirety of hagiographic stereotypes, themselves derived from sources including late antique romance.[8] Several of these saints were indeed downgraded or removed from the calendar of the Catholic Church in the reform of 1969, on the grounds of their lack of historicity.[9] This shortcoming had not, however, prevented them from functioning perfectly well for several centuries: indeed, since the very powerful group of Holy Helpers comprises fourteen such saints, it might be

---

[4] Miranda Green, *Celtic Goddesses: Warriors, Virgins and Mothers* (London: British Museum Press, 1995), pp. 196–202.
[5] Quoted in Eamon Duffy, 'The Dynamics of Pilgrimage in Late Medieval England', *Pilgrimage: The English Experience from Becket to Bunyan*, ed. Colin Morris and Peter Roberts (Cambridge: Cambridge University Press, 2002), pp. 164–77, p. 171.
[6] Jane Tibbetts Schulenberg, 'Saints and Sex, ca. 500–1100: Striding down the Nettled Path of Life', *Sex in the Middle Ages: A Book of Essays*, ed. Joyce E. Salisbury (New York: Garland, 1991), pp. 203–31, p. 205.
[7] 'Thomas of Canterbury', *Supplementary Lives*, pp. 283–320, pp. 285–6.
[8] Thomas J. Heffernan, 'Christian Biography: Foundation to Maturity', *Historiography in the Middle Ages*, ed. Deborah Mauskopf Deliyannis (Leiden: Brill, 2003), pp. 115–54, p. 130.
[9] David Hugh Farmer, *Oxford Dictionary of Saints* (Oxford: Oxford University Press, 1987), p. xxii.

surmised that fictive saints are actually the most effective intercessors and miracle-workers.[10] In Pierre Delooz's influential analysis:

> All saints are more or less *constructed* in that, being necessarily saints *for other people*, they are remodelled in the collective representation which is made of them. It often happens, even, that they are so remodelled that nothing of the real original is left, and, ultimately, some saints are solely *constructed* saints simply because nothing is known about them historically: everything, including their existence, is a product of collective representation.[11]

Many of the most popular medieval saints were of this kind. At the other end of the scale, medieval people saw contemporaries culted and canonised: indeed, sanctity was even a distinction to which an elite few might aspire.[12] Sometimes it was essential to a saint's appeal that they had been an indisputably historical person who had lived in accessible locations within living memory. *The Book of Margery Kempe* bears witness to the glamour which attached to the traces of recent saints such as Bridget of Sweden: during her visit to Rome Margery, herself arguably an aspirant saint, made a point of seeking out people who 'haddyn knowlach of hir in hir lyue-tyme' and 'þe chawmbre þat Seynt Brigypt deyd in'.[13]

Saint-cult was a continual dialogue of lay and clerical interests, and successful cults needed to satisfy both.[14] Sometimes signs of tension are apparent, as in John Mirk's introduction to the feast of Margaret of Antioch:

> And þagh hit be a ly3t holyday ... þer byn some of you þat hauen such a loue to hure, þat 3e wol fast her euyn. But þen 3e þat fastyn hur euyn, 3e quyt you not to her as 3e schuld do, but yf 3e come to chyrche on þe morrow to here a masse of her.[15]

Mirk thus envisages a popular devotion to the saint which is more enthusiastic than her status strictly warrants, and which has a tendency to express itself in forms independent of the Church. Mirk's preacher is to attempt to bring such devotion back under control. The saints were part of the fabric of everyday life, and the requirements of devotees often outweighed theological correctness. In theory, saints were persons of heroic virtue, known to be in heaven, who had

---

[10] On the Holy Helpers see Eamon Duffy, *The Stripping of the Altars: Traditional Religion in England c. 1400–c. 1580* (New Haven: Yale University Press, 1992), p. 178.

[11] Pierre Delooz, 'Towards a Sociological Study of Canonized Sainthood in the Catholic Church', trans. Jane Hodgkin, *Saints and their Cults: Studies in Religious Sociology, Folklore and History*, ed. Stephen Wilson (Cambridge: Cambridge University Press, 1983), pp. 189–216, p. 195.

[12] The papacy canonised 39 persons in the period 1198–1431, but many more were culted; André Vauchez, *Sainthood in the Later Middle Ages*, trans. Jean Birrell (Cambridge: Cambridge University Press, 1997), p. 250.

[13] *The Book of Margery Kempe*, ed. Sanford Brown Meech and Hope Emily Allen, EETS os 212 (London: Oxford University Press, 1940), pp. 94, 95.

[14] 'Cult', in this context, should not been confused with the modern use of the term to refer to controversial or minority religious organisations.

[15] John Mirk, *Mirk's Festial: A Collection of Homilies*, ed. Theodor Erbe, EETS es 96 (London: Kegan Paul, Trench, Trübner & Co, 1905), p. 199.

been canonised by the papacy or, before papal canonisation became the rule, by some other appropriate authority.[16] In practice, many of the most popular saints had never gone through any such process, either because they were fictitious or because attempts to canonise them had failed or never been presented. Papal canonisation required time, money, influence and a well-organised constituency of devotees: royal houses and monastic orders, which had all these qualifications, also had the most success in promoting their candidates for sanctity.[17] Francis of Assisi and Dominic Guzman, founders of the mendicant orders, were hence amongst the most extensively culted of the saints who had lived in the later Middle Ages.[18] However, lack of canonisation was no barrier to devotion or to the performance of miracles. Cults developed around controversial political figures such as Henry VI, Thomas of Lancaster and Richard Scrope: true to sanctity's origin as a cult of the dead, sudden death was the most important trigger of devotion to such figures, who had not necessarily been considered as exemplars of virtue during their lives.[19] Nor were ethics the main concern of some cults. Saints' patronage might result in morally questionable rewards for their devotees, such as the unashamed partisanship shown by saints such as Edmund and Werburge to their institutions, as described by Samantha Riches and Katherine Lewis in this volume. In such instances, their likeness to human patrons is not flattering to either. In theory, saints were in heaven where they exercised power by interceding with God: to worship or make offerings to the saints themselves was 'ydolatrie . . . punyschable, ʒe, and dampnable'.[20] However, popular practices such as donating personal items, including wedding rings, kerchiefs, veils and girdles, for cult statues to wear indicate that in practice not only the saints themselves but also their images were invested with a certain amount of autonomous power.[21] Several miracle stories, such as that of St Nicholas and the Jew discussed by Robert Mills in this volume, turn on the actions of images which are more like containers for saints than representations of them. The centrality of images to saint-cult made it vulnerable to charges of idolatry: as the 'Twelve Conclusions of the Lollards' argue, 'pilgrimage, preyeris and offringis made to blynde rodys [crucifixes] and to deue [deaf] ymages of tre and ston, ben

---

[16] Delooz, 'Towards a Sociology', pp. 191–2.
[17] Michael Goodich, 'Biography 1000–1350', *Historiography in the Middle Ages*, ed. Deliyannis, pp. 353–85, p. 366.
[18] Vauchez, *Sainthood*, pp. 113–23.
[19] Jonathan Hughes, *Pastors and Visionaries: Religion and Secular Life in Late Medieval Yorkshire* (Woodbridge: Boydell, 1988), pp. 299–319; Katherine J. Lewis, 'Margery Kempe and Saint Making in Later Medieval England', *A Companion to 'The Book of Margery Kempe'*, ed. John H. Arnold and Lewis (Cambridge: Brewer, 2004), pp. 195–215, pp. 206–7; Simon Walker, 'Political Saints in Later Medieval England', *The MacFarlane Legacy: Studies in Late Medieval Politics and Society*, ed. R. H. Britnell and A. J. Pollard (Stroud: Sutton, 1995), pp. 77–106: on the origins of sanctity, see Peter Brown, *The Cult of the Saints: Its Rise and Function in Latin Christianity* (Chicago: University of Chicago Press, 1981).
[20] *Speculum Sacerdotale*, ed. Edward H. Weatherly, EETS os 200 (London: Oxford University Press, 1936), p. 1.
[21] Katherine L. French, 'Women in the Late Medieval English Parish', *Gendering the Master Narrative: Women and Power in the Middle Ages*, ed. Mary C. Erler and Maryanne Kowaleski (Ithaca NY: Cornell University Press, 2003), pp. 156–73, p. 162.

ner of kin to ydolatrie'.²² Such arguments were eventually to prevail when the cults were dismantled at the Reformation, compromised by their very popularity.²³

Hagiography is only one manifestation of saint cult, and not necessarily the most important one. For devotees, a saint's identity might well be primarily based on a shrine, on the miracles performed there which showed the saint in action, and on the artworks which represented them. Anthony Bale writes of the child-martyr Robert of Bury: 'Robert's "story" was . . . that which formed the content of the performances at Robert's shrine, together with details of his *vita* which may have been known through ecclesiastical art, books of hours, rumor, and anecdote.'²⁴ The same is likely to be true of any shrine-based saint. Cultic activity and hagiography frequently reinforced one another, with shrines prominently displaying hagiographic narratives, but they could also operate independently. Visitors to shrines were primarily interested in the efficacy of saints, in their post-mortem power rather than the details of their earthly life.²⁵ Visual representations of the saints might diverge from the narratives of their lives: there is, for example, next to no textual authority for the popular scene of St Anne teaching the Virgin Mary to read.²⁶ As Lewis points out below, several contemporary figures were culted, without, so far as we know, ever being the subject of vernacular hagiography, while literary renditions of the lives of the saints, such as Geoffrey Chaucer's of St Cecilia, might be unconnected to any known cult sites or activities. Some of the most colourful narratives are of saints who had little or no active cult: the transvestites Eugenia, Margaret-Pelagien, Marina/us and Theodora, a popular group amongst modern commentators, appear in English narratives but have no known cults in medieval Britain.²⁷ Prayers of invocation to saints often concentrated on their present heavenly power and glory rather than on the details of their past earthly lives.²⁸ Or narratives might be back-formations from the relics, as in the case of the legend of St Ursula and the eleven thousand virgins, which was boosted by the discovery of the 'relics' of the saint and her companions in Cologne. What had been discovered was an ancient cemetery, containing the bodies of men and children as well

---

²² 'Twelve Conclusions of the Lollards', *Selections from English Wycliffite Writings*, ed. Anne Hudson (Toronto: University of Toronto Press, 1997), pp. 24–9, p. 27.
²³ See Duffy, *Stripping of the Altars*, pp. 407–10 on the attack on the cults as idolatrous.
²⁴ Anthony P. Bale, ' "House Devil, Town Saint": Anti-Semitism and Hagiography in Medieval Suffolk', *Chaucer and the Jews: Sources, Contexts, Meanings*, ed. Sheila Delany (New York: Routledge, 2002), pp. 185–209, pp. 188–9.
²⁵ Anneke B. Mulder-Bakker, 'The Invention of Saintliness: Texts and Contexts', *The Invention of Saintliness*, ed. Mulder-Bakker (London: Routledge, 2002), pp. 3–23, p. 12.
²⁶ Pamela Sheingorn, ' "The Wise Mother": The Image of St Anne Teaching the Virgin Mary', *Gendering the Master Narrative*, ed. Erler and Kowaleski, pp. 105–34, p. 110.
²⁷ *Golden Legend*, trans. Caxton: Eugenia, vol. II, pp. 151–2; Margaret-Pelagian, vol. V, pp. 238–40; Marina/us, vol. III, pp. 226–8; Theodora, vol. IV, pp. 48–53; they are excluded from Farmer, *Oxford Dictionary of Saints*, which includes '[a]ll saints of whom there is or was a notable cult in England', p. ix; see e.g. *Women of the Gilte Legende: A Selection of Middle English Saints Lives*, trans. Larissa Tracy (Cambridge: Brewer, 2003) for a selection which favours this group. See Bernau in this volume for further discussion of these *Lives*.
²⁸ For example, Lydgate's 'Prayer to St Edmund', *The Minor Poems of John Lydgate, Part I*, ed. Henry Noble McCracken, EETS es 107 (London: Oxford University Press, 1911), pp. 124–7.

as women, but, undaunted by the extra corpses, the cult's promoters elaborated the narratives to diversify the legendary virgins' attendants.[29]

The saints were at once models for personal conduct and patrons with access to heavenly power: the relative importance of these two functions was subject to a good deal of variance and centred upon different media. Imitation of saints, which I take to be text-based, will be discussed below. Saints were important figures in the experienced reality of many medieval people, for reasons, as Gail McMurray Gibson puts it, 'of urgent and practical utility'.[30] Eamon Duffy concludes that 'the English laity looked to the saints not primarily as exemplars or soul-friends, but as powerful helpers in time of need'.[31] Attitudes to them could be quite pragmatic: those in search of cures shopped around the shrines to compare their efficacy.[32] The miracles of Christ's ministry provided an important template for wonder-working saints; as Carole Rawcliffe argues, shrines established themselves by covering a checklist of cures for blindness, paralysis and demonic possession.[33] Even raising people from the dead was surprisingly common, at least, as one official of Thomas Becket's shrine noted, if the saint was invoked in time: once people had been dead for three days, they usually stayed that way.[34] This list was not exclusive, however, and few aspects of medieval life escaped the attention of the saints and their publicists. When not raising the dead, Becket turned to more mundane matters: his shrine-keepers recorded a miracle in which a girl forgot where she had put a newly purchased cheese, but then remembered again once she had sought the saint's aid.[35] Personal cures formed the bulk of recorded miracles, but saints might also be active in the political sphere: it was claimed that St Anne had indicated her support for Edward IV's cause by miraculously displaying her image to the king on his return to England in 1471.[36]

In addition to performing the standard list of miracles, either at their shrines or at a distance, most saints specialised in curing certain kinds of diseases or certain kinds of person. Some aspects of their patronage were based on details of their lives or deaths: hence Katherine of Alexandria, a learned woman threat-

---

[29] Farmer, *Oxford Dictionary of Saints*. The eleven thousand themselves are thought to be the product of a misreading of xi m v, meaning eleven virgin martyrs, as eleven thousand virgins.

[30] Gail McMurray Gibson, 'Saint Anne and the Religion of Childbed: Some East Anglian Texts and Talismans', *Interpreting Cultural Symbols: St Anne in Late Medieval Society*, ed. Kathleen Ashley and Pamela Sheingorn (Athens GA: University of Georgia Press, 1990), pp. 95–110, p. 95.

[31] Duffy, *Stripping of the Altars*, p. 178.

[32] Carole Rawcliffe, 'Curing Bodies and Healing Souls: Pilgrimage and the Sick in Medieval East Anglia', *Pilgrimage*, ed. Morris and Roberts, pp. 108–40, p. 117.

[33] Rawcliffe, 'Curing Bodies and Healing Souls', p. 132.

[34] Rawcliffe, 'Curing Bodies and Healing Souls', p. 129.

[35] *Materials for the History of Thomas Becket, Archbishop of Canterbury*, ed. James Craigie Robertson, 7 vols, Rolls Series 67 (London: Longman, 1875–85), vol. 2, pp. 153–5.

[36] *Historie of the Arrivall of Edward IV*, ed. John Bruce, Camden Society, 1st ser. 1 (London: Camden Society, 1838), pp. 13–14; Wendy Scase, 'Writing and the "Poetics of Spectacle": Political Epiphanies in the *Arrivall of Edward IV* and Some Contemporary Lancastrian and Yorkist Texts', *Images, Idolatry and Iconoclasm in Late Medieval England*, ed. Jeremy Dimmick, James Simpson and Nicolette Zeeman (Oxford: Oxford University Press, 2002), pp. 172–84.

ened with torture on a wheel, patronised scholars, women and wheelwrights.[37] As patron of women she helped young women hoping to find good husbands, although she was herself a virgin saint.[38] The connection between saint and power could be symbolic, paradoxical or indeed horrific: Margaret, another virgin, patronised childbirth because she had burst unharmed from a dragon's belly.[39] Some specialisations are harder to fathom: the legendary early Christian martyr Barbara came to be regarded as a protector against the much more recent danger of gunshots, and Walstan's *vita* claims that he was capable of replacing lost genitalia, though it does not mention how often this speciality was required.[40]

The cults of the saints marked out time and space. Whereas in present-day Britian a culturally inclined tourist visits locales such as 'Brontë Country', medieval travellers were aware of passing through the territories of saints. William Worcestre, for example, noted a series of locations in Cornwall and Somerset dedicated to St Michael.[41] Some were localised and specialised: the cult of Walstan did not spread far beyond his native Norfolk.[42] Saints could represent the whole nation, as when 'Seint Edwarde and Seint Lowes', symbolising the realms of England and France, were portrayed in the subtleties of Henry VI's coronation feast.[43] Or they could be attached to a region or city, as Ætheldreda was to Ely and the surrounding area, and of course to a parish or village. Many saints were markedly territorial, as Lewis's discussion below of St Werburge's defence of Chester against the Welsh demonstrates, and the importance of cult-centres was at least as much geographical as narrative. Some late medieval cults were essentially, in Anneke Mulder-Bakker's term, 'cases of topolatry', where the saint's life was a subsequent invention to explain and legitimise the sacredness of the place.[44] Saints' power was intensified in certain locations. Those with shrines may seem to lurk within them, lying in wait for the sinful, impious or merely careless. This violent and comic cautionary tale told by Gerald of Wales reminds us that saints are not invariably benign forces:

> In the north of England, just across the Humber, in Howden church, the parson's *belle amie* sat herself down without thinking on the wooden tomb

---

[37] Farmer, *Oxford Dictionary of Saints*, p. 77.
[38] Katherine J. Lewis, *The Cult of St Katherine of Alexandria in Late Medieval England* (Woodbridge: Boydell, 2000), pp. 73–7.
[39] Wendy R. Larson, 'The Role of Patronage and Audience in the Cults of Sts Margaret and Marina of Antioch', *Gender and Holiness: Men, Women and Saints in Late Medieval Europe*, ed. Samantha J. E. Riches and Sarah Salih (London: Routledge, 2002), pp. 23–35, pp. 26–7.
[40] 'Prayers to Ten Saints', *Minor Poems of John Lydgate I*, pp. 120–4, line 92; M. R. James, 'Lives of St Walstan', *Norfolk Archaeology* 19 (1917), pp. 238–67, p. 248.
[41] William Worcestre, *Itineraries*, ed. John H. Harvey (Oxford: Clarendon Press, 1969), p. 15.
[42] Duffy, 'Dynamics of Pilgrimage'; Miriam Gill, 'The Saint with a Scythe: A Previously Unidentified Wall Painting in the Church of St Andrew, Cavenham', *Journal of the Suffolk Institute of Archaeology and History* 38.3 (1995), pp. 245–54.
[43] 'The Soteltes at the Coronation Banquet of Henry VI', *Minor Poems of John Lydgate Part II*, ed. Henry Noble McCracken, EETS os 192 (London: Oxford University Press, 1934), pp. 623–4, p. 623, line 2. Claire Waters gives further examples below of political deployments of sanctity.
[44] Anneke B. Mulder-Bakker, 'Saints without a Past: Sacred Places and Intercessionary Power in Saints' Lives from the Low Countries', *Invention of Saintliness*, ed. Mulder-Bakker, pp. 38–57, p. 39: see also Woodcock below.

of Saint Osana, the sister of King Osred, which jutted out in an open space as if it were a seat. When she wanted to get up, her backside stuck tight to the wood and she was unable to wrench herself free. The people came running. They cut away her clothing until she was quite naked and kept beating her hard with lashes until the blood flowed. She wept bitterly and prayed for forgiveness. In view of her repentance and the penalty which she had paid, she was freed by divine intervention and allowed to go home.[45]

Sites which held relics, or had experienced notable occurrences in the saint's life, as in the case of Thomas Becket at Canterbury, were especially powerful. The wide dispersal of relics enabled localities to appropriate universal saints whose earthly lives had been lived thousands of miles away. Osbern Bokenham, lost in a swamp near Venice, luckily had with him a direct line to Margaret of Antioch, which he activated when he 'be-hyht the ryng,/ Wyth wych I towchyd at my partyng/ Hyr foot bare'.[46] This ring had acquired its power when Bokenham held it against a relic of (most of) the saint's foot, kept at Reading Abbey, before leaving England. He was able to call on Margaret, not because as a saint in heaven she was equally accessible from any geographical location, but because he had had the foresight to bring with him an emergency power-source which connected him to her body part and her cult site. Images could perform the same function; as Richard Marks argues, they enabled 'a disassociation of the saint from their cult centre and a relocalization in churches containing their image'.[47] Images could also take the form of symbolic references: Katherine of Alexandria is associated with hilltop locations in England because, it is thought, these mimic the distant location of her relics, Mount Sinai.[48]

The feasts of the saints marked out the passage of time. Whilst in contemporary Britain only a handful of saints' days – the patrons of the nations of the United Kingdom, plus St Valentine – are generally observed, every day of the year was and is the feast day of several saints, though not all are observed with equal solemnity, or indeed at all. Nevertheless, any given week in late medieval England would include some celebration of a saint, with a certain amount of variation according to the type and dedication of the church and to local preferences. This is a week in mid-June, according to a fifteenth-century verse calendar:

> Prayeth for us, Marcellyan and Marke,
> Wyth Geruase and Prothase, martyrs ylkone.
> This world now, Seynt Edward! wexyth darke,
> For our ynwarde sight ys al-most a-gone.
> Lede us, oure firste martyr, Seynt Albone.

---

[45] Gerald of Wales, *The Journey Through Wales and The Description of Wales*, trans. Lewis Thorpe (Harmondsworth: Penguin, 1978), pp. 84–5.
[46] Bokenham, *Legendys*, lines 167–9.
[47] Richard Marks, *Image and Devotion in Late Medieval England* (Stroud: Sutton, 2004), p. 92.
[48] Katherine J. Lewis, 'Pilgrimage and the Cult of St Katherine of Alexandria in the Later Middle Ages', *Pilgrimage Explored*, ed. J. Stopford (York: York Medieval Press, 1999), pp. 145–60.

> Etheldrede of Ely, I pray now helpe me,
> Wyth Seynt Iohn Baptist þe natiuite.⁴⁹

The grouping of the saints in the liturgical calendar would have had the effect of emphasising their common features and obscuring their different origins, flattening out the millennium-plus of Christian history into a continuous present. Medieval people referred to this calendar routinely and in secular as well as religious contexts: Margaret Paston dated an urgent note warning her husband of a rumoured indictment against him 'Wretyn at Norwiche the Weddenysday next after Seynt Mathy.'⁵⁰

The feast days of saints who were of particular importance to a parish, guild or other organisation might move out from the church into streets and greens, and were marked with a variety of activities. Procession, ceremony and drama were popular and widespread media for the representation of saints in England from at least the twelfth century, though few texts survive.⁵¹ Riches discusses below the celebration of George in Norwich by the guild which was the powerhouse of local government, but smaller-scale observations of saints happened throughout the country. The late fifteenth-century churchwardens' accounts for the parish of Snettisham, Norfolk, record the costs and profit of various communal activities, including an annual celebration of St Edmund:

> Item for washyng -yat- ageyn Sent Edmund – xd
> Item for mendyng of surples yat tyme – xijd
> Item for a lambe – xd
> Item for beryng of schaftes yat tyme – xijd⁵²

Bearing the shafts points to processional activity, the surplices to clerical involvement and the lamb to a feast, unless perhaps the animal was a kind of mascot. It is not clear exactly what was washed, but it could be that the cult image of the saint was being spruced up in honour of his feast day.⁵³ We can speculate that such activities allowed saints another form of embodied presence to that of relics, and that the event probably functioned to build a sense of community and tradition and to reinforce local social structures and customs, but there is no clue as to how and why the parish (whose church was dedicated

---

49 'Metrical Church Kalendar', *The English Register of Godstow Nunnery, Part 1*, ed. Andrew Clark, EETS os 129 (London: Kegan Paul, Trench, Trübner and Co, 1905), pp. 13–24, p. 18, lines 421–7.
50 *Paston Letters I*, ed. Davis, letter 137.
51 Clifford Davidson, 'The Middle English Saint Play and its Iconography', *The Saint Play in Medieval Europe*, ed. Davidson (Kalamazoo: Medieval Institute Publications, 1986), pp. 31–122; Darryl Grantley, 'Saints' Plays', *Cambridge Companion to Medieval English Theatre*, ed. Richard Beadle (Cambridge: Cambridge University Press, 1994), pp. 265–89; Catherine Sanok, 'Performing Feminine Sanctity in Late Medieval England: Parish Guilds, Saints' Plays, and the *Second Nun's Tale*', *Journal of Medieval and Early Modern Studies* 32.2 (2002), pp. 269–303.
52 Transcribed in James Cummings, 'Contextual Studies of the Dramatic Records in the Area around The Wash, c. 1350–1550', University of Leeds Ph.D. thesis, 2001; http://virtualnorfolk.uea.ac.uk/drama/ritual/snettisham/snettisham.html
53 Thanks to Sam Riches for this suggestion.

to the Virgin Mary) chose the Anglo-Saxon martyr, king and virgin for this purpose, and whether any saint would have done just as well.

The 'Lives' of the Saints

The saints are located at the join of textual and material cultures. As Mary Beth Long discusses below, a manuscript was itself a piece of material culture, and on some occasions a hagiographical manuscript might be treated as being not, primarily, a medium for the transmission of text, but as an efficacious object, a kind of contact relic.[54] In a self-referential moment, Margaret of Antioch prays that 'whoever writes a book on my life, or acquires it when written, or whoever has it most often in hand, or whoever reads it aloud or with good will listens to the reader, may have all their sins forgiven': reading is only one of the means of accessing the virtue of the text.[55] The corporality of saints might spill out into their texts: for example, a French legend of Margaret was made into a 'birth girdle . . . inscribed on a roll and designed to be wrapped over the body of a woman in labour'.[56] Hagiographic texts were sometimes included in sumptuously illustrated manuscripts which were precious objects in their own right, or might be inscribed in things other than books: the English verse life of Walstan was displayed on 'a triptych of wood, covered with sheets of vellum, on which the legend was inscribed'.[57] Some hagiographic texts may have been labels attached to public images. This seems likely to have been the function of John Lydgate's brief verse 'To St Ositha', where the detail, 'In thy riht hand thu heeld a litil stoon/ To bete thy brest of hool affeccioun', does not correspond to anything in the saint's legend, but may be a misrecognition of the bunch of flowers which she holds in fifteenth-century sculptures.[58]

It would be difficult to overstate the popularity of hagiography in late medieval England. Its canon has not been conclusively determined (and perhaps, given ambiguities about what should be included in the category, never can be), but D'Evelyn and Foster list 289 individual, paired or grouped saints of whom at least one English life is extant; there are multiple versions of the lives of the most popular of them, led by Katherine of Alexandria with fifteen distinct versions in a total of forty-eight manuscripts and two printed editions.[59] This one legend,

---

[54] Jocelyn Wogan-Browne, 'The Apple's Message: Some Post-Conquest Hagiographic Accounts of Textual Transmission', *Late Medieval Religious Texts and their Transmission: Essays in Honour of A. I. Doyle*, ed. A. J. Minnis (Cambridge: Brewer, 1994), pp. 39–53, p. 44.

[55] 'Saint Margaret', *Medieval English Prose for Women: Selections from the Katherine Group and Ancrene Wisse*, ed. Bella Millett and Jocelyn Wogan-Browne (Oxford: Clarendon Press, 1992), pp. 44–85, p. 79.

[56] Ruth Kennedy, 'Spalding's *Alliterative Katherine Hymn*: A Guild Connection from the South-East Midlands?', *Viator* 35 (2004), n. 103.

[57] James, 'Lives of St Walstan', p. 240.

[58] 'To St Ositha' [i.e. Sitta/Zita of Lucca], *Minor Poems of John Lydgate I*, p. 137; Francis W. Cheetham, *Medieval English Alabaster Carvings in the Castle Museum, Nottingham* (Nottingham: Art Galleries and Museums Committee, 1973), pp. 50–1. Thanks to Sam Riches for discussion of the sculptures.

[59] D'Evelyn and Foster, 'Saints' Lives'; note that this catalogue is not exhaustive and see Oliver Pickering, 'Saints' Lives', *A Companion to Middle English Prose*, ed. A. S. G. Edwards

then, circulated more widely than now better-known Middle English texts such as Chaucer's *Troilus and Criseyde* (extant in whole or part in twenty manuscripts), *The Cloud of Unknowing* (seventeen), Thomas Hoccleve's *Series* (six) and the works of the Gawain-poet (a single manuscript) put together. Hagiography occurs in prose, rhymed verse and stressed verse, varying in length from a few hundred words to several thousand lines. Its authors are often anonymous, but those who can be identified are most often male professional writers, largely clerics but also including some laymen such as Chaucer, whose hagiographic writings are part of a larger corpus.[60] The hagiographic narrator typically takes the position of mediator, both between the saint and the audience and between textual tradition and his own present day; hagiographic texts often address their audience directly, prescribing their response.[61] Knowledge of hagiography spanned the social spectrum: as Lewis points out below, 'Saints' lives were . . . one of the few literary forms to which we know that everyone would have been exposed', including the illiterate poor who heard the *Lives* of the saints read in church. Lay and ecclesiastical patrons commissioned or were presented with hagiographies; the texts may be showcased in the most elaborate manuscripts, such as BL Harley 2278, Henry VI's illuminated presentation copy of Lydgate's *Lives of Saints Edmund and Fremund*, but also appear in household compilations and circulated as inexpensive pamphlets.[62] Lydgate's account of the circumstances of the commission of *St Edmund* indicates that the gift of hagiographical narrative in a suitably luxurious format constituted the ceremonial ratification of the compact of mutual protection between the king, the saint and the abbey of Bury St Edmunds.[63] Personalised hagiographies such as those written by Bokenham, with his patrons' names woven irrevocably into the verse – he rhymes 'denston kateryne' with 'þat blyssed virgyne' – were amongst the most elite and literate manifestations of saint-cult.[64] As Long discusses below, for such patrons, hagiography could establish their credentials as pious and

---

(Cambridge: Brewer, 2004), pp. 249–70, pp. 265–70 for additional prose lives; Lewis, *Cult of St Katherine*, pp. 2, 14–25; in addition to those listed by Lewis, there is a brief life in Brian Ansley's translation of Christine de Pisan, *The Boke of the Cyte of Ladyes*, printed by Henry Pepwell in 1521, bk. 3, ch. 3; to my knowledge no catalogues or surveys of Middle English hagiography include this text, which contains yet another selection of all-female brief lives.

[60] However, three women, at least two of whom were nuns, wrote Anglo-Norman hagiography: see Jocelyn Wogan-Browne, ' "Clerc u lai, muïne u dame": Women and Anglo-Norman Hagiography in the Twelfth and Thirteenth Centuries', *Women and Literature in Britain 1150–1500*, ed. Carol M. Meale (Cambridge: Cambridge University Press, 1993), pp. 61–85. For further discussion of *The Boke of the Cyte of Ladyes*, which includes several brief lives of women saints, see Jennifer Summit, *Lost Property: The Woman Writer and English Literary History, 1380–1589* (Chicago: University of Chicago Press, 2000), pp. 93–107.

[61] Jocelyn Wogan-Browne, 'Wreaths of Thyme: The Female Translator in Anglo-Norman Hagiography', *The Medieval Translator 4*, ed. Roger Ellis and Ruth Evans (Binghampton: State University of New York Press, 1994), pp. 46–65, p. 47.

[62] See Lydgate, *St Edmund Facsimile*; Lewis, *Cult of St Katherine*, p. 175 for inclusion of Katherine's legend in household manuscripts; A. S. G. Edwards, 'The Transmission and Audience of Osbern Bokenham's *Legendys of Hooly Wummen*', *Late-Medieval Religious Texts*, ed. Minnis, pp. 157–67 on the presumed individual booklets of Bokenham's legends. See Mary Beth Long below.

[63] John Lydgate, 'St Edmund and St Fremund', *Altenglische Legenden Neue Folge*, ed. Carl Horstmann (Heibronn: Henningen, 1881), pp. 376–445, lines 160–6.

[64] Bokenham, *Legendys*, lines 1466, 1469.

cultured persons just as well as any other literary genre, but with the added advantage of constituting a claim to the saint's attention and patronage. In the Prolocutory to his legend of Mary Magdalene, Bokenham represents himself as overwhelmed by the demand for bespoke hagiographies: hearing that the countess of Oxford had commissioned a life of St Elizabeth of Hungary, Lady Bourchier requested a life of Mary Magdalene. Hagiography here is a means to access the holy, of course, but also to keep up with the de Veres; it is a very superior kind of consumer good, fittingly adorning the glamour of Lady Bourchier's Christmas party, where her family, attendants and guests dance in their finest clothes, than which 'in þe moneth of may/ Was neuyr wyth flouris whyt, blewe & grene,/ Medewe motleyid freshlyere'. In the life, Mary herself turns out to be as courtly a noblewoman as her devotee.[65] The scene is presumably polished up to advertise Bokenham's intimacy with his patron, the elegance of her household and the fashionability of his product: the lower-ranking patrons of his other lives do not merit so much detail. Nevertheless, the account would not have suited hagiographer and patron had it not been a recognisable version of the process of patronage.

Practical considerations have necessarily imposed some limitations on the material which can be considered here. One restriction is linguistic: this collection covers only hagiography in Middle English, although hagiography was a multilingual and multinational phenomenon. Nations and regions may have different emphases, but the lives of popular saints crossed such boundaries with ease: the legend of St Brendan, for example, survives in Latin, Anglo-Norman, Dutch, German, Venetian, Occitan, Catalan, Norse and English versions, as well as its native Irish.[66] Much Middle English hagiography was indeed translated, most often from Latin but also from other European vernaculars. Hagiographies in Middle English and other vernaculars could have intertextual relationships and share a bilingual audience.[67] Nor does Middle English represent the totality of insular hagiography, which was also written in Latin and in the other vernaculars of medieval Britain, Anglo-Norman, Welsh, Irish and Scots. The exclusion of hagiography in other insular vernaculars is for practical reasons only, following modern disciplinary boundaries, not medieval reading experiences, and once more attempting to address a manageable corpus of material. The exclusion of Latin means that official dossiers of canonisation, usually substantial collections of documents, will not be considered.[68] These are hugely informative, but differ in circulation and purpose from vernacular hagiographies. Excluded also are lives of Christ and the Virgin and Miracles of the Virgin, closely related literary forms, which would add an unmanageable amount of material.[69] Long lists the

---

[65] Bokenham, *Legendys*, lines 5037–75, 5026–8, 5367–73.
[66] *The Voyage of Saint Brendan: Representative Versions of the Legend in English Translation*, ed. W. R. J. Barron and Glyn S. Burgess (Exeter: University of Exeter Press, 2002).
[67] For a list of Anglo-Norman verse hagiographies, see Wogan-Browne, 'Clerc u lai', pp. 76–8; on hagiographies in the Celtic languages, see *Celtic Hagiography and Saints' Cults*, ed. Jane Cartwright (Cardiff: University of Wales Press, 2003)
[68] For an example of such a dossier, comprising Life, Miracles and letters of support, see *The Book of St Gilbert*, ed. Raymonde Foreville and Gillian Keir (Oxford: Clarendon Press, 1987).
[69] For which see Frances A. Foster, 'Legends of Jesus and Mary', *Manual of the Writings in*

major collections and authors, but elsewhere in the volume there is no attempt to discuss Middle English hagiography in its entirety: contributors have selected representative or exemplary samples. The genre was simply too popular for it to be possible to make a comprehensive study.

The date range covered by this collection is marked by linguistic change at one end and religious and political upheaval at the other. Hagiography was represented amongst the earliest English literature and forms a substantial proportion of surviving Old English poetry, including Cynewulf's *Elene*, *Juliana* and *Fates of the Apostles*, the anonymous Andreas and Guthlac poems and Ælfric's calendrical collection of the *Lives of the Saints*.[70] The Middle English, post-Conquest tradition begins with the three virgin martyr legends of the Katherine group, which, with the associated didactic texts, form one of the earliest surviving corpora of Middle English writing.[71] These lengthy, poetic and sophisticated hagiographies belie any notion of progressive development, and nor was the genre moribund when it was suddenly cut off by the Reformation. Legendaries such as William Caxton's version of the *Golden Legend* and the *Kalendre of the Newe Legende of Englande* were prominent amongst early English printed books. The genre, as it always had, was adapting to changing tastes and interests: Alexander Barclay's *Life of St George*, printed in 1515, shows a 'fusion of elements from classical rhetoric and the ideal of the Christian knight . . . a typical feature of the early sixteenth century'.[72] English hagiography continued to flourish in the early sixteenth century, and many of its tropes and themes can be seen to have survived the Reformation in some form. In this volume, Lewis's discussion of Henry Bradshaw's *Life of St Werburge* shows the uses of hagiography in the sixteenth century, and Matthew Woodcock surveys some of the channels into which hagiographical writing was diverted after the Reformation.

Hagiography has numerous subgenres. The Catholic Church recognises several types of sanctity – apostles, martyrs, confessors and virgins – all of which come with certain narrative expectations, as do the lives of kings and queens, monastic founders and leaders, prelates, mystics, warriors and widows. Early Latin writings on the saints, including Athanasius's *Life of St Antony*; Gregory the Great's *Dialogues*; Gregory of Tours's *Glory of the Martyrs*, *Life of the Fathers* and *Glory of the Confessors*; and Sulpicius Severus's *Life* of Martin of Tours developed a storehouse of motifs which hagiographers were to appropriate for the next millennium.[73] The main components of hagiographic narratives are the Life

---

Middle English 1050–1500, vol. 2, ed. J. Burke Severs (New Haven: Connecticut Academy of Arts and Sciences, 1970), pp. 447–57, 639–44.

[70] For an overview, see Michael Lapidge, 'The Saintly Life in Anglo-Saxon England', *Cambridge Companion to Old English Literature*, ed. Malcolm Godden and Lapidge (Cambridge: Cambridge University Press, 1991), pp. 243–62 and *Holy Men and Holy Women: Old English Prose Saints' Lives and their Contexts*, ed. Paul Szarmach (Albany: State University of New York Press, 1996).

[71] *Medieval English Prose for Women*, ed. Millett and Wogan-Browne; *Anchoritic Spirituality: Ancrene Wisse and Associated Works*, trans. Anne Savage and Nicolas Watson (New York: Paulist Press, 1991).

[72] Manfred Görlach, *Studies in Middle English Saints' Legends* (Heidelberg: Universitätsverlag C. Winter, 1998), p. 66.

[73] Cynthia Hahn, *Portrayed on the Heart: Narrative Effect in Pictorial Lives of Saints from the Tenth through the Thirteenth Century* (Berkeley: University of California Press, 2001), pp. 11–13;

(*vita*), the Passion (*passio*) and the Miracles, which last may include details about translation of relics or foundation of a shrine. Cults thus contributed to hagiographic writing by providing the subject matter of the Miracles as well as an audience for writing about the saint. The Passion is the oldest form: Lives of non-martyrs whose holy lives culminated in natural death developed when times became less dangerous for Christians. Thus the matter of hagiography includes the saint's human, historical life; his or her afterlife in heaven from which miracles are performed; and the often extended death-sequence which constitutes the gateway between these two states, and which, in the case of martyrs' legends, forms the bulk of the narrative and the claim to sanctity. There are also associated non-narrative forms of writing about saints, such as lyrics, liturgies, prayers and hymns, which are included within the term 'hagiography', though our interest in this collection is primarily in the narrative forms. The Lives, Passions and Miracles may appear together or separately, and are largely mixed and matched from a substantial stock of motifs: the genre is both stereotyped and almost infinitely variable. As Thomas Heffernan argues, there is a sense in which the saints share a 'collective personality'; Gregory of Tours thought they had a single 'life' because 'the saints share collectively in the luminous life of the incarnate Christ'.[74] At the level of generic convention, this means that sanctity is frequently established by demonstrating the likeness between the individual life and the lives of other saints or of Christ. Hagiography is full of conventional motifs, which can be openly transferred from one saint to another. John Capgrave, for instance, describes St Norbert as a 'very new Seynt Poule', converted when God addressed him: 'Norbert, Norbert, tende now onto me./ Why pursuest me?', a rebuke which would seem an overreaction to Norbert's unexceptional life were it not so explicitly modelled on the conversion of Paul from persecutor to leader of the early Christians.[75]

And yet the *Lives* are many and are not identical: there must have been reasons why some of the conventional motifs and not others were deployed in the construction of any given saint. Authors may insist on the individual historicity of their saint; Bokenham introduces his legend of Margaret with the claim that on his return from Rome:

> Thys blyssyd virgyne I dede visyte,
> And al the processe I dede owt wryte
> Wych I purpose now to declare
> On ynglysh, & it brout wyth me to Clare.[76]

If true, this would have been quite unnecessary, for Margaret was one of the most popular saints in England, with several English versions of her life already

---

Thomas Head, 'Introduction', *Medieval Hagiography: An Anthology*, ed. Head (New York: Routledge, 2001), pp. xiii–xxxviii, pp. xv–xviii

[74] Thomas J. Heffernan, *Sacred Biography: Saints and their Biographers in the Middle Ages* (Oxford: Oxford University Press, 1988), p. 7.

[75] John Capgrave, *Life of St Norbert*, ed. Cyril Lawrence Smetana (Toronto: Pontifical Institute of Medieval Studies, 1977), lines 146–9; Acts of the Apostles 9:4.

[76] Bokenham, *Legendys*, lines 119–22.

written.⁷⁷ However, it functions as a statement of Bokenham's scholarly credentials as a hagiographer and of the authenticity of the narrative, which takes on the status of a contact relic. In the longer narratives, where authors have the space to go beyond the essentials of establishing sanctity and intercessionary credentials, they may include various individual and idiosyncratic elements, along with details of daily life. These are most common as incidentals in miracle narratives, making them a rich source for social and cultural history, but are also present in lives, even of fictive saints: Capgrave describes in *St Katharine* a nurse's care for a newborn infant 'to lyfte it, to lulle it and to fede it eke,/ To bathe it, to wype it and to rokke it bothe', while Bokenham, an unusually intrusive narrator, includes a passage of complaints about his weariness, his blunt pen and his spectacles.⁷⁸

Contributors to this collection discuss hagiography's overlap with other medieval genres, and examples could be multiplied of its appearances in historical and geographical writing; didactic guides to political and personal conduct; romantic and epic fictions. As Woodcock argues below, it is necessary to accept 'the ill-defined edges of the genre', which mean that however conventional it may seem, hagiography in practice is capable of assimilating almost any material and becoming a vehicle for all kinds of concerns. Felice Lifshitz points out that hagiography's functions are multiple and often very practical:

> Biographies of saints provided communities and institutions with written traditions; they defended the independence of communities and institutions against those who wished to subject them; they defended property rights and territorial endowments; they fuelled episcopal rivalries; they conveyed political and theological stances; they propagated an individual author's or group's notion of 'the holy'; they served, in short, manifold purposes.⁷⁹

One could add that some of its functions are identical to those of other genres of vernacular literature in the later Middle Ages: to entertain, to edify, to contribute to the corpus of a writer or reflect on the glory of a patron. Changing forms reflect changing purposes: when the fifteenth-century version of the Latin *Sanctilogium* of British saints rearranged the narratives from calendrical to alphabetical order and omitted liturgical items, it turned a devotional manual into a dictionary of national biography.⁸⁰ And though, as Lifshitz shows, hagiography's purpose is not limited to promotion of a cult, this is of course still an important function, with many hagiographies spelling out in contractual detail how the saint should be approached and for what manner of problem.

As Claire Waters shows below, hagiography has an inherently ambivalent relationship to power; it can thus be deployed to address very current and specific areas of controversy. Sherry L. Reames argues that hagiography's very

---

77 D'Evelyn and Foster, 'Saints' Legends', pp. 606–8.
78 John Capgrave, *The Life of St Katharine of Alexandria*, ed. Carl Horstmann, with a foreword by F. J. Furnivall, EETS os 100 (London: Kegan Paul, Trench, Trübner, 1893), bk I, lines 233–4; Bokenham, *Legendys*, lines 894–908.
79 Felice Lifshitz, 'Beyond Positivism and Genre: Hagiographical Texts as Historical Narrative', *Viator* 25 (1994), pp. 95–113, p. 97, n. 7.
80 Manfred Görlach, 'Introduction', *Kalendre*, pp. 7–46, p. 9.

lack of originality makes it an especially politic vehicle for exploring controversial issues:

> the ancient saint's legend [was] a genre which provided an ideal screen for potentially dangerous ideas, in Chaucer's society, because it was so clearly identified with orthodoxy and yet so full of material that did not necessarily uphold the late medieval status quo.[81]

She reads Chaucer's version of the legend of St Cecilia as a critique of unjust contemporary rulers; in complementary analyses, David Aers and Lynn Staley interpret the same text as a critique of the institutionalised materialism of the contemporary church.[82] As Heffernan argues, hagiography is so frequently concerned with exposure of the inadequacies of earthly power that it can become a vehicle for dissent.[83] Capgrave's *St Katharine*, for example, includes a detailed discussion of whether unmarried women could exercise authority and, according to Karen Winstead's analysis, a covert critique of the rule of Henry VI.[84] Winstead and other commentators have also seen in this legend a significantly ambivalent representation of the Wycliffite critique of devotional images.[85] Sheila Delany argues that Bokenham's versions of the lives of several popular women saints constitute a rewriting of Chaucer, a defence of Augustinian aesthetics and a promotion of Yorkist interests.[86] Political comment need not be – in fact, usually was not – oppositional: Lydgate inserts a prescription of virtuous rule into his *St Albon*, claims that St Edmund protected the Church against 'Lollardis' and uses the 'Legend of St Austin at Compton' to buttress the Church's claim to tithes, a matter of perennial concern to Bury Abbey.[87] The

---

[81] Sherry L. Reames, 'Artistry, Decorum and Purpose in Three Middle English Retellings of the Cecilia Legend', *The Endless Knot: Essays in Honor of Marie Boroff*, ed. M. Teresa Tavormina and R. F. Yeager (Cambridge: Brewer, 1995), pp. 177–99, p. 199.

[82] David Aers, *Faith, Ethics and Church: Writing in England, 1360–1409* (Cambridge: Brewer, 2000), pp. 40–5; Lynn Staley, 'Chaucer and the Postures of Sanctity', David Aers and Staley, *Powers of the Holy: Religion, Politics, and Gender in Late Medieval English Culture* (University Park: Pennsylvania State University Press, 1996), pp. 179–260, pp. 198–216.

[83] Heffernan, *Sacred Biography*, p. 268.

[84] Karen A. Winstead, 'Capgrave's Saint Katherine and the Perils of Gynecocracy', *Viator* 25 (1994), pp. 361–76.

[85] James Simpson, *The Oxford English Literary History, Volume 2, 1350–1547: Reform and Cultural Revolution* (Oxford: Oxford University Press, 2002), pp. 420–9; Sarah Stanbury, 'The Vivacity of Images: St Katherine, Knighton's Lollards, and the Breaking of Idols', *Images, Idolatry and Iconoclasm*, ed. Dimmick, Simpson and Zeeman, pp. 131–50; Sarah James, 'Debating Heresy: Fifteenth-Century Vernacular Theology and Arundel's Constitutions', University of Cambridge Ph.D. thesis, 2004, pp. 80–131. My own slightly different reading is in preparation.

[86] Sheila Delany, *Impolitic Bodies: Poetry, Saints and Society in Fifteenth-Century England: The Work of Osbern Bokenham* (New York: Oxford University Press, 1998); see Caroll Hilles, 'Gender and Politics in Osbern Bokenham's Legendary', *New Medieval Literatures 4*, ed. Wendy Scase, Rita Copeland and David Lawton (Oxford: Oxford University Press, 2001), pp. 189–212 for another version of the Yorkist argument.

[87] John Lydgate, *Saint Albon and Saint Amphibalus*, ed. George F. Reineke (London: Scarecrow, 1985), bk II, lines 65–127; 'St Edmund', line 1014; 'Legend of St Austin at Compton', in *Minor Poems of John Lydgate I*, pp. 193–206. See Karen A. Winstead, 'Lydgate's Lives of Saints Edmund and Alban: Martyrdom and Prudent Pollicie', *Mediaevalia* 17 (1994), pp. 361–76 on these legends' concern with rulership.

virgin martyrs Katherine and Ursula, whose legends foreground the gulf between heavenly and earthly power, were nevertheless appropriated by earthly power in the pageant which welcomed Katherine of Aragon to London.[88]

Hagiography is usually assumed to belong to the 'realm of piety' as opposed to the 'realm of doctrine', and so to represent religious discourse at its most popular and simplistic.[89] Nicholas Watson, defining the category of 'vernacular theology' which has enabled serious analysis of numerous vernacular texts, explicitly excludes 'most narrative texts, especially saints' lives'.[90] In doing so, he reproduces a late-medieval perception that hagiography was not a sufficiently serious genre to have theological content. Certainly it is not consistently used as a vehicle for doctrinal instruction, and it is often very relaxed about theological precision. Describing Margaret's emergence from an exploded dragon, the *South English Legendary* pauses to consider the problems of demonology and plausibility raised by this encounter:

> Ac þis netelle ich noȝt to soþe [I do not tell this as truth] · for it nis
> noȝt to soþe iwrite [it is not written as truth]
> Ac weþer it is soþ oþer it nis · inot noman þat wite
> [Nobody knows whether it is true or not]
> Ac aȝen kunde [against nature] it were · þat þe deuel were to deþe
> ibroht [killed]
> For he nemei þolie nanne deþ · nemai it leue nawt
> [It is not credible that the devil should suffer death].[91]

The openly acknowledged unlikeliness of the tale does not, however, prevent it from being included in the legend: the bursting to death of the devil-dragon was too firmly established in the saint's iconography to be eliminated from her narrative.[92] In strict theological terms the saints' power was limited to intercession with God: as the *Kalendre of the Newe Legende* puts it, 'seyntys in heuyn be in suche fauoure with almyghty God þat theyre prayer is herde for suche persones as they pray for', and they could be revered, but never worshipped.[93] The headnote to Lydgate's 'Prayer to Ten Saints', however, indicates that at least some saints in practice functioned autonomously: 'these holy seyntys folwyng ar preuyledged of our lord Ihesu that what man or woman praieth to them rightfully shal haue his bone'.[94] If saints' legends could include such materials, their

---

88 Sanok, 'Performing Feminine Sanctity', p. 274; *The Receyt of the Ladie Kateryne*, ed. Gordon Kipling, EETS os 296 (Oxford: Oxford University Press, 1990), pp. 13–15.
89 Sherry L. Reames, *The Legenda aurea: A Reexamination of its Paradoxical History* (Madison: University of Wisconsin Press, 1985), p. 30.
90 Nicholas Watson, 'Censorship and Cultural Change in Late-Medieval England: Vernacular Theology, the Oxford Translation Debate, and Arundel's Constitutions of 1409', *Speculum* 70 (1995), pp. 822–64, p. 824, n. 4: James also queries this exclusion; 'Debating Heresy' pp. 82–6.
91 *SEL*, p. 297, lines 165–8. See Jocelyn Price, 'The Virgin and the Dragon: The Demonology of Seinte Margarete', *Leeds Studies in English* 16 (1984), pp. 337–57 for an explanation of the demonological problem.
92 Wendy R. Larson argues that women patrons were particularly attached to this image: 'Who is the Master of this Narrative? Maternal Patronage in the Cult of St Margaret', *Gendering the Master Narrative*, ed. Erler and Kowaleski, pp. 94–104, pp. 100–3.
93 *Kalendre*, p. 45.
94 'Prayer to Ten Saints', *Minor Poems of John Lydgate I*, pp. 120–4, p. 120. Eight of them are also included in the Holy Helpers.

authors presumably did not think that theological instruction was their priority. However, critical analyses demonstrate that at least some hagiographers did use the form to set theological concepts in narrative motion. And even if a given hagiographic text had not intentionally been written as vernacular theology, this did not mean that it could never have been read as such. When Julian of Norwich allegorised the three wounds of St Cecilia to pray for 'the wonnde of contricyoun, the wonnde of compassyoun and the wonnde of wylfulle langynge to god', she took hagiography seriously as a genre which could answer her questions about how she might live for God.[95]

It is a commonplace that one function of hagiography was to function as a model for imitation. In a monastic context, such imitation might be exact and literal. Capgrave describes his intent in the *Life of St Norbert*, 'Of þis same seynt to telle þe lyf real,/ Both of his diete and eke of his wede'.[96] Such details then form the basis of a rule of life for the members of Norbert's order, who are to form themselves by imitating him. Hagiography could, though probably exceptionally, shape a lived life, as it is represented as doing in *The Book of Margery Kempe*, in which Margery is explicitly shown to imitate several kinds of saints, including virgin martyrs, apostles and contemporary mystics and confessors.[97] For most laypeople, however, imitation was of the kind rather than the degree of the saints' virtues. Hagiography taught daily conduct and obedience to prevailing social values more often than it taught heroic virtue: best documented is the use of legends of the virgin saints as examples for girls, who were thought likely to identify with the narratives of other girls like themselves.[98] Lewis argues that the virginity of Edmund of East Anglia was held up as a model to Henry VI in the expectation that he would imitate it in the less inconvenient form of sexual moderation.[99] Barclay's message to the 'englysshe youth' he envisaged as readers of his *Life of St George* was that they should imitate the saint's 'manly doughtynes' by eschewing 'thriftles game', a moral to which much of the action-packed narrative is quite irrelevant.[100] Imitation of the saints did not have to include every aspect of their lives: like replicas of the Holy Sepulchre, any point of contact was sufficient.[101]

---

[95] *A Book of Showings to the Anchoress Julian of Norwich*, ed. Edmund Colledge and James Walsh (Toronto: Pontifical Institute of Medieval Studies, 1978), vol. I, p. 206.

[96] Capgrave, *St Norbert*, lines 30–1.

[97] See Lewis, 'Margery Kempe and Saint Making' for a summary of readings of *The Book of Margery Kempe* in the context of hagiography and Woodcock in this volume for a brief discussion. The *Book* has otherwise been largely excluded from the current collection as it is thoroughly covered in Arnold and Lewis's volume: see also A. C. Spearing, 'Margery Kempe', *Companion to Middle English Prose*, ed. Edwards, pp. 83–97.

[98] Katherine J. Lewis, 'Model Girls? Virgin-Martyrs and the Training of Young Women in Late Medieval England', *Young Medieval Women*, ed. Lewis, Kim M. Phillips and Noel James Menuge (Stroud: Sutton, 1999), pp. 25–46; Kim M. Phillips, 'Desiring Virgins: Maidens, Martyrs and Femininity in Late Medieval England', *Youth in the Middle Ages*, ed. P. J. P. Goldberg and Felicity Riddy (York: York Medieval Press, 2004), pp. 45–59.

[99] Katherine J. Lewis, 'Edmund of East Anglia, Henry VI and Ideals of Kingly Masculinity', *Holiness and Masculinity in the Middle Ages*, ed. P. H. Cullum and Lewis (Cardiff: University of Wales Press, 2004), pp. 158–73, pp. 166–7.

[100] Alexander Barclay, *The Life of St George*, ed. William Nelson, EETS os 230 (London: Oxford University Press, 1955), lines 323–5.

[101] On replica sepulchres, the appearance of which could vary considerably, see Richard

However, devotion to saints was not always primarily based on identification. As Jacqueline Jenkins argues, when secular women enjoyed the narratives of virgin saints who rejected the womanly concerns of marriage, motherhood and household, they 'returned again and again to texts addressing the lives of their spiritual opposites'.[102] Devotion could mimic heterosexual romance, as when Bokenham claims that his friend Thomas Burgh had 'a synguler deuocyoun/ To thys virgyne of pure affeccyoun', Margaret of Antioch.[103] Bokenham's version of her life is a carefully packaged gift which confirms his love for his friend, uniting the men in devotion to the saint.[104] Women, likewise, could have a special affection for male saints: Bokenham's life of Elizabeth of Hungary refers to what appears to be a recognised custom of young girls picking their 'valentines' from among the male saints. Elizabeth herself picks John the Evangelist as 'kepere of hyr uirgynyte', thus forming a relationship like saintly unconsummated marriage, or indeed mystic marriage, in which gender difference is probably less important than shared virginity.[105]

Hagiography was the most common, though not the only, form of biography in the later Middle Ages, and arguably the dominant model, for medieval secular biography shares its representations of exemplary persons and moralisations.[106] The form of the legendary has a secular equivalent in collections of exemplary biographies, such as *The Fall of Princes* or Capgrave's *Illustrious Henries*. Hagiography seems on first acquaintance quite other than modern lifewriting. It makes no pretence of objectivity or judiciousness: a saint is by definition always in the right, and hagiography's task is to stir up affective engagement with them, as Bokenham puts it:

> to excyte
> Mennys affeccyoun to haue delyte
> Thys blyssyd virgyne to loue & serue.[107]

There are, however, some modern examples of engaged and exemplary lifewriting, such as David Halperin's *Saint Foucault*, which rehabilitates what he takes to be the essence of hagiography along with the subject of the biography.[108]

Krautheimer, 'Towards an Iconography of Medieval Architecture', *Journal of the Warburg and Courtauld Institutes* 5 (1942), pp. 1–33, pp. 3–20; Veronica Sekules, *Medieval Art* (Oxford: Oxford University Press, 2001), pp. 17–19.

102 Jacqueline Jenkins, 'Reading Women Reading: Feminism, Culture and Memory', *Maistresse of My Wit: Medieval Women, Modern Scholars*, ed. Louise D'Arcens and Juanita Feros Ruys (Turnhout: Brepols, 2004), pp. 317–34, p. 321.

103 Bokenham, *Legendys*, lines 179–80.

104 On virgin saints as gifts, see Jocelyn Wogan-Browne, *Saints' Lives and Women's Literary Culture c. 1150–1300: Virginity and its Authorizations* (Oxford: Oxford University Press, 2001), pp. 57–90.

105 Bokenham, *Legendys*, line 9608; on unconsummated marriages see Bernau in this volume.

106 Goodich, 'Biography 1000–1350', p. 358. See Julia Boffey, 'Middle English Lives', *The Cambridge History of Medieval English Literature*, ed. David Wallace (Cambridge: Cambridge University Press, 1999), pp. 610–34 for an overview of hagiography in the context of Middle English lifewriting.

107 Bokenham, *Legendys*, lines 127–9.

108 David M. Halperin, *Saint Foucault: Towards a Gay Hagiography* (New York: Oxford University Press, 1995).

There are modern parallels too for the use of formulae: Angela Jane Weisl details medieval hagiography's likeness to a sub-genre of modern lifewriting, the sporting biography.[109] Sarah Churchwell's study of biographies of Marilyn Monroe reveals a combination of elaborated narrative, moralised incident and truth-telling corpse quite familiar to students of hagiography.[110] The ancient and the modern genres share a certain tension, for the very act of writing a life requires that its subject be unfailingly significant both as extraordinary individual and as imitable exemplar.

Scholarship

Recent scholarship has found it necessary to rehabilitate hagiography. The genre was formerly dismissed as too crude and too stereotypical to be truly artistic or historically informative. Much Middle English hagiography was edited in the late nineteenth century, by Carl Horstmann and by contributors to the Early English Texts Society, but at that period interest in the genre was primarily philological and it was not uncommon for owners and editors to make disparaging remarks on its content. Horstmann sadly acknowledged that 'most Englishmen' regarded hagiography as 'worthless stuff, without any merit'; one such was the nineteenth-century owner of Mirk's *Festial* who commented that 'The stories in this book are so extravagant that it may be supposed they were invented to try how far human credulity could be extended.'[111] It does not help that the intervention of the Reformation broke off the mainstream of the tradition of hagiography in England, meaning that non-Catholic modern British readers encounter it as an alien genre. Secular readers may resist its piety, pious ones its sexual and violent content. At first acquaintance, the genre can look static and derivative to literary scholars, and so unpromising material to search for either authorial originality or social engagement. Often anonymous and existing in multiple redactions, hagiography fits awkwardly with a literary canon based on named authors and discrete texts. In a still-current introduction to the literature of medieval England, hagiography is very largely ignored.[112] To historians, meanwhile, hagiography could appear to be a genre which systematically contaminated historical evidence by mixing it with formulaic and fantastic materials.

However, hagiography has now joined the critical mainstream, as can be seen by consulting the Hagiography Society's directory of researchers and research events.[113] Some hitherto obscure texts have been, or are about to be, published in

---

[109] Angela Jane Weisl, *The Persistence of Medievalism: Narrative Adventures in Contemporary Culture* (New York: Palgrave, 2002), pp. 33–120.
[110] Sarah Churchwell, *The Many Lives of Marilyn Monroe* (London: Granta Books, 2004). Indeed, Donald Spoto has written biographies both of Monroe and of Francis of Assisi.
[111] Carl Horstmann, 'Introduction', *The Early South-English Legendary*, ed. Horstmann, EETS os 87 (London: Trübner, 1887), pp. vii–xii, p. xi; Thomas E. Marston, 'An Early English Bestseller', *Yale University Library Gazette* 46.1 (1971), pp. 86–8, p. 87.
[112] *New Pelican Guide to English Literature: Medieval Literature 1*, ed. Boris Ford, rev. edn (Harmondsworth: Penguin, 1982).
[113] Run by Sherry L. Reames: see http://mendota.english.wisc.edu/~hagio/

scholarly editions; the publication of several paperback anthologies of saints' lives has made it easier to introduce this material into curricula. Those of us who teach the saints in undergraduate courses have found that students respond with enthusiasm and insight to this apparently alien genre. Historical records of saints' cults – of dedications, processions, shrines and pilgrimages – have proved to be invaluable sources for cultural historians. As Lewis discusses, historians have learnt to use hagiography as evidence for mentalities, and discovered it to be an excellent source for social and cultural histories. Peter Brown points out, 'In studying both the most admired and the most detested figures in any society, we can see, as seldom through other evidence, the nature of the average man's expectations and hopes for himself.'[114] Some of the more eye-catching oddities of the saints and their cults – such as the theory of relic-theft or the cult of St Guinefort, the holy greyhound – have been the subjects of histories which participate in the rediscovery of medieval alterity.[115] The genre has been particularly useful to studies on the borderlines of history, art history and literature. Because hagiographic narratives often exist in parallel textual and visual forms, the variations between the two can shed light on the relation of medieval visual and verbal cultures.[116]

Medievalists have adopted the techniques of cultural studies to read our own less-than-respectable popular literatures. Literary scholars have become more cunning at reading hagiography's restricted code and tracing its variations through time and space: as Reames puts it, hagiographies may be adapted to address 'a surprisingly wide array of purposes, intended audiences, notions of decorum and kinds of religious and socio-political teaching'.[117] Historicist readings such as those detailed above show that hagiography was engaged in the conversations and debates of its own day. Winstead's *Virgin Martyrs* is a sustained demonstration of how seemingly minor differences between even very conventional narratives and motifs may be significant when considered along with broader historical changes. One driver of hagiography's literary rehabilitation has been provided by the methods of gender studies. In an influential article, Jocelyn Wogan-Browne applied Janice Radway's study of modern women's reception of popular romance to hagiography.[118] Both genres, frequently dismissed as sub-literary, are thereby restored as vehicles for

---

114 Peter Brown, 'The Rise and Function of the Holy Man in Late Antiquity', *Journal of Roman Studies* 61 (1971), pp. 80–101, p. 81.
115 Patrick J. Geary, *Furta sacra: Thefts of Relics in the Central Middle Ages* (Princeton: Princeton University Press, 1978); Jean-Claude Schmitt, *The Holy Greyhound: Guinefort, Healer of Children since the Thirteenth Century*, trans. Martin Thom (Cambridge: Cambridge University Press, 1983); Paul Freedman and Gabrielle Spiegel, 'Medievalisms Old and New: The Rediscovery of Alterity in North American Medieval Studies', The American Historical Review 103 (1998), pp. 677–704.
116 Hahn, 'Portrayed on the Heart'; Barbara Abou-el-Haj, *The Medieval Cult of Saints: Formations and Transformations* (Cambridge: Cambridge University Press, 1994).
117 Reames, 'Artistry, Decorum and Purpose', p. 178.
118 Jocelyn Wogan-Browne, 'The Virgin's Tale', *Feminist Readings in Middle English Literature: The Wife of Bath and All Her Sect*, ed. Ruth Evans and Lesley Johnson (London: Routledge, 1994), pp. 165–94; Janice A. Radway, *Reading the Romance: Women, Patriarchy and Popular Literature* (Chapel Hill: University of North Carolina Press, 1984); the connection is further discussed in Jenkins, 'Reading Women Reading'.

encodings of the discontents of women living under patriarchy. Thus feminist and queer analyses have led one strand of the recovery of hagiography, often noting that the genre makes space for versions of gender and sexuality which medieval norms of conduct forbid.[119] Gendered histories of canonisation patterns complement such analysis. To date most gendered analysis has concentrated on women saints, authors and patrons of hagiography, but the recent wave of medieval masculinity studies has recognised it as a valuable resource, and gendered analyses of male saints and masculine involvement with cults have begun to appear.[120]

There are numerous single-authored and collaborative histories of sainthood generally and of specific aspects of the cults, some concentrating on Christian medieval Europe and some enabling cross-cultural comparisons with other times, places and faiths.[121] The lives of saints and holy persons who lived in the later Middle Ages have been rich sources for studies of medieval spirituality.[122] Several major saints have been the subject of their own histories, a format which requires unpicking hagiography to rewrite it as biography or cultural history, and which is flexible enough to work both for historical saints such as Bridget of Sweden and fictional ones such as Anne.[123] A fruitful variant on this method is the interdisciplinary and collaborative study of individual figures, covering some combination of hagiographic writings, visual arts, liturgy and performance and cultic activities.[124] Collaborations allow the use of a wider range of knowledges and methodologies than most individual scholars can muster; the examination of a cult is an ideal exercise in interdisciplinary methodology. Editors of recent collections on Anne and Katherine of Alexandria remark on the multi-functionality of their saints; further comparative studies of other saints will show whether this is peculiar to certain kinds of saint or a trait of all successful cults.[125] Virtual archives have great potential to enable interdisciplinary analysis of representations of saints and their cults in text and art,

---

[119] See references in Bernau below.
[120] *Holiness and Masculinity*, ed. Cullum and Lewis.
[121] In addition to those already cited: Donald Weinstein and Rudolph M. Bell, *Saints and Society: The Two Worlds of Latin Christendom, 1000–1700* (Chicago: University of Chicago Press, 1982); *Saints of Europe: Studies towards a Survey of Cults and Culture*, ed. Graham Jones (Donington: Tyas, 2003).
[122] Such as Caroline Walker Bynum, *Holy Feast and Holy Fast: The Religious Significance of Food to Medieval Women* (Berkeley: University of California Press, 1987); Richard Kieckhefer, *Unquiet Souls: Fourteenth Century Saints and their Religious Milieu* (Chicago: University of Chicago Press, 1984).
[123] Bridget Morris, *Saint Birgitta of Sweden* (Woodbridge: Boydell, 1999); Virginia Nixon, *Mary's Mother: Saint Anne in Late Medieval Europe* (University Park: Pennsylvania State University Press, 2005); see also Kathleen Ashley and Pamela Sheingorn, *Writing Faith: Text, Sign and History in the Miracles of Sainte Foy* (Chicago: University of Chicago Press, 1999); Samantha Riches, *St George: Hero, Martyr and Myth* (Stroud: Sutton, 2000).
[124] In addition to those cited elsewhere, Antony Bale is currently editing a collection of essays on Edmund of East Anglia; *St Edmund, King and Martyr: Contexts and Interpretations* (Medieval Institute Publications, forthcoming).
[125] Kathleen Ashley and Pamela Sheingorn, 'Introduction', *Interpreting Cultural Symbols*, ed. Ashley and Sheingorn, pp. 1–68, p. 2; Jacqueline Jenkins and Katherine J. Lewis, 'Introduction', *St Katherine of Alexandria: Texts and Contexts in Western Medieval Europe*, ed. Jenkins and Lewis (Turnhout: Brepols, 2003), pp. 1–18, p. 3.

making it possible for researchers from all over the world to view unique artworks, and enabling analysis of large bodies of data. Numerous attempts have been made to process materials for these purposes, but most remain as yet under development.

The chapters of this collection largely read hagiography in ways which its medieval authors probably did not anticipate, and would not necessarily approve. Contributors have consolidated work on themes which are most prominent in current criticism. Riches and Long take an exterior view of hagiography, Riches describing the cultic activities within which it occurs and Long its material existence in manuscripts. Late medieval concerns often appear in hagiography in fantastic, disguised and reversed forms. Waters, Mills, Bernau and Lewis explore some of hagiography's deployments in conversations about politics, nation, Church, personal identity, family, past and present. Saints are found to be figures around which local, national and international communities are imagined, though the sheer number of saints means that their operations vary widely. Common themes include the adaptability of hagiography to varying forms and functions; the multiplicity of readings and contexts of reception; the flexibility of a genre which combines the authority of truth-claims with the responsiveness of fiction. Finally, Woodcock explores the rough edges of hagiography, the generic impurities and crossovers which enabled many of its constituent parts to survive the Reformation.

1

Hagiography in Context: Images, Miracles, Shrines and Festivals

SAMANTHA RICHES

All historical evidence – written, visual, archaeological or folkloric – comes into being within a specific context. As historians, whether professional academics or amateur enthusiasts, it is vital that we try to reconstruct as much of the context of production and usage as we can so that we are able to engage with this evidence appropriately. Middle English hagiography is now almost exclusively experienced as printed, bound volumes, often read silently and alone, but this is very different from its original form and purpose. Fundamentally, we must appreciate that these saints' lives were not composed in order that future students of religious history and literature would be able to read them in edited, printed versions. Modern editions are often compiled and translated from a number of variant sources, so that what may appear to be the 'true', 'real' or 'only' version of a text is often little more than a compromise between conflicting versions, rendered into contemporary language with inevitable loss of nuance. Increasingly, editions of lives of the saints are becoming available on the internet, and this is a welcome development in terms of ease of access. However, many of the same caveats apply: these versions are often merely transcriptions of printed editions (sometimes simply scanned and digitised, with the result that typographical errors often creep in), so the reader still needs to make a conscious effort to develop awareness of the ways in which the text would have originally been used. Furthermore, this heightened awareness needs to encompass some consciousness of the fact that written saints' legends will originally have formed just one aspect of devotion to particular saints; they may actually have been less significant at the time of their composition than shrines, relics, visual imagery, ritual, liturgy, oral narrative and other elements of a saint's cult. These physical and performative aspects are often fugitive, with the consequence that written hagiography can be unduly privileged by the simple fact of its survival and publication.

The specific reason why a piece of hagiography was composed or copied usually cannot be retrieved but sometimes we can establish the patronage of an individual text. A good example of a clear rationale for composition is Osbern Bokenham's dedication of his 'Life of St Anne' to Katherine Denston, who hoped that the saint, who had herself suffered from childlessness, would help her and her husband John to conceive a son.[1] This kind of record is unusual, but it indicates a wider context where all hagiography had a level of functionality: a saint's life was written in order that it could be read, and (crucially) *read to others*, to the glory of God and the saint concerned.[2] Saints were perceived as powerful advocates for their venerators: they could intercede with God on behalf of their devotees and also intervene directly in the lives of people, curing illness, offering protection from danger and answering requests made in the form of prayers. In most cases, though, these favours had to be earned: there is considerable evidence that saints' cults in the medieval period operated on a *quid pro quo* basis, as 'payments' in the forms of offerings, pilgrimage and other actions were made either in the hope of prayers being answered or in thanks for aid received. The written life of a saint thus operated within a much wider context of veneration, and needs to be set within a panoply of other means of glorification and supplication, both public and private.

Individuals could become devotees of a specific saint for a wide variety of reasons, relating to their given name, their profession, or the place they lived, to state but a few of the most obvious. However, we should not think of medieval people acting purely as individuals in relation to the saints they venerated: both historical and contemporary religious practice can be usefully characterised as a largely communal activity, where people choose to join together on some level with others to engage in acts of veneration, contrition and so forth. Thus, for example, whilst it was perfectly possible for a medieval Christian to commune with God, or any of the saints, within their own home or alone in an open space, it seems to have been far more common for people to meet together within a church or other sanctified setting to perform communal acts of worship. However, people need not always have physically met together in order to be identified as a group: they can be seen as sharing common understandings of the legend and powers of a specific saint, for example. The phenomenon of the saint cult thus seems to reside in a mental rather than temporal space, to form an imagined community rather than one with physical boundaries: devotees could be spread across a wide geographic area, but they tended to share a considerable amount of common belief and practice, often formulated into actual communal activities within particular localities.

For modern historians of religion, it is generally accepted that whilst this tendency towards commonality is crucial, a grouping (whether localised or scattered) with a common interest in a saint, or a quasi-saintly figure, is not necessarily to be defined as a *cult*. It seems that a genuine cult, as opposed to a simple grouping of devotees, requires certain attributes, such as the ability to display some physical or performative focus, and the potential to attract further adherents. The Appendix presents a list of elements which have been identified as strongly associated with saints' cults, both formal and informal; not all of these factors need to have been present in any given location, and it is certainly possible for a medieval saint's cult to have existed in the absence of quite a few

---

[1] Bokenham, *Legendys*, lines 1466, 2092–7.
[2] On medieval reading practices, see Michael Clanchy, *From Memory to Written Record: England 1066–1307* (London: Arnold, 1979), especially pp. 175–231.

of these components. However, it forms a useful guide to the range of cultural markers associated with saints' cults, and it clearly indicates that written hagiographies formed just one aspect of a cult, working alongside physical evidence such as relics and healings, celebratory practices such drama and feasts, and supplicatory activities such as pilgrimage and prayer before an image.

This chapter focuses primarily on evidence for the medieval cults of two saints, St George and St Edmund of East Anglia, outlining cultic practices in order to demonstrate that hagiographic texts formed just one aspect, and perhaps even a marginal aspect, of devotion. Both were very popular figures; George's cult was widespread in the Middle Ages, with evidence of veneration in many parts of Europe, whilst Edmund had more than sixty churches in England dedicated to him, and also a notable medieval cult at Toulouse, based on relics allegedly stolen by French soldiers defeated at the battle of Lincoln in 1217.[3] George was primarily associated with the traditions of the Latin Church, and ultimately a saint of the Eastern Mediterranean, but he shares common ground with Edmund, a product of the pre-Conquest English Church, for both have strong associations with England. Edmund was evidently identified as an 'English' saint, even though he was alleged to be of German birth and identified specifically as the ruler of the kingdom of East Anglia, rather than England generally.[4] The evidence for claiming George as an 'English' saint is even more complicated, and it is likely that he was not truly considered a patron of the English people until the post-medieval period.[5] However, both saints were frequently invoked as patrons of the English monarchy in the later Middle Ages; Edmund's role as an 'English' king made him eminently suitable for this role on one level, although his martyrdom at the hands of an enemy of England, which left his kingdom vulnerable to invaders, meant that his actual abilities as a king were rather less than first-rate. Meanwhile, George was a handy cipher for concepts of chivalry and martial ability: his usefulness as a patron of the English monarchy relied upon an identification with these abstract concepts rather than upon any historical link with England.

Here we will concentrate on evidence for these cults in eastern England; in Edmund's case this relates to the geographical area in which he lived and died: the final resting place of his tomb, at Bury St Edmunds (Suffolk) formed the central locus of his cult. Meanwhile, George has no known historical link with this part of Britain: it is merely an accident of history that good records of observances relating to this saint have survived for the city of Norwich. In this way these two figures indicate that the presence of a saint in a particular geographical area – whether in the form of their physical remains or the existence of stories about the individual's life within the locality – can be an important influence on the development of a cult, but the absence of such locators need not be a particular hindrance.

---

3 David Hugh Farmer, *The Oxford Dictionary of Saints* (Oxford: Oxford University Press, 1978) p. 121.
4 On the cult of St Edmund see: *St Edmund, King and Martyr: Contexts and Interpretations*, ed. Anthony Bale (Medieval Institute Publications, forthcoming).
5 On the medieval English cult of St George generally see: Samantha Riches, *St George: Hero, Martyr and Myth* (Stroud: Sutton, 2000).

This chapter is illustrated with a range of visual imagery created as an expression of the English cults of both George and Edmund, including works which were displayed in publicly accessible places, such as sculpture and wall painting, as well as images which would have been privately owned, such as manuscript illumination and pilgrim badges. We are also presented with a variety in monetary terms: pilgrim badges were sold very cheaply whilst illuminated manuscripts were the preserve of a financial elite. This fact reminds us that although poorer people may have been able to listen to the legend of a saint being recited from a manuscript life, the ownership and control of this text was likely to be restricted to a much higher, and necessarily smaller, class of person: the ways in which manuscript lives are formulated may well reflect the concerns of this social elite rather than the understandings of the wider range of people interested in the specific saint. Evidence suggests that many medieval people would have sought to own, or at least look at, images of the saint as a token of their veneration, and sometimes also as a kind of talisman against disaster, so understanding the role that images played in medieval saints' cults can help us to broaden out from the restricted reading provided by a simple focus on written sources.

Figure 1 shows a pilgrim badge of St Edmund, which would have been bought quite cheaply by a visitor to his shrine at Bury. The possession of such an object would have declared the devotee's allegiance to this saint, formed a tangible symbol of the pilgrimage they had undertaken – or perhaps had arranged to be undertaken on their behalf – and also allowed an awareness that the saint was physically present with them in some sense. In certain respects a parallel situation pertains in our own times, when people often carry around photographs of their loved ones in a wallet or purse. Clearly this is not simply a question of being unable to remember what the loved one looks like: the photograph allows the holder to feel some aspect of the presence of that person. Viewing a wall painting or public sculpture could have carried similar sets of meanings, and reminds us of the extent to which medieval people believed that imagery was invested with real power. We know, for example, that looking upon an image of St Christopher was thought to protect against sudden death and misadventure for the rest of the day, and for this reason wall paintings of the saint are often handily positioned within English parish churches so that they could be seen from the south door, obviating any need to enter the building to gain this advantage, and hence reducing the time and effort required from individual venerators. Examples of this location for late-medieval images of St Christopher include Bledlow (Buckinghamshire), Baunton (Gloucestershire) and Troston (Suffolk). Some versions are given an inscription articulating this belief, usually a variation on *Cristofori faciem die quacunque tueris/Illa nempe die morte mala non morieris* ['Whoever looks on the face of Christopher shall not that day die an evil death'].[6]

---

[6] J. C. Salmon, 'Saint Christopher in Medieval Art and Life', *Journal of the British Archaeological Association* 61 (1936), pp. 76–115, p. 80. Grateful thanks to Eleanor Pridgeon for her advice on imagery of St Christopher. Her doctoral thesis 'Saint Christopher in English Medieval Wall Painting, c. 1250–1500' is currently in preparation at the University of Leicester.

Figure 1. Pilgrim badge of St Edmund, fifteenth century, pewter. Museum of London, MoL 78.13. Photograph: Museum of London

Another aspect worth considering of wall painting and other publicly accessible forms of imagery is that they could have provided a vehicle for the patron to broadcast his or her views of the saint to all who saw the image, and hence perhaps shape their own understandings of the saint. Given that any patron would by definition need to have some level of disposable income, he or she would be likely to occupy a position of higher status than other members of his or her community. In consequence, it could be argued that the understandings of saints found in public art forms such as wall painting and sculpture should be read as nuanced in some of the same ways that the understandings presented in written hagiography are nuanced: they are the product of the veneration of an elite minority of the population. With this in mind it thus becomes even more important that we seek to discover and interpret the elements of saints' cults which were reflective of a wider social base, albeit that in many cases – public ritual, for example – we are potentially looking once more at evidence of the imposition of the belief system of only the upper echelons of any one community.

In a few cases we have very full contemporary descriptions of the events which took place on a saint's day in a specific location, and this kind of evidence can help us to reimagine some of the practices which may have taken place elsewhere, both in relation to the named saint and on other saints' feast days. The Guild of St George at Norwich kept good records of its activities on St George's day, 23 April.[7] This was a large and important guild, so not all of its activities will have been mirrored by other guilds, nor indeed in locations where the devotees of George (let alone other saints) did not organise themselves into a recognised or official grouping such as a guild. However, it is clearly not entirely atypical, because many of the elements found at Norwich are recorded even for saints with fairly small-scale, localised devotions. Thus we routinely find evidence of Masses said in honour of a saint, sometimes in a chapel or at an altar carrying that dedication, as well as the veneration of relics and images. However, it is likely that processions, the re-enactment of parts of legends, and large-scale feasts may have been restricted to the cults of saints with a significant following, particularly in terms of the financial resources which they were able to command.

George himself is a deeply problematic saint: whilst he is universally recognised as a Christian soldier and dragon-slayer, there is no solid evidence that he ever really existed. His earliest narratives portray him as a martyr who was tortured and executed for his refusal to abjure the Christian faith, and in some versions he is not even presented as a soldier, but simply as a holy man. By the twelfth century he had become widely venerated as a dragon-slayer – a motif which was ultimately based on allusion to Christ overcoming the devil – but he was highly revered as a martyr throughout the medieval period, with his cult gaining popularity across virtually the whole of Europe, both east and west. As we have already noted, George was strongly associated with the English monarchy, and his usefulness to them as a symbol of chivalry and authority seems to have mirrored the role he played for the membership of the English guilds devoted to him, which was often drawn from social elites, particularly in towns. In fact it is possible that George's attraction for an urban patriciate was founded in the trope of the knight (an inevitably high-status man) overcoming the dragon, a concept which is often associated with chaos and wild places. George can thus be read as a form of the city itself, prevailing over the wilderness which threatens to encroach upon it. Figure 2, a late fifteenth-century English wooden sculpture of George overcoming the dragon, formerly stood in one of the gate chapels on the city walls at Coventry: the liminal location is perfectly suited to this reading of the saint as personification of the town itself.[8]

The St George Guild at Norwich is particularly well attested, but it seems to have been typical of the urban guilds devoted to this saint. It was deeply enmeshed in the political life of the city, and sometimes seems to have acted as a branch of the city council itself. The Guild worshipped in the cathedral, where there was an altar or small chapel dedicated to St George, on the south side at

---

[7] On the Norwich Guild of St George see: Riches, *St George*, pp. 128–35, also *Records of the Gild of St George in Norwich, 1389–1547*, ed. Mary Grace, Norfolk Record Society 9 (Norwich, 1937).

[8] On the Coventry sculpture see: Samantha Riches, 'St George and the Dragon', *Gothic: Art for England 1400–1547*, ed. Richard Marks and Paul Williamson (London: V&A Publications, 2003), p. 137, cat. no. 284.

Figure 2. St George and the Dragon, late-fifteenth-century polychromed wooden sculpture. Herbert Museum and Art Gallery, Coventry. Photograph: Dr Jenny Alexander

the east end, below the high altar. It is not known if the chapel and altar belonged exclusively to the Guild, but Mass was said here daily by the Guild priest. A bell in the cathedral, known as St George's bell, tolled for the use of the Guild. The inventories of the Guild tell us that it had its own Mass vestments, also chapel and altar furniture. The list of property includes a ceremonial sword, banners, and an elaborate reliquary, a silver and gilt statue of an angel 'berying þe Arme of Seynt George'.[9] There was also an image of the saint himself, recorded in 1444/5 and 1461/2, and two secondary relics of the saint, stained cloths from his martyrdom, are also claimed.[10] The possession of a number of relics of their patron is indicative of the prestige of this guild, but we should note that it is also testament to the very healthy trade in relics which characterised medieval religion as well as the importance of relics as a focal point of saints'

---

[9] *Records of the Gild of St George*, pp. 30–2, p. 31.
[10] *Records of the Gild of St George*, pp. 15, 32.

cults (see Appendix). Another arm of George is noted amongst the many relics of a large number of saints recorded at Christchurch Canterbury in an inventory of 1315.[11] It is likely that both here and at Norwich a fragment of bone, reputed to be from the arm of the saint, was kept in a substantial reliquary. However, it is by no means impossible that the compilers of these inventories were writing about entire arms. It is well known that many saints appear to have a superfluity of body parts – no fewer than five heads of St George are recorded, for example, some of which were certainly entire skulls – and this underlines both the financial aspect of the trade in relics, for large profits could be made from the invention (meaning 'discovery') of sought-after relics, and a belief system which seems to have allowed that the power of a genuine relic could migrate into other objects, such as ordinary bones, and hence make them equally worthy of honour.[12]

We know that the St George Guild took part in a great annual procession of Norwich guilds and crafts on the feast of Corpus Christi, and that there was a Guild feast at Christmas, but the most important date in their calendar was undoubtedly St George's Day (23rd April). Indeed, the celebration of this day was a highlight of the year for the whole city. Sadly there seem to be no visual records of these festivals, but the documentary evidence at Norwich does at least allow us some sense of the splendour and pageantry associated with the marking of St George's Day. The chief ceremony of the celebration was a procession or 'Riding' in which a player dressed as George, in silver armour and a fur-trimmed robe, paraded on horseback with another actor dressed as the 'Margaret', a name quite possibly borrowed from another dragon-slaying saint but here almost certainly referring to the princess the saint is said to have rescued.[13] They were accompanied by all the Guild members who could attend, wearing their Guild livery and also on horseback. The mayor of Norwich paraded too, in full robes of office, and the senior members of the Guild were each required to pay for a priest to accompany the party, some wearing red robes and others in white.[14] Various poor men were paid to carry banners and torches; a cross, the banner of St George's Guild and other images and ornaments were also carried in the procession, as well as a stoup containing holy water. There are also records of payments to minstrels and cantors – cathedral clerks whose function was to sing the church services. This large group of people on foot and on horseback was accompanied by a dragon – a large puppet carried by a man who could

---

[11] On the Canterbury inventory, London BL MS Cotton Galba E iv, fols 122–127v, see J. Charles Wall, *Shrines of British Saints* (London: Methuen, 1905), pp. 13–16 and J. Wickham Legg and W. H. St John Hope, *Inventories of Christchurch Canterbury* (Westminster: Constable and Co., 1902), pp. 28–9; the full inventory is printed in this latter work at pp. 78–94.

[12] Riches, *St George*, p. 17.

[13] *Records of the Gild of St George*, pp. 32, 140. Evidence of the assimilation of St Margaret into the cult of St George is patchy and late, but one possible example occurs in a carved panel on the sixteenth-century court cupboard at Cotehele (Cornwall), where the princess is uniquely depicted with both a lamb and a dragon on leashes. St Margaret is associated with both sheep and a dragon, but the iconography of this panel is too unusual to allow a firm identification to be made. The Cotehele court cupboard is the subject of ongoing research by Nicholas Riall in association with Karen Watts and the current author (publication forthcoming).

[14] *Records of the Gild of St George*, p. 34.

snap its mouth open and closed, doubtless to the terrified delight of onlookers. On occasion gunpowder was used to heighten the effect (and evidently the danger: it was only recorded once, in 1429).[15] The actor playing George was expected to engage the dragon in combat as the Riding progressed, so there was plenty of opportunity for entertaining the spectators.[16] Throughout the procession the bells of the cathedral were rung, and the thought of the bells combining with the waits' music, the cantors' singing, the colourful robes, as well as the fighting between the George and his dragon, evokes a wonderfully dramatic event. These types of performative activities were a significant part of medieval cultural and communal life. Indeed, Alexander Barclay's account of the life of St George of 1515 was so imbued with contemporary celebrations of the saint that – in a remarkable piece of anachronistic projection from his own times back to the fourth century – he even claimed that the parents of the rescued princess ordained plays of the events to be performed:

> Also to kepe / in mynde this noble dede
> They ordeyned playes / of all the hole hystory
> Whiche theyr ofspryng / that after shuld succede
> Shulde yerely play / to kepe it in memory.[17]

The ceremonies began on the eve of the feast with evensong in the cathedral, which all members of the Guild were expected to attend. The feast day itself began with a breakfast of wine, bread and cheese, refreshments which were also provided by the Guild during the main focus of the day's events, the Riding itself. The procession through the city streets, starting out from the cathedral, was followed by a re-enactment of the story of the combat between St George and the dragon, which took place in a wood outside the city.[18] This choice of location underlines the contention that a representation of George's victory could be used to signify the *urbs* overcoming the wilderness. The procession then returned to the cathedral, which was newly strewn with rushes to receive them; Guild members would then offer up wax to be burned at the high altar during a feast in honour of the Trinity, the Virgin Mary and St George, then a Mass was held in honour of St George, the king, and the whole Guild. Following the Mass, the feast, or jantaculum, took place. Sadly no details survive of what food was served, but a record from 1535 shows that access was allowed to kitchens, pantries and other facilities of the Bishop's Palace, where the jantaculum was held, for eight days before and six days after the feast, so we can assume that the meal provided was little short of spectacular.[19] There was considerable opportunity for largesse to the local poor, again reinforcing the social and economic superiority of the Guild and its members. George was one of a small handful of saints whose cults were not suppressed in England by

---

[15] *Records of the Gild of St George*, p. 17
[16] *Records of the Gild of St George*, p. 67.
[17] Alexander Barclay, *The Life of St George*, ed. William Nelson, EETS os 230 (London: Oxford University Press, 1955), p. 53, lines 1156–9.
[18] *Records of the Gild of St George*, p. 72.
[19] *Records of the Gild of St George*, pp. 18–19.

Henry VIII in 1536: as a non-Biblical saint George was decidedly anomalous within this group, and the likelihood is that it was the political utility of his cult to the social and economic elite which led to the officially sanctioned retention of the cult until the mid sixteenth century. However, even an edict from the Bishop of London in 1552 outlawing the observance of St George's Day was insufficient to end the Norwich Riding, which continued in various forms, despite the eventual absence of George himself, almost into the modern era. There is written evidence that the Norwich dragon was still being paraded in the city during the nineteenth century, and even photographic evidence of a Riding performed by a St George Guild from nearby Costessey in 1887.[20]

At the conclusion of the feast, the brethren returned to the cathedral to pray for the souls of Henry V, thought of as the founder of the Guild, all benefactors and departed 'brethren and sustren' – all former members, both male and female, who had died. The next day, the Guild assembled again. The entire fraternity was expected to attend an early requiem Mass in honour of the founder of the Guild, benefactors, departed brethren and sustren and all Christian souls. The St George bell tolled in the cathedral in memory of the departed.[21] The requiem Mass was followed by what amounts to the Annual General Meeting of the Guild, which saw the elections of the masters, twenty brethren for common council, and other officers including the feast-makers for the following year, who would perhaps have been expected to start their planning whilst the events of that year's feast were still fresh in their minds.[22]

Whilst we must admit that this scale of festivity is unlikely to be entirely representative – the Guild of St George at Norwich was a rich and powerful organisation with a marked political dimension operating within a conurbation of considerable economic and social significance, and it is unlikely that other saints' days were marked even in the same town with a similar degree of display – it can be seen as a concrete example of many of the factors which are associated with medieval saints' cults. Comparison with the Appendix indicates that the records of the St George Guild at Norwich contain references to many of these components. As a martyr of the early Church, George was never formally canonised, and there was certainly no tomb in England, but the Norwich Guild held one of many recognised corporeal relics of the saint, as well as the secondary relics of cloths stained with his blood. They also owned images of the saint and evidently commemorated both his (alleged) deeds and the date ascribed to his death in the annual procession and dramatic re-enactment, and quite possibly had a special song or dance of St George, given the documented presence of musicians in the Riding.[23] The chapel of St George and its altar in the cathedral are also testimony to local interest in the saint, and we can certainly envisage

---

[20] See Riches, *St George*, fig. 4.17.
[21] *Records of the Gild of St George*, p. 19.
[22] *Records of the Gild of St George*, p. 40.
[23] There are no recorded songs of St George in England, although one is known in Normandy, reflecting a localised story of the saint linked to a holy well. See Jean Fournée, 'Le Culte de Saint Georges en Normandie', *Annuaire des Cinq Départements de la Normandie* (Association Normande et les Assises de Caumont, Congres de Louviers, 1986), pp. 105–27.

offerings being made before his image there in order to ask for his intercession.[24] Whilst we have no record of a specific hagiographic text of St George linked to Norwich, we do know that Barclay's *Life of St George* was dedicated to Thomas, Duke of Norfolk, and Nicholas West, who was consecrated as Bishop of Ely in 1515: this may indicate that this specific version of the legend would be known locally. Furthermore, there are another six versions of his life in Early and Middle English known, plus one version in a Scots dialect, so there was plenty of opportunity for devotees of George to access textual versions of his legend.[25] In the same way, whilst no English play-text survives, there is good evidence of performance of the legend of George, not only in relation to processions such as the Norwich Riding, but also apparently to independent plays, such as the one recorded at Lydd (Kent) between 1526 and 1534, and staged over four days in 1532–33.[26] We have little sense of what this play at Lydd would have involved, but some evidence can be even less substantial. For example, a letter of 16 April 1473 from Sir John Paston, a Norfolk landowner, to his younger brother, also named John, makes reference to problems with a number of servants who wished to leave his employment, including one who had been retained 'thys iij yere to pleye Seynt Jorge and Robynhod and the shryff off Notyngham'.[27] Given that Robin Hood and his enemy the Sheriff of Nottingham both appear in eminently secular stories, the mention of St George in the same context may perhaps tell us that the plays in which the servant portrayed these characters were all essentially worldly rather than religious. Alternatively, it may simply tell us that Sir John was fearing the loss of an actor who gave good performances in both saints' legends and secular stories. It is impossible to deduce how frequently these plays were staged, or how important they were as cultural markers, although it is tempting to conclude that performances were both frequent and popular, and that the Pastons' sponsorship of such events indicates elite investment in the cult of St George.

The medieval cult of St Edmund provides an interesting comparison to the evidence for devotion to George, not least because his cult had a clear focus around the saint's body and tomb at Bury St Edmunds (Suffolk) whereas George's English venerators had only a few scattered relics to capture their attention. This royal saint was an historically authentic figure – albeit that the narrative of his life was heavily embroidered – who had evidently spent time on English soil, in contrast to George, who was never credited with visiting England until post-Reformation narratives were developed to explain his status as patron of the country. The name of Bury St Edmunds is a perfect example of a

---

[24] Sadly there are no records of miracles credited to St George at Norwich, but elsewhere he was linked with the healing of a number of ailments. He was particularly associated with scaly skin conditions such as herpes, presumably because of his victory over the scaly dragon.

[25] The various medieval versions of St George's legend in English and Scots are listed in Riches, *St George*, p. 227 and their correspondences and differences tabulated in tables 1–3.

[26] Ian Lancashire, *Dramatic Texts and Records of Britain: A Chronological Topography to 1558* (Cambridge: Cambridge University Press, 1984), p. 224, entry 1164. There is also a record of a St George play staged in Lydd in July 1456; entry 1162.

[27] *Paston Letters and Papers of the Fifteenth Century*, ed. Norman Davis, 2 vols (Oxford: Clarendon Press, 1971–76), vol. 1, letter 275.

toponym reflecting interest in a saint's cult (see Appendix): formerly known as Bedericesworth, or Beodricsworth, the town's current name means literally 'St Edmund's borough', and reflects the translation of his relics there in 903. Edmund was so popular as to be the subject of six Latin and Middle English hagiographies, most of which relate directly to the Abbey of Bury St Edmunds.[28] He was an enormously popular saint, particularly significant in England because he was identified as an English king; yet his royal status was not his only important role. Like George and many other medieval saints he was perceived as a martyr, a holy figure who had physically suffered for his faith, and like all saints he was considered to have the potential to be an active agent in the lives of people who venerated him. There are numerous contemporary medieval records of posthumous miracles and other interventions by Edmund that give us a great deal of information about the ways in which he was perceived by his devotees, and there is also a considerable amount of visual evidence surviving, in the form of wall paintings, manuscript illuminations, stained glass and so forth. In consequence, it is possible to develop a good sense of the context in which his hagiographies were written and read.

St Edmund was a king of East Anglia who was killed by Danish raiders on 20th November 870, following a battle near Thetford. A few lines in the Anglo Saxon Chronicle (c. 890) and Asser's *Life of Alfred* (893), telling us briefly of the death of the king, comprise all the genuinely contemporary information that exists, but this was evidently no bar to celebrating him as a both a royal and a martyr saint. Abbo of Fleury, the composer of one of the earliest lives of Edmund, lived three generations after his subject but it is claimed (by Aelfric of Eynsham, in the preface to his Anglo-Saxon version of Abbo) that he had been able to consult with St Dunstan, who had in turn spoken with an armour bearer of Edmund at the court of Athelstan.[29] This type of oral culture may well have underlain much of the written hagiography which we now have, and again needs to be understood as part of the context of both composition and reception of legends. Whilst Edmund was undoubtedly a genuine historical character, the reality of his life is difficult to discern within the complex web of myth that built up around him, much of it designed to give echoes of other saints' stories, and the bare facts of his death at the hands of Vikings were embroidered with romantic idiom to put the king in the best light possible. The legend seems to have been fully developed by the fourteenth century, and it can be distilled down to the following essential elements.[30]

---

[28] *Memorials of St Edmund's Abbey*, ed. Thomas Arnold, 3 vols, Rerum Britannicarum Medii Aevi Scriptores (London, 1890–96), vol. 1, pp. ix–x, which also notes the existence of a metrical version in Old French by Denis Piramus, c. 1240, possibly relating to the cult at Toulouse.

[29] An accessible modern English translation of Aelfric's version of Abbo's *Life*, by Professor Kenneth Cutler, is available in the Medieval Sourcebook at: http://www.fordham.edu/halsall/source/870abbo-edmund.html [accessed 23/03/05].

[30] On the development of the complex narrative of St Edmund see *Memorials of St Edmund's Abbey*, ed. Arnold, vol. 1, pp. xv–xvi, and Dorothy Whitelock, 'Fact and Fiction in the Legend of St Edmund', *Proceedings of the Suffolk Institute of Archaeology* 31 (for 1969), pp. 217–33. The version of St Edmund's life given here is derived ultimately from Abbo's *Life*. This version is notable for a number of reasons, not least that it was written at Ramsey Abbey (Cambridgeshire) and hence may reflect localised East Anglian traditions.

Edmund was identified the younger son of a Saxon king, and the chosen heir of the pious yet childless Offa, king of East Anglia, a character who seems to have no historical authenticity. On Offa's death Edmund travelled to his new kingdom, making landfall at a place named as Maydenebure – the Maiden's Bower, an apparent reference to the Virgin Mary. Here Edmund prayed for his adopted country, whereupon twelve springs miraculously welled up out of the ground.[31] This naming of the place where Edmund is reputed to have landed seems to indicate a desire to underline his sanctity by linking him directly with the Virgin Mary, but it possibly also acts as a reference to his own physical chastity. At the conclusion of Abbo's hagiography of Edmund there is a reference to the incorruption of Edmund's flesh as evidence of his virginal purity, and other writers also comment on this aspect of his life. In reality, chastity was an enormously problematic issue for a king – one of the primary functions of a monarch was to secure the throne for his lineage by producing a legitimate male heir – but a rejection of sexual activity was virtually a necessity for a truly saintly figure.[32]

Edmund was accepted as king by all the East Anglians, and proved to be a wise and just Christian ruler. However, his land was subject to incursions by the Vikings, one story claiming that this was an attempt at revenge for the murder of a Viking ruler, Lodbrok, which had been unfairly blamed on the innocent Edmund, whilst another tradition claims that it was simple rivalry which drew the Vikings to attack the 'Saxon conqueror' of East Anglia.[33] It is reasonably certain that a Viking army engaged with the East Anglians near Thetford (Norfolk) in 869, after which Edmund was killed, but the hagiographic accounts make little reference to the battle and instead maintain that he was captured at a place usually identified as Hoxne (Suffolk) and taken to a nearby wood. The Vikings demanded part of his kingdom, something that hagiographers present him as willing to give up if his enemies would convert to Christianity, but he absolutely refused to abjure his own faith. As with the problematic issue of royal chastity, the hagiographers' emphasis on Edmund's disdain for his earthly treasures is not congruent with the real pressures on medieval kings: the loss of control of parts of a kingdom was obviously to be avoided at all costs, but voluntary poverty is another trope associated with sanctity. In consequence of his refusal to recant his Christian beliefs the king was stripped, tied naked to a tree, shot with arrows and then beheaded. There seem to be two distinct trends in accounts of how Edmund actually died. The 'clerical' model, put forward by writers such as Abbo and William of Malmesbury (d. 1143), states that Edmund made no resistance to his enemies, and this clearly seeks to model him on Christ, whose Passion is characterised by patient suffering; indeed, Abbo makes a direct allusion to the legend of St Sebastian, a martyr of the early Church, whose

---

[31] The discovery of wells and springs is a common marker of sanctity, and this episode may well reflect the drive to make this saint conform to the conventional idea of saintliness.

[32] The application of the trope of chastity in relation to kingship and sanctity is explored by Katherine J. Lewis in 'Becoming a Virgin King: Richard II and Edward the Confessor', *Gender and Holiness: Men, Women and Saints in Late Medieval Europe*, ed. Samantha J. E. Riches and Sarah Salih (Routledge: London, 2002), pp. 86–100.

[33] A number of variants on the legend of St Edmund are discussed in *Memorials of St Edmund's Abbey*, ed. Arnold, vol. 1, pp. xvi–xix.

Figure 3. The Martyrdom of St Edmund, fourteenth-century wall painting. Stoke Dry (Northamptonshire). Photograph: Anne Marshall, www.paintedchurch.org

suffering is clearly modelled on Christ's. Meanwhile, the 'secular' model, found in the Anglo Saxon Chronicle and accounts including that of Asser in his life of King Alfred, contends that Edmund fought stoutly against his enemies – 'atrociter pugnavit'.[34] This version seems to have better evidence in terms of what actually happened, but it was less useful than the clerical model in terms of the construction of Edmund as a recognisable saint.

Interestingly, visual accounts of this event are equally inconsistent, even though they tend to focus on the motif of the passive death of the king. Figure 3 depicts a fourteenth-century English wall painting of the martyrdom of St Edmund at Stoke Dry (Northamptonshire). Here he is indeed shown naked and filled with arrows, but we see him fully dressed in figure 4, an illustration from

---

[34] *Memorials of St Edmund's Abbey*, ed. Arnold, vol. 1, p. xx.

Figure 4. The Martyrdom of St Edmund, early-twelfth-century manuscript illumination attributed to the Alexis Master. New York, Pierpont Morgan Library MS M. 736, fol. 14.
Photograph: Pierpont Morgan Library

an early twelfth-century account of his life, probably created at Bury St Edmunds, whose illustrations are attributed to an English artist known as the Alexis Master. The parallel with the suffering Christ – a motif which regularly appears in medieval imagery of martyred saints, both written and visual – is made much more obvious in figure 3 than figure 4, which opts instead to maintain Edmund's kingly dignity by keeping him fully clothed. In the same way, the Stoke Dry wall painting is far closer than the Alexis Master's work to imagery of St Sebastian, for he too is almost always depicted in a state of near nudity. This type of variation between different visual forms is not unusual: it underlines the

Figure 5. The Relics of St Edmund on a Narrow Bridge, early-twelfth-century manuscript illumination attributed to the Alexis Master. New York, Pierpont Morgan Library MS M. 736, fol. 20v. Photograph: Pierpont Morgan Library

extent to which designers and artists were able to deviate from the standard account in order to meet a patron's requirements, and it is paralleled in written hagiography which may also show variations from established versions in order to meet a particular agenda.

Edmund's body was eventually recovered from the wood by Christian followers, and buried reverently. His head was subsequently discovered when a heavenly voice guided the searchers to a wolf who was guarding it reverently, calling 'here, here'. The head was then buried along with the rest of the body, and was believed to have rejoined itself to the neck – there are several accounts of subsequent exhumations when the body was found to be intact, and incorrupt, with only a thin red line around the neck showing where the head had been severed: tropes of regenerated and incorrupt flesh both function as markers of sanctity. In 903 Edmund's relics were translated to a more fitting resting place at Bedericesworth, later renamed Bury St Edmunds, but they were temporarily removed to London for safety, in view of ongoing Viking raids, in 1010. Figure 5 is another of the Alexis Master's illustrations for a hagiography of Edmund. It shows Egelwin, or Ailwin, the custodian of the shrine, moving the loculus, or chest, of relics on a cart: the blessing hand of God significantly gestures towards the relics rather than the custodian taking them to safety, and this underlines the enormous importance attached to corporeal relics. The decision to create an image of the relics in addition to the story of the life of the saint in itself reflects the primacy of relics. It reminds us that relics were thought to contain the corporeal essence of the saint, and guaranteed that the saint remained on earth in some form whilst simultaneously inhabiting heaven, thus ensuring that saints were able to remain accessible to their devotees in a physical way whilst also being able to intercede for those devotees with God.

The saint's body remained in London for three years in the church of St Gregory, by St Paul's Cathedral, before being returned to Bury St Edmunds in a triumphal procession. A great abbey was founded around his tomb in 1020 on the orders of King Cnut (Canute), and this became a site of continuing royal interest. Edward the Confessor, who himself was recognised as a royal English saint, was a frequent pilgrim to Edmund's tomb, and it is recorded that he habitually travelled the last mile on foot, a significant gesture of humility in a king.[35] Richard Coeur-de-Lion made a pilgrimage to Bury before going on crusade, and gave land to maintain a perpetual light before the shrine; in thanks for his safe return to England he also gave the banner of Isaac, king of Cyprus, to beautify it.[36] However, despite this level of veneration, the saint could not to be relied upon to help even a royal devotee in any circumstance. When Richard was being held captive and treasures were being collected throughout England for ransom, the Abbot of Bury refused to despoil Edmund's shrine for fear of the wrath of the saint. Edmund had already given ample evidence of his displeasure against those who were less than respectful to his remains, so the abbot may have had just cause. When Egelwin took the body to London he was inhospitably received by a priest in Essex, whose house then burned down. According to the chronicle of Joscelin of Brakelond, which covers the period 1173–1202, Edmund was so dissatisfied with the level of care bestowed on his relics that he caused a fire in order that a new shrine would have to be built, using King Richard's own gift to this purpose. Joscelin claimed that on the night of the vigil of St Ætheldreda (another British royal saint, and one particularly associated with East Anglia), 22 June 1198, the custodians fell asleep, and one of the torches kept burning between the shrine and the high altar, in accordance with Richard's instructions, set a table on fire. When the blaze was eventually put out much of the woodwork of the shrine was found to have been burned, but the jewels with which it

---

[35] Wall, *Shrines of British Saints*, p. 219
[36] Wall, *Shrines of British Saints*, p. 218.

was adorned were mysteriously even more beautiful than before.[37] Samson, the abbot of Bury at the time, told the monks that the fire had less to do with Edmund's concern about his relics, and more to do with the fact that the community was sinful, particularly in their complaints about the food and drink they were given, and proposed that all members of the convent should resign their pittances for a year so the money could be put towards the reconstruction of the shrine. However, the tomb was soon discovered to have been beautified without the aid of human hands, with the miraculous appearance of a new reliquary made from white doeskins and silver nails. The sacrist is said to have commented that 'St Edmund could well repair his shrine [himself]',[38] and the project to fine the monks was abandoned. This understanding that the saint was able to work from beyond the grave even to enrich his own shrine is indicative of the way that many medieval people seem to have thought about the objects of their devotion: they were in awe of saints and their power, and their love was mixed with fear, and, on occasion, a measure of pragmatism.

The accounts of Edmund's posthumous deeds certainly show that he was not a saint to be trifled with: there are several records of people who were insufficiently respectful coming to a bad end. For example, it is recorded that in 1341 a certain John de Beaumont exclaimed one day how much the confiscation of the gold and jewels at the shrine would help the king in the wars; soon afterwards he was killed in a tournament, whilst William de Gislingham, after making a similar speech in the Black Chamber at Westminster, immediately fell down and expired.[39] A long account of the translation of the saint's relics in 1095 tells us that all three witnesses present at the exhumation were dead within a year because of their presumption in handling the incorrupt body (1.168–73). Some other accounts speak of people who tried to steal offerings left at the shrine. In one case, a Flemish man approached the shrine under the pretence of devotion and tried to bite away a gold piece attached to it (1.373–4). His teeth became stuck fast, and he was only released when he made a full confession. Meanwhile, a thief who tried to make off with a peacock from the abbey at Bury came to an even worse end: he was drowned, presumably because of the saint's intervention; the peacock escaped unharmed and returned to its rightful owners (1.365–6). These latter stories are rather transparent attempts to demonstrate that Edmund was perceived as a powerful saint with both the means and the motivation to protect the material interests of his abbey, and this type of belief system allows even clearly unrelated events to be attributed to the power of the saint in the cause of self-justification. Another episode recounted at some length concerns the unsuccessful attempts made by Bishop Bateman of Norwich in 1345–46 to undermine the legal privileges of the abbey (3.320–7); the argument went before both the English king and the pope, and the subsequent death of the bishop was claimed, according to the anonymous chronicler, as a sign of

---

[37] Wall, *Shrines of British Saints*, pp. 223–5.
[38] Wall, *Shrines of British Saints*, p. 220.
[39] *Memorials of St Edmund's Abbey*, ed. Arnold, vol. 2, pp. 367–8. Subsequent volume and page references are given in brackets in the text.

Edmund punishing this persecutor, even though he lived for nine years after the settlement of the dispute.

There is an evident understanding that a saint could be vengeful towards those who behaved inappropriately towards him or his devotees, yet there also seems to be a frequent expectation that the saint will intervene on behalf of those who honour him even if they may have done little to warrant such help. Thus when Deorman, a rich London merchant who visited Bury to sell silks and spices, fell victim to a cutpurse – the medieval equivalent of a pickpocket – whilst visiting Edmund's shrine he remonstrated with the saint for allowing this to happen (1.183–5). The saint responded by ensuring that as Deorman left the church he walked straight into the culprit, who promptly confessed her sin and restored his goods to him. Deorman, much impressed by this, later became a monk within the abbey. Another story is even more illuminating: Robert of Banham, one of a number of men apprehended for a murder, vowed the best of his four oxen to Edmund if he could be allowed to escape the threat of ordeal by water (1.367). The saint responded: Robert's name was found to have been miraculously removed from the list of malefactors and he was set free. Does this mean he was innocent of the crime? The record we have is quite ambiguous on this point; the purpose of the account is to demonstrate the power of the saint and his ability to intervene in the lives of those who venerate him, even if they are not truly deserving.

In the same way, there are many records of Edmund coming to the aid of a devotee who calls upon him in time of crisis, with no mention of any specific bargain made in terms of an offering or pilgrimage to be made despite our generalised understanding that there was an expectation of such a compact. For example, when a clerk of Lichfield was voyaging to Jerusalem – presumably on pilgrimage but clearly not to the shrine of Edmund – his ship foundered and began to sink (1.195–6). Struggling in the water, the man invoked St Edmund, who seized him by the hair and brought him safely, although perhaps rather painfully, to dry land. This is an interesting example of a corporeal intervention by a saint, in comparison to the more usual miracles of healing, changing weather and so forth which do not require the saint to appear in person. The clerk then went to Bury and told the monks what had happened, but this does not seem to be the result of any particular bargain at the time of the rescue, for there is no record of the clerk offering to undertake a new pilgrimage if he is saved. Rather, the implication is perhaps that any request to the saint which meets with success will automatically lead to some sense of obligation to make a *quid pro quo*, with pilgrimage and offering being the most obvious 'payment'. Furthermore, the very act of recounting the miracle, which can lead to it being recorded for posterity, will result in greater veneration of the saint and hence form a reward in itself.

On other occasions though, the records speak clearly of a bargain being entered into. Another account of Edmund intervening in a case of a sinking ship, this time when travellers to Rome were returning to England, tells us that a collection of money was made as well as prayers offered to Edmund (1.162–4). In consequence of this the level of water in the hold decreased, the ship came safely into port and the offerings were brought to Bury. The fact that two members of the abbey at Bury, Wulfward the priest and Robert, were present among the pilgrims may suggest a reason why a collection was taken up: they would have been able to guarantee to bring it safely to the shrine, and doubtless knew how much their fellow monks would have valued the offering. However, the presence of these men does not in itself explain why it was Edmund who was called upon, rather than St Nicholas or even St Christopher, both of whom are associated with protecting travellers, particularly seafarers in the case of Nicholas. There are a remarkable number of miracles recorded in the *Memorials of St Edmund's Abbey* that involve sailors or people saved from shipwreck, and it is quite likely that Edmund was identified in England, or perhaps primarily in East Anglia, as a patron of voyagers. In the same way, there are a number of miracles associated with the freeing of prisoners, and this too may indicate a special patronage. Alternatively it could be the perception that Edmund was powerful in all circumstances which is the crucial issue: if calling on Edmund failed then a more specialist saint might be applied to, such as Sts Christopher or Nicholas for endangered travellers, or Sts Barbara, Faith or Dismas, or even Nicholas again, for prisoners.

A record of 1374 tells us that an infant of one year, named Alice, was believed to be dead (3.328); she was saved when her parents bent a penny over her and made a vow to St Edmund.[40] This final example is one which is particularly indicative of the role of saints in medieval society. In a time when modern medicine was in its very early infancy, a belief in the power of saints formed a kind of health insurance policy: you asked them to keep you well, and turned to them for help when sick. There are many accounts of people being cured after drinking from St Edmund's cup (for example, 1, 203; 374),[41] a secondary relic kept at Bury, but his role as a thaumaturge – or healer – was one which was shared with many other saints. Some saints were associated with particular ailments, such as St Lucy for eye complaints and St Roche for the plague, but there is no clear evidence that Edmund was perceived in this way. He is credited with curing a range of problems including blindness, ague, fever, paralysis, swellings and an unspecified 'painful disease' (1.371; 377; 202; 374; 167; 373), and again he may have been the first resort for people living near his shrine who would then have turned to a more specialist thaumaturgical saint if their usual patron failed.

This chapter can present only the most superficial overview of the full range of medieval saints' cults, yet the evidence considered here clearly demonstrates that Sts George and Edmund – in common with many other saints – were

---

[40] The practice of bending a penny over a sick, dying or dead person whilst invoking the saint is often recorded in medieval records: the bending of the coin seems to signify a formal promise to offer the money at the saint's shrine, and hence forms a 'contract' between venerator and saint, as discussed above. A similar ritual was 'measuring' a person to a saint: if the individual recovered, a candle with a wick the same length as the person would be offered at the saint's shrine in thanks. On these types of practice see Eamon Duffy, *The Stripping of the Altars: Traditional Religion in England, c. 1400–c. 1580* (New Haven: Yale University Press, 1992), pp. 183–6.

[41] See also Carole Rawcliffe, 'Curing Bodies and Healing Souls: Pilgrimage and the Sick in Medieval East Anglia', *Pilgrimage: The English Experience from Becket to Bunyan*, ed. Colin Morris and Peter Roberts (Cambridge: Cambridge University Press, 2002), pp. 108–40, p.121.

perceived as powerful supernatural figures who could intervene in the lives of humans both positively and negatively, according to the reverence they were shown. Their written hagiographies formed just one part of the means of glorifying them and seeking their intervention, and worked alongside relics, visual imagery and many forms of performance to praise and invoke the saint.

Appendix: Typical components of a saint's cult in the medieval period[42]

Physical Presence of the saint
Body/tomb in recognised location
Corporeal and/or secondary relics: may be widely distributed in reliquaries[43]

Celebration of the Saint
Formal/informal recognition of sanctity: canonisation or popular acclamation
Hagiography
Visual images of the saint and their legend
Marking of feast day in calendars
Commemoration in liturgy, sermons, hymns etc.
Processions, especially on the saint's feast day
Songs, dances and drama

Actions performed by devotees
Visits to local shrine, may include touching/kissing relics or images
Pilgrimage over longer distance, often with veneration of relics or images
Offerings at shrine or image, both as requests for intercession and in thanks
Recording of miracles attributed to the saint
Acquisition of pilgrim badges and other imagery depicting the saint
Commissioning of images for display on altar or other location linked to the saint
Request for burial near the saint's shrine or altar
Rituals intended to obtain the favour of the saint, often focused on the tomb or shrine
Establishment of guilds and other organisations in the name of the saint
Specific mention of saint in wills, especially commendation of the soul to their charge
Naming of children in honour of the saint

Commemoration in religious buildings
Dedication of churches and chapels

---

[42] This list is based on that given by Graham Jones in his introduction to *Saints of Europe: Studies Towards a Survey of Cults and Culture*, ed. Jones (Donington: Tyas, 2003), p. 11. I am grateful to Dr Jones for his advice on the reformulation of this material.
[43] Secondary, or contact, relics are objects which are venerated because they have been in contact with the corporeal relics of the saint. An example would be a cloth which had been used to wrap the bones of the saint, or one which has absorbed some oil excreted by the bones.

Dedication of altars, lights
Presence of visual imagery of the saint

Commemoration in the wider community
Toponyms relating to the saint, such as towns, hills, woods and holy wells[44]
Folklore, especially pseudo-historical stories about the saint
Fairs held on or near the saint's feast day

---

[44] Toponyms, or placenames, may reflect a tradition of a saint visiting a particular place, or making a posthumous miraculous appearance there, but the dedication of a nearby church or chapel may also lead to the (re)naming of physical features in the landscape.

2

Corpora and Manuscripts, Authors and Audiences

MARY BETH LONG

Manuscripts and Miscellanies

The inscription in the back of the British Library's mid-fifteenth-century manuscript Harley 4012 reads, 'Thys ys the boke of dame anne wyngefeld of harlyng', a statement that both suggests its writer's pride in ownership of so beautiful a book and reminds any borrower of the book that it must be returned, and to whom. The manuscript is certainly visually impressive. For a book that belonged in a woman's private collection, it is a sizeable volume, approximately 25 by 16cm, despite having been cropped on all sides. The manuscript's enlarged initials are often elaborate: gilt letters shimmer with quill work, and plum, blue and green designs swoop over both top and left margins, sometimes with tiny gilded fruits painted in the foliage. Other initials are less intricate, but no less impressive: gilt accents two tones of blue, with decorative inkwork surrounding the text up to the binding. A few initials, less extravagant, are simply painted blue and red and left ungilded. Highlighted sentences may be enlarged or rubricated red; new paragraphs are marked with red or blue. The varying hands may indicate that several different scribes helped copy the book, but the colours and style of the artwork are consistent throughout, suggesting it was a planned compilation. The vellum pages seem spacious: the lines never look cramped, and margins appear generous, perhaps partly because they are free of marginalia. The book was clearly well planned – and expensive. It is easy to imagine the mixture of pride and anxiety suggested by the inscription upon the author's loan of the book to another reader. We might even read into the inscription an awareness that the borrower keeps multiple books, perhaps borrowed from multiple literate friends, and needs help to keep straight which one goes back to Anne Wyngefeld of Harlyng.[1]

This article derives in part from my Ph.D. thesis, 'Reading Female Sanctity: English Legendaries of Women, c. 1200–1650', University of Massachusetts Amherst, 2004. I thank Ann Higgins and Sarah Salih for their generous and helpful advice on early drafts.

[1] For more on this manuscript and its owner, see Anne Dutton, 'Piety, Politics and Persona: London, British Library MS Harley 4012 and Anne Harling', *Prestige, Authority and Power in Late Medieval Manuscripts and Texts*, ed. Felicity Riddy (York: York Medieval Press, 2000), pp. 133–46; Jacqueline Jenkins, 'St Katherine and Laywomen's Piety: The Middle English Prose Life in London, British Library, Harley MS 4012', *St Katherine of Alexandria: Texts and Contexts in Late Medieval Europe*, ed. Jenkins and Katherine J. Lewis (Turnhout: Brepols, 2003), pp. 153–70.

There are no such identifying marks on another British Library manuscript, Arundel 168, a contemporary of Harley 4012.[2] It is even larger than Harley 4012, approximately 32 by 22cm, but it is not nearly as colourful or as well designed. The manuscript appears to have been executed in haste and with an eye toward completing it cheaply rather than achieving legibility: its pages are crowded, with two columns of text heavy on abbreviations and very narrow margins. Vellum pages are mixed with somewhat thick (cheaper) paper ones. The writing is not especially neat; often the lines are crooked and crammed together, and the letters are stylistically inconsistent and often illegible. The scribe uses little, if any, punctuation. Lines do not extend completely to the right margin, and occasional large gaps in the text suggest that the scribe's blocking of pages (still visible on some folios) was not careful enough to ensure a pleasing layout. The manuscript's only decorations are the inkwork on letters A–F of an alphabet poem on the first page; the letters G–Z are not even drawn in. While Harley 4012's inscription hints at the presence of a proud owner and a community of readers, Arundel 168's lack of one, together with its unfinished initials and lack of legibility, raises the question of whether its owner read it much at all, much less lent it out.[3]

At first glance, these two books appear to have different agendas: one is clearly meant to please the eye as well as the intellect, while the other seems to function only as a medium to hold as many texts as possible, without regard to eyestrain. When we look at the texts contained in the two manuscripts, however, it seems fair to infer that they served similar purposes, or at least that their readerships shared similar interests. Among other non-hagiographical texts, each of the manuscripts contains three complete saints' lives. Harley 4012 contains the prose lives of saints Katherine of Alexandria, Margaret, and Anne, as well as a fragment of the life of St Patrick. Arundel 168's *vitae* are William Paris's verse life of Christine, a verse life of Dorothy, and John Capgrave's *vita* of Katherine of Alexandria.[4] Arundel 168 also contains a fragment of John Lydgate's *Life of Our Lady*, along with prayers to the Virgin Mary, Dorothy and Katherine. These two mid-fifteenth-century manuscripts are different enough in appearance and execution for this similarity in content to demand attention, especially because both include the life of the popular Katherine of Alexandria, along with at least one other virgin martyr's life.[5]

---

[2] Richard Beadle lists Arundel 168 as being copied by a Norfolk scribe in 'Prolegomena to a Literary Geography of Later Medieval Norfolk', *Regionalism in Late Medieval Manuscripts and Texts*, ed. Felicity Riddy (Cambridge: Brewer, 1991), pp. 89–108, p. 104.

[3] Ann Higgins points out to me that Arundel 168 may have been copied for personal use by the scribe, hence the lack of attention to aesthetics and design. Such a scribe might have been a pious reader who could not afford to pay for professional transcription of her favorite *vitae*, or a professional scribe who merely wanted to have a working copy of the texts handy.

[4] The *vitae* of Christine and Katherine are the most legible texts of Arundel 168. In contrast, the script of the life of Dorothy is messy, with obvious changes of ink, crowded lines, and more corrective insertions, crossings-out, and abbreviations than might be expected; it seems to have been completed either in a great hurry or by an inexperienced scribe.

[5] See A. S. G. Edwards, 'Fifteenth Century English Collections of Women Saints' Lives', *The Yearbook of English Studies* 33.1 (2003), pp. 131–41 for codicological descriptions of other collections of female saints' lives.

It is difficult for us to conceive what these textual parallels might have meant to a fifteenth-century reader, who would have taken the appearances of the books at least as seriously as their contents. Just as the individuality of each manuscript 'implies a unique material act of production potentially localizable in time and space', so does it suggest a unique reading experience: each manuscript's particular layout, order of texts, and material construction provides for its reader a distinctive literary encounter.[6] To ignore the physical context in which hagiographical texts are found – pictures, page material and thickness, and ink colour, as well as the content of accompanying texts and marginalia – is to miss a vital piece of the interpretative experience medieval readers would have of the individual *vitae*. Hagiographical books in particular are important as physical entities because people tended to think of them as being holy objects. As Alain Boureau writes:

> The dual nature, theological and magical, of the hagiographical book made it a sacred object that one could manipulate. Like a cult object, it could be possessed in common and be endowed with sacred power, but like devotional materials, it was an individual continuation of cultic activities and the mark of a religious practice. It took its place among medals, pious images, and pilgrimage tokens. It signalled, recalled, evoked a vow or a past or ongoing practice. When it was read, leafed through, or put on display it became a spiritual guide, along with breviaries, missals, and books of hours.[7]

Manuscripts can also offer clues about who their readers may have been, although determining medieval ownership of saints' narratives is an inexact science. Inscriptions and dedications are as close as manuscript evidence gets to being definitive, and marginalia by the scribe or the reader can be telling. Even when such textual indicators are absent, however, the manuscript as a physical entity reveals much about its readership. A book's construction can provide basic information about its production: physical details such as the script, the style of miniatures and other artwork, and, later in the period, watermarks on paper, often suggest the region (if not the exact site) of its origin and by extension its original readership. Sometimes we can make guesses about readership by the size of a manuscript: the smaller the book, the more likely it was to be owned by an individual (often, in cases of legendaries, a woman) and read privately; larger books tended to stay on monastic and conventual library tables for reading or reference. The ornateness of a book is also revealing: the size as well as the quality of the decorations suggest whether it was meant for public or private reading and can offer hints about the degree to which the owner could spend money on books.

The intertextual context of the saints' lives in a given manuscript can offer clues about the book's ownership or intended audience. For example, the juxta-

---

[6] Ralph Hanna, *Pursuing History: Middle English Manuscripts and Their Texts* (Stanford: Stanford University Press, 1996), p. 7.

[7] Alain Boureau, 'Franciscan Piety and Voracity: Uses and Strategies in the Hagiographic Pamphlet', *The Culture of Print: Power and the Uses of Print in Early Modern Europe*, ed. Roger Chartier, trans. Lydia G. Cochrane (Princeton: Princeton University Press, 1989), pp. 15–58, p. 19.

position of dozens of saints' narratives with two chapters on the theory and practice of penance, such as we find in *Speculum Sacerdotale*, would seem entirely logical and practical to a parish priest, who would need regular access to both types of texts. A manuscript on a topic as specific as continental beguine spirituality, such as Douce 114, would likely be owned by a woman of some material means: she was almost certain to have already had a psalter, perhaps a few more conventional saints' lives and probably at least one or two other devotional texts before acquiring something like Douce 114. (Harley 4012 and Arundel 168, with their less idiosyncratic, more popular texts, were each somewhat more likely to be the central or even sole manuscript in a fifteenth-century reader's possession.[8]) The variety of texts in a manuscript such as BL Cotton Titus A xxvi, best known for its French and Italian song lyrics and musical notation, whose lives of saints Alexis, Mary Magdalene, Katherine, the Seven Sleepers and Julian are accompanied by naval sketches (such as a windmill, several elaborate ships, an unidentifiable pulley contraption, and a bridge) and texts on topics ranging from botany to physiognomy to the siege of Rhodes, implies a broadly educated, probably male, reader with interests both secular and sacred.[9] More generally, we can look at the language of a text for guesses at ownership; books known to be owned by laypersons (especially women) are almost always in the vernacular, and prior to the mid fourteenth century those including Anglo-Norman or Latin texts generally indicate readers of higher social status and education than readers of English texts.[10] As we will see later in this discussion, however, even priests were likely to own vernacular texts later in the period, when most of the legendaries we now know of were written.

Of course, any one book might have had a plurality of readers at a given time. While this is particularly true of conventually owned books, it was also the case for books of laypersons who had wide networks of social and familial connections with other readers. Further, because books containing saints' lives were often passed from one generation or family or even social class to another, the

---

[8] That a book contains the lives of only female saints is in itself not necessarily a guarantee of female ownership: for example, a priest who regularly confessed women would have found an all-female legendary especially handy – although in the case of the two manuscripts described above, we know that Anne Harling Wingfield owned Harley 4012, and there is no immediately obvious reason to doubt A. S. G. Edwards' attribution of Arundel 168 to a 'lay female pious audience'. Edwards refers to the manuscript in passing as an 'anthology of female saints' lives' in mentioning Capgrave's and Lydgate's pieces; A. S. G. Edwards, 'The Transmission and Audience of Osbern Bokenham's *Legendys of Hooly Wummen*', *Late-Medieval Religious Texts and Their Transmission*, ed. A. J. Minnis (Cambridge: Brewer, 1994), pp. 157–67, p. 164.

[9] The male reader on whom I speculate here – who may simply be Robert Cotton himself – would have read Cotton Titus A xxvi sometime during or after the seventeenth century, when the various MSS of the volume were bound together. Additionally, all known owners of the volume's several parts, including the saints' lives, were (lay)men. See for examples Daniel Leech-Wilkinson, 'Il libro di appunti di un suonatore di tromba del quindicesimo secolo (London, British Library, Cotton Titus A.xxvi)', *Rivista italiana di Musicologia* 16 (1981), pp. 16–39, and Richard Leighton Green, *The Early English Carols* (Oxford: Clarendon Press, 1977), p. 297.

[10] But see Ann Higgins's forthcoming Ph.D. thesis ('The Mark of the Hero: Language, Identity and the Middle English Romance', University of Massachusetts Amherst), particularly her chapter on the Auchinleck MS, for the argument that texts addressed to readers (rather than hearers) indicate status more clearly than the particular vernacular used.

viewpoints and values of their readers changed several times over the course of the manuscript's public life as an actively read book. For example, Osbern Bokenham wrote individual saints' lives for various lay patronesses in the mid fifteenth century, but the compiler of Arundel 327, a collection of Bokenham's *vitae*, put the manuscript together for his sister's convent. Like their readership, the production and reproduction of many legendaries evolved over the course of their public lives; many of the larger collections (such as the *South English Legendary* and the *Northern Homily Cycle*) therefore appear in redactions that suit the purposes of later scribes better than did the original compilations. As might be expected, most manuscripts of legendaries were written by the religious enclosed, often for their own or for other religious houses. Some copies of saints' narratives may have been produced at the command of a superior, as the compiler of Douce 114 claims of its origins, or at the request of the recipient, as we can infer of the Katherine Group. Of the major legendaries described below, all have monastic or conventual associations in either their production or ownership, and nearly half are conceived both by and for religious. An increase in demand for lay devotional reading, such as saints' lives, devotional texts and spiritual instruction, occurred after the Fourth Lateran Council's mandate of lay education in 1215; this meant more legendaries were produced – and by extension that more people became hagiographers. That laypersons such as Geoffrey Chaucer began writing saints' lives in the later Middle Ages is evidence of the genre's growing popularity. Andrew Taylor points out that by the fifteenth century, laypeople were commissioning their household chaplains to write lives that other members of the household were recruited to copy, as was the case with BL MS Harley 2253, a substantial miscellany of saints' lives, religious and secular lyrics and other items.[11] Later in the period, scriptoria may have kept booklets of certain popular saints' lives 'in stock' so that readers could purchase them for inclusion in a collection or miscellany.[12] Thus by the time print culture established itself in England, legendaries were readily available for purchase as collections or, often, by the piece.[13]

It is difficult to tease out the relationship between the literature of sanctity and the larger phenomenon of the medieval cult of saints (e.g. the building of large churches for pilgrims, the reading of the *vitae* in church, the commissioning of the narratives), but the fact that people invoked the saints in prayer makes

---

11 Andrew Taylor, 'Manual to Miscellany: Stages in the Commercial Copying of Vernacular Literature in England', *The Yearbook of English Studies* 33.1 (2003), pp. 1–17.
12 This theory, based on the existence of manuscripts of booklets produced by different scribes, was put forth by Pamela R. Robinson in her Ph.D. thesis, 'A Study of Some Aspects of the Transmission of English Verse Texts in Late Medieval Manuscripts', Oxford University, 1972. See also her 'The "Booklet": A Self-contained Unit in Composite Manuscripts', *Codicologica* 3 (1980), pp. 46–69. However, A. I. Doyle and M. B. Parkes have argued that book dealers may have outsourced text copying to various scribes on demand rather than maintaining a stock of booklets; see their 'The Production of Copies of the *Canterbury Tales* and the *Confessio Amantis* in the Early Fifteenth Century', *Medieval Scribes, Manuscripts and Libraries: Essays Presented to N. R. Ker*, ed. Parkes and Andrew G. Watson (London: Scolar Press, 1978), pp. 163–210.
13 See A. S. G. Edwards and Carol M. Meale, 'The Marketing of Printed Books in Late Medieval England', *The Library* 6th ser., 15 (1993), pp. 95–124.

clear that hagiography's uses go beyond those of other literature. Originally, the existence of a *vita* had served as the first official step toward establishing its subject's sanctity, but most of the lives extant from the medieval period are old narratives recast for a new audience. The uses to which saints' narratives and legendaries were put varied widely, depending on the form they took. Several collections, such as the *Northern Homily Cycle*, John Mirk's *Festial* and *Speculum Sacerdotale*, were intended for priests to use as references in sermon preparations; they offer nearly exhaustive coverage of the saints. Others, such as Douce 114, are more idiosyncratic and were meant for a specific class of lay devotional readers. The life of Margaret of Antioch often appears in medical texts because it was read to labouring women, of whom Margaret is patron saint. Prayers to her were even carved into apples for pregnant women to eat.[14] Lay people often mentioned legendaries in their wills, indicating that they valued their texts of saints' lives – and, possibly, considered their mention in wills a kind of shorthand to indicate the extent of their piety. Carol Meale points out that religious books could serve a 'commemorative function' for their owners: bequeathing a devotional text increased the likelihood they would be remembered and prayed for.[15] More than any other kind of text, saints and their narratives were embedded in people's daily lives, so that books containing them took on more functions than those containing other types of literature.

We can guess best at readership and uses of these texts when we examine the contents of the manuscripts in which they appear. Some manuscripts were clearly planned as pious or hagiographical books; others contain a saint's life seemingly by happenstance.[16] Individual saints' lives appear in schoolbooks, in medical texts and in apparently random bindings of personal papers. For example, BL MS Sloane 2569 includes texts copied from the fifteenth to the late seventeenth centuries, in Greek, Latin, English and French, in a variety of hands on several different types of page materials, including advertisements. Tucked among 'a x-mass carole, made on x-mass day', an instruction slip for a cure-all powder, and 'the Sad Story of Adam & Eve, And their being turn'd out of Paradice & Concerning ye Fruites of Paradice' is a neatly-copied *vita* of Mary the Egyptian. A fifteenth-century manuscript, BL Royal 17 C xvii, includes Latin lessons (with four columns of someone's Latin-English crib), seven penitential Psalms, and prayers with the *vitae* of Mary Magdalene, Anthony and Jerome. The lives of Katherine of Alexandria and Dominic appear in the thirteenth- or early-fourteenth-century BL Cotton Titus D xviii, which also includes an alphabet crib of several languages.[17] Oxford's Corpus Christi College MS 237

---

[14] For more details on the use of Margaret's narrative see Jocelyn Wogan-Browne, 'The Apple's Message: Some Post-Conquest Hagiographic Accounts of Textual Transmission', *Late Medieval Religious Texts and Their Transmission: Essays in Honour of A. I. Doyle*, ed. A. J. Minnis (Cambridge: Brewer, 1994), pp. 39–53.

[15] Carol M. Meale, ' "... alle the bokes that I haue of latyn, englisch, and frensch": Laywomen and Their Books in Late Medieval England', *Women and Literature in Britain, 1150–1500*, ed. Meale (Cambridge: Cambridge University Press, 1993), pp. 128–58, p. 130.

[16] Hanna has demonstrated that the composition of some volumes was always in flux in his study of booklets in his *Pursuing History*.

[17] Among those alphabets listed in the Latin table of contents of the crib are Hebrew, Greek (in several versions), Chaldean/ Syrian, Gothic, Persian, Runic, Nortmannorum and English.

contains Athanasius's *Katherine*, the *Margaret* from the *South English Legendary*, Lydgate's *Life of Our Lady*, a list of towns, churches and administrative details, *The Maner of Offering in the Cyte of London*, medical recipes, dream visions and many poems. The Auchinleck Manuscript (National Library of Scotland MS Advocates 19.2.1) contains the lives of Pope Gregory, Margaret, Katherine, Mary Magdalene, Adam and Eve, and the Virgin Mary, along with a handful of prayers and other spiritual texts, but it contains many more romances and secular texts. Lives that appear in miscellanies such as these are likely to have been specially requested by their readers: we might assume they represent favourite narratives or saints. As scriptoria developed, and later in the period as print commerce began to take hold, readers could buy fascicles or booklets of individual lives. Few of these have survived, probably in part because they were heavily used. An exception is the *Lyf of Saint Katherin of Senis*, translated from extracts of Raymond of Capua's *vita*, which appears in BL MS Royal 17 D v and was printed by Wynkyn de Worde in 1493.

Vitae also appear in collections alongside religious devotional literature such as that by Richard Rolle and Walter Hilton. Particularly in the fourteenth and fifteenth centuries, devotional miscellanies began to circulate and, occasionally, to be modified or copied. The largest and most impressive of these is the Vernon manuscript (Oxford Bodleian, MS. Eng. poet. a.1), a massive volume thought to have been commissioned by a Cistercian convent towards the end of the fourteenth century.[18] It contains dozens of devotional texts, including Aelred of Rievaulx's *De Institutione Inclusarum*, *Ancrene Wisse*, *Piers Plowman*, Walter Hilton's *Scale of Perfection*, several of Richard Rolle's letters, *Cursor Mundi*, *The Prick of Conscience* and translations of *Estorie del Euangelie* and Edmund Rich of Abingdon's *Speculum Ecclesie*; its legendaries include copies of the *Northern Homily Cycle*, the *South English Legendary*, the first English translations of nine lives from the *Legenda aurea* and several 'Miracles of Our Lady'. Smaller collections such as Harley 4012 and Arundel 168 may be more representative of those that were privately owned: Harley 4012 contains, along with its *vitae*, devotional texts such as 'The Clensynge of Man's Sowle', a selection from the *Poor Caitiff*, 'Mirror of Sins', the vision of 'Sent Moll' (or Mechtild) and the 'Mirror of St Edmund'. Arundel 168 contains texts such as Benedict Burgh's translation of Cato's 'Morals' and Lydgate's 'Dietary' (later printed by William Caxton as 'Medicina Stomachi'). Custom-made legendaries allowed affordable access to a reader's favorite *vitae*; stories could be chosen or shortened to fit the number of pages a patron could afford. For example, Cambridge University Library Addit. MS 4122 contains verse lives of Margaret and Dorothy and a treatise on the Virgin Mary's marriage in its 162 folios, and BL MS Cotton Faustina B iii binds the lives of Edith and Ætheldreda with unrelated materials.[19]

---

[18] For more on the Vernon MS, see *Studies in the Vernon Manuscript*, ed. Derek Pearsall (Cambridge: Brewer, 1990) and *The Vernon Manuscript: A Facsimile of Bodleian Library, Oxford, MS. Eng. Poet.a.1*, with an introduction by A. I. Doyle (Cambridge: Brewer, 1987).
[19] Edwards, 'Fifteenth', pp. 131–3, 137.

Legendaries

The conventional critical understanding of 'legendary' as a freestanding collection of several saints' lives tends to exclude pious miscellanies such as those mentioned above, perhaps because such manuscripts are thought to be one-offs, privately commissioned and remaining under the owner's control rather than texts that were widely circulated and copied.[20] Although readers sometimes commissioned or requested copies of individual saints' lives, and *vitae* were occasionally composed by or for a saint's community, they were more often written or translated as part of a freestanding legendary. One effect of the Fourth Lateran Council's mandate of lay education was a renewed interest in the creation and distribution of portable legendaries and other religious texts. (The *Golden Legend*, for example, is thought to have been the second-most-read book of the medieval period.[21]) This interest fuelled something of a literary celebrity for freestanding legendaries and their compilers: as a collection began to circulate in a region, it would be copied in whole or in part into other manuscripts and added to private and communal libraries. Texts included in such legendaries were considerably more stable than those that included other non-hagiographical texts. As Manfred Görlach has suggested, *vitae* that were part of legendaries tended to be revised less than those that circulated individually.[22] In the company of several other *vitae*, these lives were not as susceptible to individual readers' control: the context lent the whole collection authority as an entity.

The collections described below are the best-known of those that were written, copied and circulated during the medieval period. In discussing the corpora and manuscripts of medieval saints' lives, we should keep in mind that the extant manuscripts are probably not representative of all those that were kept and read during the medieval period. Those that were truly dog-eared with use are simply less likely to have survived. Compilers of the *Index of Middle English Verse* note that 'it is really long books that are found in the largest number of manuscripts', and we can reasonably surmise that 'really long books' were not those read most frequently.[23] With the possible exception of the Katherine Group, the largest collections do tend to be the ones to which scholars

---

[20] But see Margaret Connolly, 'Books for the "helpe of every persoone þat þenkiþ to be saved": Six Devotional Anthologies from Fifteenth-Century London', *The Yearbook of English Studies* 33.1 (2003), pp. 170–81, which discusses the idea that devotional miscellanies did circulate for copying.

[21] Among myriad sources of this speculation, see 'Introduction', *Golden Legend*, trans. Ryan, vol. 1, p. xiii.

[22] Manfred Görlach, 'Middle English Legends, 1220–1530', *Hagiographies: Histoire internationale de la littérature hagiographique latine et vernaculaire en Occident, des Origines à 1550*, vol. 1, ed. Guy Philippart (Turnhout: Brepols, 1994), pp. 429–85, p. 439.

[23] Kate Harris, 'Patrons, Buyers and Owners: The Evidence for Ownership and the Rôle of Book Owners in the Book Production and the Book Trade', *Book Production and Publishing in Britain 1375–1475*, ed. Jeremy Griffiths and Derek Pearsall (Cambridge: Cambridge University Press, 1989), pp. 163–99, p. 166.

have paid the most attention; because so much information is readily available about these legendaries, I have provided relatively less information about them.

The history of Middle English legendaries begins in about 1200 with the three saints' lives of what is known as the 'Katherine Group'. Found together in two extant manuscripts, Bodley 34 and BL MS Royal 17 A xxvii, the lives form the collection Wogan-Browne has called a 'specialized miniature female legendary'.[24] In both manuscripts, the prose *passio* of Katherine of Alexandria appears first, followed by those of Margaret of Antioch and Juliana. Because of the emphases and style of the lives – for example, they include several oral 'tags' addressing listeners – they are thought to have been originally used as sermons. E. J. Dobson dates the *passio* of Katherine to between 1200 and 1210 and the narratives of Margaret and Juliana to between 1190 and the first years of the thirteenth century.[25] Such dating suggests one reason this collection continues to intrigue scholars: at the apex of Anglo-Norman language and culture, the appearance of the all-English Katherine Group demonstrates that some readers still wanted their saints' lives in English – or that, having heard them preached in English, they wanted to read them in the same form.

The first owners of the Katherine Group texts were probably a group of anchoresses during the early thirteenth century; Dobson suggests the sisters for whom the original legendary was intended may have been named for Katherine, Margaret and Juliana, hence the choice of these three saints in their legendary.[26] There is little doubt that anchoresses spent considerable time reading, and that the anchoritic life's emphasis on devotional reading created a demand for anchoritic literature. An anchoritic audience would not seem one that would influence other readers. Bricked into a small room, committed to silence for much of the day, and supported by alms in exchange for prayers, the anchoress considered herself dead to the living world, and was expected to have as little social interaction as possible. Yet scholars have long known that the Katherine Group texts eventually reached several different audiences, including nuns, laywomen, men and royalty, and have suggested they were intended to do so – which implies the anchoritic readers must have shared their reading with someone.[27] *Ancrene Wisse*, an early-thirteenth-century guide for anchoritic living, accompanies several extant copies of some of the Katherine Group lives (although not Bodley 34 or Royal 17 A xxvii) and is our best source of information about the Katherine Group audience and its reading habits. Scholars are in consensus that the Katherine Group hagiographer was likely *not* the author of *Ancrene Wisse*, but the texts are associated by manuscripts, language, and tradition. To judge from what *Ancrene Wisse* reveals about anchoritic life, the original audience of the Katherine Group was probably more diverse than it initially

---

24 Jocelyn Wogan-Browne, *Saints' Lives and Women's Literary Culture c. 1150–1300: Virginity and its Authorizations* (Oxford: Oxford University Press, 2001), p. 6.
25 E. J. Dobson, *The Origins of* Ancrene Wisse (Oxford: Oxford University Press, 1976), p. 166.
26 Dobson, *Origins of* Ancrene Wisse, p. 138.
27 For example, Bella Millett notes that Henry VIII saved a Latin copy of *Ancrene Wisse* for his own library at the Dissolution; Ancrene Wisse, *the Katherine Group, and the Wooing Group,* Annotated Bibliographies of Old and Middle English Literature (Cambridge: Brewer, 1996), p. 53.

seems. In addition to the aural social interaction with passers-by that her cell window provided, the anchoress could have had two or more servants and occasional important out-of-town visitors, along with regular visits from her confessor. She probably maintained contact with other anchoresses, as suggested by the reference in *Ancrene Wisse* to the use of messengers for that purpose. In some cases, an anchoress would share living quarters with one or two other anchoresses.[28] Further, we know from the examples of Hildegard of Bingen and Christina of Markyate that young women considering anchoritism themselves often lodged temporarily with established anchoresses for an apprenticeship of sorts, and anchoresses sometimes taught girls how to read.[29] Given so many potential readers and listeners of the Katherine Group texts, it does not seem so unusual that they were frequently recopied throughout the thirteenth century, and the possibility that they influenced writers of other *vitae* does not seem so far-fetched.

Larger legendaries intended as reference books have had a better-documented impact on insular literary history, as more physical copies remain extant and more hagiographers have borrowed heavily from them. In particular, the *South English Legendary*, *Northern Homily Cycle* and English translations of the *Golden Legend* influenced compilers of legendaries and devotional miscellanies and authors of individual lives. It may not be possible to overstate here the influence of Jacobus de Voragine's *Legenda aurea*, or the *Golden Legend*, on English hagiographers after the thirteenth century. Jacobus's style is that of a scholar: he cites over 130 sources, opens most *vitae* with an etymology of the saint's name and often closes them with an evaluation of the story's authenticity. Completed around 1260, his encyclopaedic Latin collection of over 160 lives was organised according to the church calendar; about one thousand copies are extant. The *Legenda aurea* was perhaps the most widely distributed text of the Middle Ages and was certainly consulted, copied, translated and mimicked more than any other legendary before or since.[30] Even when they did not translate directly from Jacobus's Latin text, English compilers of legendaries such as the *South English Legendary* and *Northern Homily Collection* would have found escaping its influence difficult.

Almost an exact contemporary of Jacobus's text, the *South English Legendary* was composed anonymously toward the end of the thirteenth century (1270–80), in the Worcester/ Gloucester area. Its short, lively narratives in septenary couplets feature simplified plots that are heavy on action and drama and light on the long prayers and theological arguments that appear in the Katherine

---

[28] Elizabeth Robertson mentions a group of rooms including separate bedrooms and 'servants' quarters that housed two maids and a kitchen boy'; *Early English Devotional Prose and the Female Audience* (Knoxville: University of Tennessee Press, 1990), p. 27.

[29] *Jutta and Hildegard: The Biographical Sources*, trans. Anna Silvas (University Park: Pennsylvania State University Press, 1999); *The Life of Christina of Markyate*, trans. C. H. Talbot (Toronto: University of Toronto Press, 2000). The possibility that the Katherine Group texts may have been used to teach reading to children is not one I have seen mentioned in the scholarly literature, although warnings against teaching in *Ancrene Wisse* suggest the practice was common enough to warrant mention.

[30] 'Introduction', *Golden Legend*, trans. Ryan, vol. 1, pp. xiii–xiv.

Group – editorial choices that would have helped ensure the collection's appeal among laypersons. As Görlach has noted, the *SEL* also lacks the potentially confusing etymologies, expressed scepticisms and multiple narrative variations that are characteristic of its contemporary, the *Legenda aurea*.[31] Not surprisingly, this accessibility helped *SEL* achieved the widest popularity of any Middle English verse legendary; it more or less became *the* standard legendary in the south-west and Midlands until at least the end of the fourteenth century.

The *SEL* began as roughly one hundred saints' lives and festival readings arranged in heptameter couplets in the order of the ecclesiastical year. Its purpose was to provide homiletic material for all the feast days. That material was drawn from a variety of sources. The *SEL*'s origin is not definitively known; it may even have been a group effort at the Gloucester monastery. By 1290, the collection underwent a significant revision (also anonymous) that was strongly influenced by the *Legenda aurea*.[32] After 1330, the *SEL* continued to be copied, but was no longer revised; it was by then considered a stable entity.[33] The oldest known manuscript of *SEL* is Bodley's Laud 108, which has been dated 1280–90; the legendary also appears in the late-fourteenth-century Vernon Manuscript and in many fifteenth-century manuscripts, including Bodleian MS Tanner 17, BL MS Stowe 949 and MS Bodley 779.

At the beginning of the fourteenth century, a legendary of 20,000 lines in octosyllabic couplets was produced anonymously, possibly near Durham. The prologue of what is now known as the *Northern Homily Cycle* explains that the text provides 'Sunday gospels' in the vernacular in order to supplement sermons preached to laypersons.[34] Each homily begins with a few verses of the day's gospel passage from the Vulgate, followed by a rhyming tetrameter couplet translation, an often-allegorical interpretation of the passage, and, usually, an exemplum, narrative or tale to illustrate the gospel passage's lesson. It is in these illustrations that the saints' lives are found. Scholars have not yet determined *NHC*'s source legendary; it is possible that the *Legenda aurea* was used.

The *NHC* did not reach as wide an audience as the *SEL*, but it circulated sufficiently in the north to merit two later expansions by different poets, one a translation into the Midlands dialect toward the middle of the century (which appears in the Vernon Manuscript and in the related Simeon Manuscript, BL MS Add. 22283) and another in the northern dialect around 1400. This latter expansion may have been compiled at York, one of the few northern locations that allowed access to a large library. It is extant in two manuscripts, BL Harley 4196 and BL Cotton Tiberius E vii. These have 28–32 homilies that include legends to be read on saints' feast days, also in octosyllabic couplets, that appear as the *Tractatus de Legenda Sanctorum*. Along with the Sunday and daily homilies on the

---

[31] Görlach, 'Middle English Legends'.
[32] Görlach has suggested that even the original took *Legenda aurea* into account in the second half of the collection; 'Middle English Legends', p. 450.
[33] Görlach, 'Middle English Legends', p. 456.
[34] For a modern edition, see *The Northern Homily Cycle: The Expanded Version in MSS Harley 4196 and Cotton Tiberius E vii*, ed. Saara Nevanlinna, 3 vols, Mémoires de la Société Néophilologique (Helsinki, 1972–84).

gospels, Harley 4196, which dates to 1400, also includes the *Prick of Conscience* (which also appears in the Vernon and Simeon MSS) and the *Gospel of Nicodemus*. Tiberius E vii, somewhat older than Harley 4196, has in addition to the homilies: *Speculum Vitae*, a verse dialogue between Mary and St Bernard on the Passion that also appears in Vernon, a verse paraphrase of Richard Rolle's *Form of Living* (a prose version of which is in the Vernon and Simeon MSS), *The Gast of Gy* (also appearing in both Vernon and Simeon) and a poem about the Magi's visit to Bethlehem.

The collection known as the *Scottish Legendary*, compiled in c. 1400, consists of fifty legends and a prologue in rhyming couplets, and survives in a single manuscript, Cambridge University Library Gg 2 6.[35] It is ultimately derived from the *Legenda aurea*, supplemented from various other Latin sources, and it confidently addresses an audience of some literary knowledge, citing Cato's maxims and, surprisingly, *The Romance of the Rose* in its opening lines.[36] Its Scottishness is evident in its Lowland dialect rather than its choice of saints, of which only Andrew and Machor (or Mochumma), a monk and disciple of the better known Columba, are of local interest. The collection begins with the legends of the apostles and evangelists and ends with ten legends of virgins, with a mixed selection in the middle: it thus appears to have been assembled from other, smaller legendaries specialising in the subcategories of sanctity, a type of collection of which there are no extant examples. The author of (at least) the prologue and the legends of the apostles describes himself as a priest of 'gret eld and febilnes', which may be a literary topos and does not enable him to be identified.[37]

Considering the importance of the *Legenda aurea*, it seems odd that, although a few of its lives appear in the Vernon Manuscript in mid-fourteenth-century East Midlands dialect, the first complete English-language translation of it, the *Gilte Legende*, did not appear until 1438. Translated from Jean de Vignay's *Légende dorée* rather than directly from the Latin, the *Gilte Legende* sometimes sacrifices clarity in favour of fidelity to the French. The translator is unknown, although the 178-item work has occasionally been attributed to Bokenham.[38] The first revision of this 1438 translation added a number of English and British saints' *vitae* reworked from *SEL*: Edmund the Bishop, Bridget, Edmund the King, Frideswide, Edward the Martyr, Alphege, Austin, Oswald the Bishop, Dunstan, Aldhelm, Swithun, Kenelm, Chad, Cuthbert, Brendan and Leger.[39] In addition, the reviser reworked or added several non-English legends. The *Golden Legend* is extant in whole or in part in Middle English in eight

---

[35] W. M. Metcalfe, 'Introduction', *Legends of the Saints in the Scottish Dialect of the Fourteenth Century*, ed. Metcalfe, 3 vols (Edinburgh: Blackwood, 1896), vol. 1, pp. vii–xxxiii.
[36] *Legends of the Saints in the Scottish Dialect*, ed. Metcalfe, vol. 1, lines 1–5.
[37] *Legends of the Saints in the Scottish Dialect*, ed. Metcalfe, vol. 1, line 35.
[38] A recent occurrence of this speculative attribution occurs in Sheila Delany, *Impolitic Bodies: Poetry, Saints, and Society in Fifteenth-Century England: The Work of Osbern Bokenham* (New York: Oxford University Press, 1998), p. 23. However, Görlach has recently agreed with Richard Hamer's attribution of the translation to an unidentified monk at St Albans; 'Middle English Legends', p. 475.
[39] For an edition of these English lives, see *Supplementary Lives*.

mid-fifteenth-century manuscripts. In 1483, Caxton also translated the *Golden Legend* from the French, using the *Legenda aurea* and *Gilte Legende* as additional sources; his 880–folio *Golden Legend* had several printings at Westminster. Like *SEL*, the *Golden Legend* emphasises the saints' autonomy rather than God's power, focusing on action, rather than didactic aspects such as prayers and theological arguments. According to the prologue in BL MS Harley 4755, the *Gilte Legende* was meant 'to excite and stere symple-lettrid men and women to encrese in virtue bi the offten redinge and hiringe of this boke'. The legendary now known as the *Golden Legend* generally *was* popular among lay readers. We know, for example, that Cecily Neville left a copy of the *Legenda aurea* (along with a life of Saint Catherine of Siena and 'a boke of Saint Matilde') to her granddaughter Brigitte; Anne Neville Stafford owned an English *Legenda sanctorum*.[40] Because not every '*Golden Legend*' or '*Legenda aurea*' mentioned in a will indicates that of Jacobus or his translators – for example, the colophon of MS Lambeth Palace 223 refers to itself as *Legenda aurea*, although we know it as *SEL* – it is not always clear just who owned or read Jacobus's text during the medieval period. Judging from the number of extant copies, however, it is safe to assume that English translations of the *Gilte Legende* were widely distributed and read.

The compilers of two other near-comprehensive collections, Mirk's *Festial* and *Speculum Sacerdotale*, envisioned audiences of parish priests rather than lay readers. Their prose legendaries therefore share common content in fifty-four of approximately seventy chapters, and both begin in Advent, the start of the church year. Despite the fact that they were intended for a pastoral rather than lay audience, both are heavily dependent on the *Golden Legend*, borrowing its content and sometimes its presentation style. Seeking to articulate differences between the two collections, Theodor Erbe finds *Festial* somewhat more 'narrative' and *Speculum Sacerdotale* more 'expository' in approach.[41] For many scholars, however, the two are similar enough to merit discussion in tandem.

Mirk's *Festial* has been called 'an early English best-seller' with good reason: there are at least twenty-six manuscripts extant, fourteen of them complete; Caxton printed eighteen editions between 1483 and 1532; a manuscript was made of the printed text; it was translated into Welsh and eventually made its way to Ireland.[42] The *Festial*, which was completed by 1415, is a homily-and-legend cycle of sixty-nine items, some of which include multiple narratives.[43] Mirk, an Austin canon and Prior of Lilleshall (Shropshire), intended

---

[40] For both these see Karen K. Jambeck, 'Patterns of Women's Literary Patronage: England, 1200–c. 1475', *The Cultural Patronage of Medieval Women*, ed. June Hall McCash (Athens GA: University of Georgia Press, 1996), pp. 228–65, pp. 240–1.
[41] Edward H. Weatherly, 'Introduction', *Speculum Sacerdotale*, ed. Weatherly, EETS os 200 (London: Oxford University Press, 1936), pp. xv–xliv, p. xli.
[42] *Mirk's Festial: A Collection of Homilies*, ed. Theodor Erbe, EETS es 96 (London: Kegan Paul, Trench, Trübner & Co, 1905); Thomas E. Marston, 'An Early English Bestseller', *Yale University Library Gazette* 46.1 (1971), pp. 86–8. A. I. Doyle has more recently referred to *Festial* as an 'early printed best-seller'; 'Publication by Members of the Religious Orders', *Book Production and Publishing in Britain, 1375–1475*, ed. Jeremy Griffiths and Derek Pearsall (Cambridge: Cambridge University Press, 1989), pp. 109–23, p. 115.
[43] Martyn Wakelin, 'The Manuscripts of John Mirk's Festial', *Leeds Studies in English* s.s. 1 (1967), pp. 93–118.

the *Festial* to be a reference book for parish priests, especially those who did not have physical access to Latin sermon collections or could not read Latin with ease. He used the *Golden Legend* loosely as a source, but abridged and altered its text considerably, adding his own commentary. He borrowed as well from *Gesta Romanorum*, the popular collection of Latin tales, ultimately creating a collection of very short, overtly didactic homilies. A. I. Doyle has suggested that Mirk meant to offer his *Festial* as an alternative to the Lollard homily cycles.[44]

About three-quarters of the extant manuscripts are organised by the order of the church calendar and are prefaced with a prayer and introduction to the texts. These manuscripts are thought to be copies of Mirk's original. The remaining one-quarter or so, thought to be copies of a redaction, separate homilies for Sundays and major feasts from those of saints' days, which are grouped together in the collection's second half. These 'redaction copies' are generally much shorter than the others, excluding the prayer, textual prologue and several of the feast days and saints' homilies. *Festial* occurs in several manuscripts as a stand-alone text (e.g. BL MS Harley 2247, Bodleian MS Royal 18 B xxv), but also appears bound in medieval books alongside copies of Mirk's *Instructions for Parish Priests* (BL Cotton Claudius A ii, Bodleian Douce 60); with other lives and/or homilies (BL Harley 2250, BL Royal 18 B xxiii, and Bodleian Hatton 96, which last conflates Mirk's narratives with another set of otherwise unknown festial sermons); and with poetry (Cambridge University Library Ee 2 15) or romance (Cambridge University Library Ff 2 38). However, in most manuscripts, *Festial* is bound with other texts that priests would find useful, such as services, prayers and explanations of ritual and doctrine.

Like *Festial*, *Speculum Sacerdotale* was written in the early fifteenth century (c. 1425) and includes some seventy homiletic addresses on the seasons of the ecclesiastical year and feast days of the apostles, the major saints and several English saints. Most of the chapters include saints' *vitae*, with a dozen legends of the Virgin Mary and several gospel narratives of the life of Christ. In the section devoted to Lent, two chapters focus on the theory behind penance and how it should be practised. The author uses the *Legenda aurea* extensively – as the collection's modern editor Edward Weatherly notes, it is a source in forty-seven chapters, sometimes almost verbatim – but not exclusively: the Bible and several Church fathers' writings also feature prominently as sources.[45] The style of *SS* emphasises the miraculous, presenting narratives of miracles somewhat less critically than do other collections. Like *Festial*, *SS*'s primary purpose was to provide an abundance of expository and narrative materials from which non-Latinate priests could choose for their sermons. Unlike that of *Festial*, *SS*'s authorship is unknown, and it exists only in one manuscript, BL Additional MS 36791. Corrections for skipped lines and similar mistakes in the manuscript indicate that this is a copy and not autograph. Weatherly describes the language as 'standard' with southern West Midland influence; the extant copy's scribe may have standardised it somewhat from the original dialect.

---

[44] Doyle, 'Publication', p. 115.
[45] *Speculum Sacerdotale*, ed. Weatherly, p. xxx.

In the Low Countries, from the late twelfth century, women who derisively referred to as 'beguines' took informal, temporary vows, kept their own property, and took on work to support themselves, participating fully in the social, commercial and religious aspects of urban life. Bodleian Douce 114, a fifteenth-century manuscript, stands as the chief medieval English-language witness to the beguine movement, containing translations of the lives of the beguines Elizabeth of Spalbeek, Christina *mirabilis* and Mary of Oignies, along with a letter supporting the canonisation of Catherine of Siena and a translation of Henry Suso's *Orologium Sapientiae*.[46] How the beguine *vitae* first travelled to England from their Belgian origins is somewhat mysterious. We know from manuscripts in England and Belgium that a literary exchange of sorts occurred between the two regions; several English women saints' lives appear in Bibliothèque Royale MS 7917, and a psalter known to belong to beguines is in the British Library.[47] Douce 114 is the only known Middle English manuscript that contains the beguine lives of Elizabeth, Christina and Mary, but several Latin versions of the *vitae* are extant in England, suggesting that the narratives were fairly accessible to clergy.[48]

Douce 114 measures approximately 16cm by 14cm and is about 2.5cm thick; it is a comfortable size to hold in one's hands for reading. The manuscript's narratives were probably first described or told to a woman by the confessor who eventually translated them for her. Given contemporary caution about heresy, this woman's chaplain doubtless felt that her reading about the controversial beguines would not lead her astray, so we might assume that she had a fairly sophisticated understanding of spiritual practice and could in the chaplain's view handle beguine *vitae* freshly translated from the linguistic, geographical and temporal unfamiliar. The last folio (150v) bears the inscription: 'Iste liber est domus belle valle ordinis carthusiensis in comitatu Notyngham.' The 'shorte Apologetik of þis englisshe compyloure' that appears after the letter on Catherine of Siena describes the translator as 'vnsuynge of englyshe, as vmwhile soþeren, oþere-while norþen'.[49]

---

[46] The beguine *vitae* and the letter on Catherine of Siena (fols 1–88) are in a separate quire from Suso's treatise (fol. 89ff). The Suso treatise is also in a different hand from that of the *vitae* and letter, although the inkwork seems to have been completed by the same artist. Both the letter and the treatise appear widely in medieval texts and in print during the fifteenth century. The letter on Catherine of Siena appears along with the beguine lives in Carl Horstmann, 'Prosalegenden: Die legenden des ms. Douce 114', *Anglia* 8 (1885), pp. 103–96, pp. 119–34. Horstmann also edited Suso's treatise, in 'Orologium Sapientiae or The Seven Poyntes of Trewe Wisdom, Aus MS. Douce 114', *Anglia* 10 (1887), pp. 323–89. Page numbers given here correspond with Horstmann's editions.

[47] The psalter is Add. MS 21114. See Judith H. Oliver, *Gothic Manuscript Illumination in the Diocese of Liège (c. 1250–c. 1330)*, 2 vols (Leuven: Uitgeverij Peeters, 1988), vol. 1, pp. 110ff.

[48] Patricia Deery Kurtz, 'Mary of Oignies, Christine the Marvelous, and Medieval Heresy', *Mystics Quarterly* 14.4 (1988), pp. 186–96; Jennifer Brown also notes that all three lives exist in Oxford St John's College MS 182, from the Carthusian house at Witham; 'A Critical Edition of and Commentary on MS Douce 114: The Middle English Vitae of Elizabeth of Spalbeek, Christina Mirabilis, and Marie D'Oignies', CUNY Ph.D. thesis, 2003. The order of the lives is reversed in 182 from that in Douce 114. Kurtz posits that both 182 and Douce 114 were owned by Carthusian houses and dates Douce 114 to the second quarter of the fifteenth century; p. 187.

[49] Horstmann, 'Prosalegenden', p. 195.

In 1495, Wynkyn de Worde printed Caxton's translation of *Vitas Patrum*, a fifth-century collection of saints' lives, exempla, moral treatises and related miscellanea that is usually attributed to Jerome. Caxton's translation was based on the French printed text *La Vie des Anciens Pères Hermits* (Lyon, 1486–87). At 347 folios in double columns, *VP* is the second longest work Caxton ever translated, second only to *GL*. In the first of five parts, we find 132 *vitae*, mostly of desert fathers but including Mary of Egypt and Pelagia. Some of the texts that appear in *VP* had first been translated into Middle English in the Vernon collection; others appear in *NHC*, Mannyng's *Handlyng Synne* (1303), BL MS Harley 2253 and the *Scottish Legendary*. However, Caxton was the first to produce the entire text in Middle English.

The *Kalendre of the New Legende of Englande* is an abridgement and translation of a Latin legendary of 168 saints associated with the British Isles. Printed by Pynson in 1516 along with Walter Hilton's 'Epistle on the Mixed Life', *Kalendre* was the last English legendary published before the Reformation. Its source text, the *Nova Legenda Angliae*, formerly attributed to Capgrave, was based on a fourteenth-century collection of Latin legends assembled by John of Tynemouth from various sources.[50] The *Kalendre* does not in fact function as a calendar, for the saints are arranged in alphabetical order, with the exception of Edgar and Bridget of Sweden, who are added on at the end. The inclusion of Bridget has led to the plausible suggestion that the legendary was compiled and printed for the Brigittine nunnery of Syon.[51] The *Kalendre* and its predecessors are undoubtedly attempts to compile a national legendary, presumably, as Görlach suggests, as an alternative or complement to the international selections of the *Golden Legend* and *South English Legendary*.[52] Though the *Kalendre*'s selection comprises saints from all parts of the British Isles, its address is to the English: its preface explains that while the Scots, Irish and Welsh celebrate their national saints, 'in this realme of Englonde . . . fewe people in comparison of the multitude haue deuoycon to any of these blessyd sayntes that haue laboured for the welthe of the people in this realme in tyme paste'.[53]

Authors and Single Lives

The distinction between legendaries and single lives is an imperfect one: some of the authors discussed below wrote several *vitae*, and it is not always clear to what extent they and their readers considered them as part of a single project. Many extant single *vitae* were or are anonymous; several have been mentioned

---

[50] Manfred Görlach, 'Introduction', *Kalendre*, pp. 7–46.
[51] See Rebecca Krug, *Reading Families: Women's Literate Practices in Late Medieval England* (Ithaca NY: Cornell University Press, 2002), pp. 153–206 on the literary culture of Syon Abbey.
[52] Görlach, 'Introduction', p. 31. For a later attempt at a national legendary that also draws heavily from Tynemouth, see Ralph Buckland, *The Lives of Women Saints of our Contrie of England, also Some Other Liues of Holie Women Written by Some of the Auncient Fathers*, ed. Carl Horstmann, EETS os 86 (London: Trübner, 1886).
[53] *Kalendre*, p. 45.

above, and lists can be found in other sources.[54] Some saints, such as Alexis, of whom there are four independent anonymous verse lives, seem to have been considered especially suitable for literary treatment; some anonymous texts, such as the alliterative poem which narrates a miracle of *St Erkenwald*, are of considerable literary interest. [55] However, I focus here on the *Lives* of known authors, of which the social and cultural contexts are easier to trace. Those translators and authors of saints' lives whose names we know with certainty – Chaucer, Paris, Symon Wynter, Bokenham, Lydgate, Capgrave, Caxton, Henry Bradshaw and Alexander Barclay – are not an especially homogeneous group. To take the most obvious distinction, Wynter, Bokenham, Lydgate, Capgrave, Bradshaw and Barclay were religious; Chaucer, Paris and Caxton were of the laity. Their hagiographical production also varies widely: we have only one *vita* each from Chaucer and Paris, while Lydgate wrote several thousand lines' worth of saints' lives. Paris's *Life of St Christine* is his only known work, but most of the other authors are celebrated for the texts they wrote in addition to the saints' lives and legendaries described below.

This is especially true of Chaucer, whose name does not often come into discussions of medieval hagiography. Chaucer did not write a religious legendary, but the success of his *Legend of Good Women* depends partly on his audience's familiarity with that genre, and it has been argued that the *Canterbury Tales* contains up to four stories of hagiographical type.[56] Chaucer's *Retraction* suggests that he wrote several lives of women saints, but the only one to have surfaced thus far is that of St Cecilia, 434 lines of rhyme royal found in the *Canterbury Tales* as the *Second Nun's Tale*. Chaucer's life of Cecilia was already written before he began the *Canterbury Tales*. Mary Giffin has suggested that he wrote it for the Benedictines of Norwich to honour Adam Easton's being named Cardinal Priest of Sancta Cecilia in Trastevere in the early 1380s.[57] The scholarly consensus has been that Chaucer simply inserted this life as the *Second Nun's Tale* without revising it or, as Sherry L. Reames suggests, considering all the implications of its inclusion.[58] It appears with his *Prioress's Tale*, but apart from the other tales and alongside Lydgate's *Life of Our Lady*, in BL Harley 2382 and Manchester, Chetham's Library MS 6709.[59] Because his version of St Cecilia

---

54 D'Evelyn and Foster; anonymous independent prose lives are described in Oliver Pickering, 'Saints' Lives', *A Companion to Middle English Prose*, ed. A. S. G. Edwards (Cambridge: Brewer, 2004), pp. 249–70.
55 D'Evelyn and Foster; *St Erkenwald*, ed. Clifford Peterson (Philadelphia: University of Pennsylvania Press, 1977).
56 These are the *Man of Law's Tale*, the *Clerk's Tale*, the *Prioress's Tale*, and the *Second Nun's Tale*, as discussed especially by Laura Braswell, 'Chaucer and the Art of Hagiography', *Chaucer in the Eighties*, ed. Julian N. Wasserman and Robert J. Blanch (Syracuse: Syracuse University Press, 1986), pp. 209–21. I concur with the general scholarly consensus that only the *Second Nun's Tale* is a true saint's life.
57 Mary Giffin, 'Hir House the Chirche of Seinte Cecilie Highte', *Studies on Chaucer and His Audience* (Québec: Éditions 'L'Éclair', 1956).
58 Sherry L. Reames, 'The Cecilia Legend as Chaucer Inherited It and Retold It: The Disappearance of an Augustinian Ideal', *Speculum* 55.1 (1980), pp. 38–57. See also her 'The Second Nun's Prologue and Tale', *Sources and Analogues of* The Canterbury Tales, vol. 1, ed. Robert M. Correale and Mary Hamel (Woodbridge: Brewer, 2002).
59 This inclusion perhaps suggests that the compiler of those manuscripts considered the *Prioress's Tale* a saint's life as well. Edwards has noted that Lydgate's *St Margaret* also

follows his sources so closely, its presence in the *Tales* has stimulated more discussion about his work as a translator than as a hagiographer. Reames argues that Chaucer used two different sources, noting that lines 85–344 correspond closely to the *Legenda aurea*, while the remainder of the narrative is based on what she calls a 'Franciscan abridgement', a somewhat skimpy version of Cecilia's *passio* found in manuscripts such as Bibliothèque Nationale MS latin 3278 and Arsenal MS 596.[60] Chaucer's translation of these texts has been called the best saint's life in Middle English, but this praise is with respect to his verse, not to any significant changes to the plot.

The second named hagiographer of the Middle English period wrote a lively verse *Life of St Christine* which, though it was its author's only work, has been compared in quality to Chaucer's hagiography. William Paris was an accidental hagiographer, a squire who in 1397 found himself imprisoned with his master, the Earl of Warwick, and turned to writing the *Life*, we can surmise, both to relieve the tedium and to appeal to a saint who had herself spent a significant period of her legend imprisoned.[61] As Karen Winstead remarks, the writer's identification with the saint is unusually strong, and the final prayer addresses their situation directly:

> Seint Cristyn, helpe thorought thi prayere
> That we may fare the better for thee,
> That hath ben longe in prison here.[62]

John Lydgate (c. 1370–1450), a Benedictine monk of Bury St Edmunds (Suffolk), was famous in his own lifetime for his didactic and devotional writing. The most prolific of any English poet of his day, Lydgate had a formidable output: 145,000 lines of verse and some prose texts total around 200 works. His Latinate style is notoriously verbose, with his *vitae* sometimes reaching a length of 6000 lines. He wrote several lives of saints, including those of Alban and Amphibal, Austin, Edmund and Fremund, George, Giles, Margaret, and Petronilla.[63] Lydgate's most popular text, the *Life of Our Lady*, was written around 1415–16 and survives (often as the central text) in 50 manuscripts.[64]

---

appears in the Chetham's manuscript, and two of the complete *Canterbury Tales* manuscripts also contain Lydgate's *St Margaret*; 'Fifteenth', p. 141.

[60] Sherry L. Reames, 'The Sources of Chaucer's "Second Nun's Tale" ', *Modern Philology* 76 (1978), pp. 111–35. For a correction of one argument put forth in 'Sources' and details of the Franciscan abridgement, see her 'A Recent Discovery concerning the Sources of Chaucer's "Second Nun's Tale" ', *Modern Philology* 87.4 (1990), pp. 337–61.

[61] William Paris, 'Life of St Christine', *Middle English Legends of Women Saints*, ed. Sherry L. Reames with Martha G. Blalock and Wendy R. Larson (Kalamazoo: Medieval Institute Publications, 2003).

[62] *Chaste Passions: Medieval English Virgin Martyr Legends*, ed. and trans. Karen A. Winstead (Ithaca NY: Cornell University Press, 2000), p. 61; Paris, 'Life of St Christine', lines 497–9.

[63] *The Life of Saint Alban and Saint Amphibal*, ed. J. E. van der Westhuizen (Leiden: Brill, 1974); 'St Austin at Compton', pp. 193–206; 'St George', pp. 145–54; 'St Gyle', pp. 161–73; 'St Margaret', pp. 173–92; 'St Petronilla', pp. 154–9, *The Minor Poems of John Lydgate*, Part 1, ed. Henry N. McCracken EETS es 107 (London: Oxford University Press, 1911); 'St Edmund and St Fremund', *Altenglische Legenden Neue Folge*, ed. Carl Horstmann (Heibronn: Henningen, 1881), pp. 376–445.

[64] *A Critical Edition of John Lydgate's* Life of Our Lady, ed. Joseph A. Lauritis, Ralph A. Klinefelter and Vernon F. Gallagher (Pittsburgh: Duquesne University Press, 1961).

Lydgate draws heavily from the *Legenda aurea*, and as Winstead has argued, he 'restore[s] . . . the long passages of prayer and teaching' that Jacobus omitted.[65]

Bury St Edmunds was an imposing institution in Suffolk, with its hand in economic, legal, ecclesiastical and civic matters. As a monk there, Lydgate had considerable interaction with the outside community and was relatively free to travel for business or personal reasons (e.g., he earned a degree at Oxford and spent time in London and Paris). His patronage reflects his and his monastery's relations with the wealthy lay public, with several of his works commissioned by upper- and middle-class readers. Lydgate dedicated his *Legend of St Margaret* to 'My lady March' (Anne Stafford, countess of March, d. 1432), and an *Invocation to St Anne* and possibly an accompanying *vita* to 'my Ladie Anne Countasse of Stafford' (Anne Woodstock, countess of Stafford, d. 1438).[66] He wrote the Lives of Ss. Edmund and Fremund as a gift from the monastery to King Henry VI, who visited Bury for several months during his childhood reign; it is extant in the presentation copy Harley 2278, with 120 illuminations.[67] The abbot of St Albans, John Whethamstede, commissioned Lydgate's *Lives of Ss Alban and Amphibal* in 1439; these, too, were heavily illustrated. Winstead argues that fifteenth-century authors such as Lydgate and Bokenham were writing for genteel readers who had a 'preoccupation with good breeding', but that Lydgate wanted his life of Margaret to 'transcend class lines' and circulate among all women.[68]

Approximately ten miles south-east of Bury, a contemporary of Lydgate's composed a number of women saints' lives in verse. Bokenham, an Austin friar at Clare Priory in Suffolk, mentions fellow hagiographers Chaucer, Capgrave and Lydgate in prologues to the lives that are extant in BL Arundel 327. Bokenham was fairly prolific, composing in addition to the saints' lives *Mappula Angliae*, a geographical text meant to supplement his lives of saints, and possibly up to three other works: a translation of Claudianus's fifth-century *De Consulatu Stilichonis*, a genealogy of Joan of Acre known as the Clare Roll or 'Dialogue at the Grave', and, according to some scholars, the *Gilte Legende*.[69] Bokenham's lives are often based on the *Legenda aurea*; even those from other sources retain the name etymologies that are characteristic of this source.

Bokenham wrote the *vitae* of Arundel 327 between 1443 and 1447 for several gentle and aristocratic readers and patrons, largely (but not exclusively) female. But according to the endnote on folio 193 of the manuscript, it was the dedicatee

---

[65] Karen A. Winstead, *Virgin Martyrs: Legends of Sainthood in Late Medieval England* (Ithaca NY: Cornell University Press, 1997), p. 124.
[66] Jambeck, 'Patterns of Women's Literary Patronage', p. 247.
[67] Doyle points out that dedications in copies of this *vita* made after Lydgate's death were changed to Edward IV; 'Publication', p. 117; see Lydgate, *St Edmund Facsimile*.
[68] Winstead, *Virgin Martyrs*, p. 121.
[69] Speculation on Bokenham's authorship of the *Gilte Legende* derives partially from his mention in *Mappula Angliae* of having written a large legendary; see Delany, *Impolitic Bodies*, p. 23. Alternatively, Serjeantson suggests Arundel 327 may have been part of this legendary, which has otherwise been lost. Edwards notes that the *Gilte Legende* is the only other Middle English legendary to include all of the lives that appear in Arundel 327; 'Transmission and Audience', p. 167.

of the first *vita* of the collection, Thomas Burgh, who actually had the lives copied and compiled into one codex for his sister's convent:

> Translatyd in to englys be a doctor of dyvyni
> te clepyd Osbern Bokenam a suffolke man. frer Austyn of the
> quent of Stokclare, and was dun wrytyn i[n] cane
> bryge by hys sou[n] ffrer Thomas Burgh. The yer of our lord
> a thousand four hu[n]dryth sevy[n] & fourty whose expence dreu
> thretty schyligys & yafe yt on to this holy place of nun[n]ys
> that þei shulde haue mynd on hym & of hys systyr Dame
> Betrice Burgh. Of þe wych soulys ihu haue mercy. Amen.[70]

The endnote reveals a relative wealth of implications about the web of connections among author, compiler and readers and identifies the influences on the manuscript besides the author and patrons of the original texts. The compiler's personal relationship with the author would certainly have been a factor as he organised the manuscript that is today the only surviving copy of Bokenham's saints' lives; it is probably not a coincidence that the life Bokenham wrote for Burgh appears first in the collection. Additionally, Burgh was putting together the manuscript for his sister's convent, perhaps at her request, and would have had in mind the general needs of conventual readers as well as the specific needs of his sister.[71] The production of Arundel 327 thus had influences from multiple sources: in addition to the primary textual contribution of Bokenham and the influence of his patrons, Burgh's relationships with Bokenham and with the conventual readers, particularly his sister, would have affected the arrangement and emphases of the manuscript.

The codex itself tells us a good deal about its own origins, purpose and use. Small enough to be suitable for private reading, the book is approximately 15cm high, 10cm wide, and 3cm (193 folios) thick. It appears to have been designed with care: each margin and line is ruled, and the compiler's instructions to the artists are still intact. The decoration of the manuscript confirms its status as a presentation copy; the similarity of the colours and design to other monastic books suggests its designer wanted this convent book to confirm to monastic standards. The collection is untitled, but the endnote and a table of contents at the end of the manuscript indicate that it is a work meant to stand alone. Burgh's compilation of Bokenham's work contains thirteen lives of women saints: Margaret, Anne, Christine, Ursula and the 11,000 virgins, Faith, Agnes, Dorothy, Mary Magdalene, Katherine, Cecilia, Agatha, Lucy and Elizabeth of Hungary. The book is now known as *Legendys of Hooly Wummen*, a phrase cobbled together from lines in the prologue to Mary Magdalene's *vita* and affixed to the legendary

---

[70] In the second line, 'a suffolke man' appears in a later hand. The spelling in my transcription of the note differs slightly from Serjeantson's; *Legendys*, p. 289.

[71] A. I. Doyle has suggested that the nuns in question were the Franciscans of Aldgate and Denny, situated just north-east of Cambridge; 'Books Connected with the Vere Family and Barking Abbey', *Transactions of the Essex Archaeological Society* n. s. 25.11 (1958), pp. 222–43, p. 236, n. 8.

in Mary Serjeantson's 1938 edition and more recently in Sheila Delany's modern English translation.[72]

Bokenham's *vitae* include far more detail about his patrons than do other texts, often providing information about them in the form of prayers or explanations of his relationships with them. In addition to Thomas Burgh, Bokenham specifically names several of his patrons and readers, most of them wealthy and influential women: Elizabeth de Vere (countess of Oxford, d. 1475), Isabel Bourchier (countess of Eu, sister to Richard duke of York, d. 1484), John and Katherine Denston (d. after 1445), Isabel Hunt, Katherine Howard (d. 1465), Agatha Flegg (d. after 1446). Much of the scholarly interest in Bokenham's readership has focused on these readers who are mentioned by name in the individual lives, rather than on those who would have read his work in the conventual manuscript Arundel 327. Bokenham actively encourages such interest by his claims that these readers were directly responsible for the geneses of the *vitae*.

There is no evidence in the manuscript, however, that Bokenham intended the individual lives to stand as a whole.[73] As I have noted above and as A. S. G. Edwards confirms, Thomas Burgh had the primary role in arranging the legendary. From his codicological examination, Edwards suggests that 'the creation of this manuscript was in some respects a rather piecemeal affair', concluding that Burgh's copyists were working from several booklets of Bokenham's *vitae* rather than a complete legendary.[74] Edwards argues that the booklets (perhaps containing only one life each) probably circulated widely – and independently of one another – before Burgh compiled the legendary.[75] With respect to readership, Burgh's motivation and purpose in compiling the manuscript for a convent were doubtless quite different from Bokenham's in composing the individual lives.

Capgrave (1393–1464), prior of Lynn, Norfolk, and provincial of the Austin friars, wrote a handful of individual saints' lives toward the middle of the fifteenth century, including those of Katherine of Alexandria, Augustine, Norbert and Gilbert of Sempringham, for a wide range of patrons. Doyle has found that most of Capgrave's texts survive only in

---

[72] *A Legend of Holy Women: Osbern Bokenham, Legends of Holy Women*, trans. and ed. Sheila Delany (Notre Dame: University of Notre Dame Press, 1992).

[73] Scholars have often based readings of the legendary on the assumption that Bokenham himself arranged it. For example Delany puts forth an extensive argument that Bokenham's choice and order of texts are meant to follow the model of Chaucer's *Legend of Good Women* (1386), to 'rehabilitate the original' generic form that Chaucer parodies; *Impolitic Bodies*, p. 32. Delany suggests further that the saints are grouped in the legendary according to the physical body parts that are most important to their *vitae*; p. 71. Such an argument may be plausible in light of Burgh's having arranged the legendary, but probably necessitates at least some recasting.

[74] Edwards, 'Transmission and Audience', p. 158.

[75] The miscellany BL Add. 36983, the last folio of which contains the beginning of Bokenham's life of Dorothy, stands as evidence of Edwards' theory. Mary Erler and Winstead concur with Edwards' findings, agreeing that Burgh, not Bokenham, was the compiler. See Mary C. Erler, *Women, Reading, and Piety in Late Medieval England* (Cambridge: Cambridge University Press, 2002), p. 120; Winstead, *Virgin Martyrs*, p. 119. Add. 36983 contains romances, lyrics, a text by Richard Rolle and other devotional texts.

autographs and apographs corrected by himself, with dedications to eminent laypeople (Henry VI, Edward IV, Duke Humphrey, Sir Thomas Tuddenham of Norfolk), churchmen (the archbishop of Canterbury and bishop of Ely), other religious superiors (the Premonstratensian abbot of Wester Dereham, Norfolk and the Master of the Gilbertine order, for his nuns) and an unnamed lady.[76]

Capgrave wrote his prose life of Gilbert c. 1440 for the nuns at Sempringham, who wanted an English version of their founder's life; the autograph is extant in BL MS Add. 36704. His life of St Augustine is dedicated to 'a noble creatur, a gentill woman' who remains unidentified.[77] Capgrave's rhyme royale life of St Katherine, written around 1450, is something of an anomaly among his works.[78] It is not dedicated to anyone, and is extant in a handful of East Anglian manuscripts not showing the author's hand, suggesting its relative success in the area. Doyle suggests its popularity was boosted by the strength of Capgrave's 'Austin brethren' in the region. It appears in four manuscripts, including Arundel 168, and Arundel 396, owned by Katherine Babington, Austin nun and sub-prioress of Campsey in Suffolk.

Symon Wynter, another fifteenth-century writer, may have been either a hagiographical specialist like Bokenham, or one of a group of clerics producing lives of the saints for lay devotees. In the second quarter of the fifteenth century Wynter, a priest of the Bridgettine Abbey of Syon, wrote a prose *Life* of St Jerome, adapted from the *Golden Legend* and other sources, for 'the hyghe princesse Margaret, Duchesse of Clarence', a patron of the abbey.[79] Claire Waters finds such a context especially appropriate, imitating as it does Jerome's own commitment to writing for and in dialogue with pious women.[80] The *Life* is associated with contemporary prose *Lives*, of Katherine of Alexandria, Barbara, Dorothy, a putative Bridget of Sweden and a double *Life* of John the Baptist and John the Evangelist, which are similar in style and structure, and appear to be connected with both Syon Abbey and the Lancastrian court.[81]

Barclay (c. 1484–1552), a scholar, priest and schoolmaster whose career spanned the Reformation, wrote a verse *Life of St George*, based on the Latin life of the Mantuan Baptista Spagnuoli, and printed by Pynson in 1515.[82] If John Bale is to be believed, hagiography formed a significant proportion of his oeuvre, but the lives of Katherine, Margaret and Ætheldreda which Bale attributes to him

---

[76] Doyle, 'Publication', p. 118.
[77] *John Capgrave's Lives of St Augustine, St Gilbert of Sempringham and a Sermon*, ed. J. J. Munro, EETS os 140 (London: Kegan Paul, Trench, Trübner, 1910), p. 1.
[78] John Capgrave, *The Life of St Katharine of Alexandria*, ed. Carl Horstmann, EETS os 100 (London: Kegan Paul, Trench, Trübner, 1893).
[79] Symon Wynter, 'The Life of St Jerome', ed. Claire Waters, *Cultures of Piety: Medieval English Devotional Literature in Translation*, ed. Anne Clark Bartlett and Thomas H. Bestul (Ithaca NY: Cornell University Press, 1999), pp.232–49, p. 232.
[80] Symon Wynter, 'The Life of St Jerome', intr. and trans. Claire Waters, *Cultures of Piety*, ed. Barlett and Bestul, pp. 141–63, pp. 145–6.
[81] Pickering, 'Saints' Lives', pp. 252–3. *Virgins and Scholars: A Fifteenth-Century Compilation of the Lives of John the Baptist, John the Evangelist, Jerome, and Katherine of Alexandria*, ed. Claire M. Waters, is forthcoming.
[82] Alexander Barclay, *The Life of St George*, ed. William Nelson, EETS os 230 (London: Oxford University Press, 1955), pp. ix–x.

have not survived.[83] The *Life* of George, treated as an exemplar of virtue and good conduct, suited Barclay's preference for serious and didactic writing.

We do not know whom Henry Bradshaw had in mind as his original audience when he wrote the *vita* of St Werburge in 1513, the last year of his life.[84] Werburge was the patron saint of Chester and of the Benedictine monastery at which Bradshaw resided from his childhood, so her story would likely find an appreciative local audience. Bradshaw's *vita* is over five thousand rhymed lines long, in seven-line stanzas, and is wide ranging in scope. It includes a history of the city of Chester, a description of Werburge's homeland Mercia and the genealogy of its royal house, and histories of Ermengild and Sexburge, Werburge's mother and grandmother, who were abbesses of Ely. The work has been criticised for its lack of rhythm, although Bradshaw was described in the prologue by a fellow monk as the 'styrpe of eloquence'.

Pynson's 1521 edition of Bradshaw's life of Werburge (BL c.21.c.40) opens with the following on the first folio:

> Here begynnth the holy lyfe and history
> of Saynt Werburge very frutefull
> for all chriten people
> to rede.

This introduction appears above a woodcut of a woman seated at a desk with an angel perched on her shoulder. Because Werburge herself is not portrayed in the text as a reader or scholar, the picture apparently depicts one example of what 'chriten people' reading her *vita* might look like. That the woodcut is of a woman suggests the printer had women in mind as the book's chief audience.

Given the variety of authorship, periods of origin and readership of the present hagiographical corpus, it is striking that the image in Pynson's woodcut is one that would work equally well for the intended readers of the Katherine Group, Douce 114, Burgh's compilation of Bokenham's *vitae*, or – perhaps with a change of gender – any of the legendaries described above. The medieval writers of these texts would naturally consider their hagiography 'very frutefull for all chriten people to rede', and would have probably delighted in envisioning an audience of a solitary reader with divine guidance, be it a pious laywoman exercising private devotions or a priest conducting research for a public sermon. The solitary figure of a twenty-first-century scholar poring over a legendary might also accord with this image of the intended reader, even though the reasons for our own devout attentions to these texts would not have entered medieval hagiographers' imaginations.

---

[83] Barclay, *St George*, p. xxv.
[84] *The Life of Saint Werburge of Chester, by Henry Bradshaw*, ed. Carl Horstmann, EETS os 88 (London: Trübner & Co., 1887). Bradshaw also wrote a *Life of St Radegund*, printed by Pynson in c. 1525: the rare modern edition is by Fred Brittain (1925).

3

Power and Authority

CLAIRE M. WATERS

At first glance, medieval saints' lives seem to have a fairly clear attitude toward power and authority: they value the latter over the former, frequently pitting a saint who has only faith and the ultimate *auctoritas* of God on his or her side against a representative of coercive, worldly power and showing the saint's decisive triumph. Seemingly unprotected against the full onslaught of governmental, parental or purely aggressive power, the saint manages, with God's help in the form of spiritual support, miracles, angelic aid and other unexpected resources, ultimately to beat those powers at their own game. As such victories suggest, however, medieval saints and, even more, medieval hagiographers were actually in a somewhat awkward position with regard to power and authority. On the one hand, saints in their pursuit of moral perfection tended ostentatiously to renounce all earthly goods, including secular power, and to regard them as corrupting. On the other hand, saints are inevitably depicted as exercising considerable spiritual authority, usually even before their deaths, and could invoke the awesome power of God through miracles of punishment, destruction and healing. A good number of them also held earthly power, or influenced those who did.[1] Thus the claim that 'Saints in this life were meek, humble and powerless. After death the situation is reversed' points to a certain ideal of Christian reversal – that the last shall be first, that strength lies in weakness – but hardly represents accurately the hagiographic depiction of saints during their lives.[2] Quite often a saint, while explicitly, indeed ostentatiously, despising the trappings of earthly power, proves able to exploit the implications of that power and even usurp it.

One reason for the complexity of power and authority as they are represented in saints' lives is that the two terms are closely linked, yet potentially in opposition. While they had distinct meanings in medieval political theory, and retain these to some degree in modern usage, their relationship could be represented in

---

I am grateful to Anke Bernau and Fran Dolan for their thoughtful responses to this chapter, and to Anne Salo for her research assistance.

[1] Donald Weinstein and Rudolph M. Bell point out that the majority of saints throughout the Middle Ages were of high social status: *Saints and Society: The Two Worlds of Western Christendom, 1000–1700* (Chicago: University of Chicago Press, 1982), pp. 194–219.

[2] Margaret Hurley, 'Saints' Legends and Romance Again: Secularization of Structure and Motif', *Genre* 8.1 (1975), pp. 60–73, p. 64.

a variety of ways. Thus 'power' might most straightforwardly designate the ability to produce physical actions or effects, while 'authority' refers to the ability to influence actions, effect moral persuasion or inspire belief; medieval political theory tends to associate the former with earthly rulership, the latter with spiritual leadership.[3] But as any survey of scholarship on medieval power and authority will demonstrate, it was equally possible to associate power with sanctity and authority with kingship, and medieval hagiography presents the same overlap. In negotiating between the values of this world and those of the next, saints and their biographers had to reckon with the power of their earthly rulers and readers while asserting the authority of sainthood. While all saints exercised some form of power after their deaths, since the power to intercede with God was a *sine qua non* of sainthood, most of them also exerted influence on earth, and made spiritual authority an instrument by which they affected their world.[4] The ways in which they did so both shed light on Christian attitudes toward power and authority and suggest some of the political and social uses of Middle English hagiography.

For there is also, of course, the matter of context: these lives have something to tell us about power and authority not only within their narratives but with regard to their audiences. '[A]ttempts to define and, inevitably, appropriate the holy underlay medieval attempts to image authority', giving depictions of conflict in saints' lives a natural topicality and making the cultural authority of hagiography a tool that could critique or uphold various kinds of earthly power and authority.[5] This is particularly visible in late-medieval England, where continual upheavals – from the Norman Conquest, to the baronial uprisings of the thirteenth century, through the depositions of Edward II in 1327 and Richard II in 1399 and the ongoing struggles of the Hundred Years War – made political legitimacy a valuable commodity, and stories of the holy dead one well-tried means of attaining, as well as of challenging it.[6] The linguistic diversity of England and the battles over religious literature in the vernacular in this period also mean that lives written in Middle English have a certain political implication in their very form: the writer has chosen to compose in or (more often) translate into the common vernacular rather than the court's language of

---

3   On the origins of medieval political uses of these terms, see Walter Ullmann, *The Growth of Papal Government in the Middle Ages: A Study in the Ideological Relation of Clerical to Lay Power*, 3rd edn (London: Methuen, 1970), pp. 14–31, esp. pp. 20–2.
4   Weinstein and Bell, *Saints and Society*, p. 141.
5   David Aers and Lynn Staley, *The Powers of the Holy: Religion, Politics, and Gender in Late Medieval English Culture* (University Park: Pennsylvania State University Press, 1996), p. 262.
6   The prophetic dream of Edward the Confessor, discussed below, offers one example. See also Shelagh Mitchell, 'Richard II: Kingship and the Cult of Saints', *The Regal Image of Richard II and the Wilton Diptych*, ed. Dillian Gordon, Lisa Monnas and Caroline Elam (London: Harvey Miller, 1997), pp. 115–24, and Jill Frederick, 'The *South English Legendary*: Anglo-Saxon Saints and National Identity', *Literary Appropriations of the Anglo-Saxons from the Thirteenth to the Twentieth Century*, ed. Donald Scragg and Carole Weinberg (Cambridge: Cambridge University Press, 2000), pp. 57–73. Use of the saints to reinforce entrenched power was met by equally strong efforts in the other direction; see for example Carroll Hilles, 'Gender and Politics in Osbern Bokenham's Legendary', *New Medieval Literatures* 4, ed. Wendy Scase, Rita Copeland and David Lawton (Oxford: Oxford University Press, 2001), pp. 189–212, p. 190.

Anglo-Norman or the church's lingua franca, Latin.[7] The political stakes of such a decision became ever more evident in the fifteenth century, when Archbishop Arundel outlawed many kinds of vernacular spiritual literature (though not saints' lives).[8] Even before that, though, Chaucer and other English poets were choosing, for various reasons, to write in their native tongue and make their texts available to an audience that may not have known the higher-status languages. Their decision to do so was no doubt influenced in part by the growth of an audience eager for vernacular religious instruction, and this audience, most of which had considerably less worldly power, and certainly less spiritual authority, than the saints, also inflected the ways in which power and authority came to be represented in hagiography.

The saint's authority derives in part from his or her own holiness but ultimately, of course, relies on his or her relationship and devotion to God, the ultimate source of all holiness. It is also frequently emphasised that any power the saint exercises is God's power: miracles are responses to the saint's intercession, but are of course performed by God. This is important not only from a theological point of view (since it highlights the error of worshipping the saint him- or herself, which would be idolatry) but also from that of the lives' reception. The interactions of power and authority that we see in saints' lives are usually emphatically divorced from any real-world implications: saints are to be admired, not imitated.[9] That this principle had to be stated suggests, of course, that the temptation to imitation was always available. The lives themselves seldom foster such a reading, preferring to centre on God as a way to discourage any attempts on the part of their audiences to adopt the spiritual authority of sanctity by any means other than an earnest effort to live a pious and God-fearing life. The power and authority remain with the saint and, ultimately, with God; rather than being transferred to the audience, they are exercised on its behalf, as the prayers for intercession that end many saints' lives indicate. The saint can be an agent of God's power, but the lay reader is not granted such a role – such, at least, would seem to be the message of most lives that address 'a formal type of power, that is, one that makes overt claims to institutional authority'.[10]

---

[7] Some hagiographers and lives make even more emphatic use of English; see Frederick, 'South English Legendary', pp. 63–4, and, more generally, Nicholas Watson, 'The Politics of Middle English Writing', *The Idea of the Vernacular: An Anthology of Middle English Literary Theory, 1280–1520*, ed. Jocelyn Wogan-Browne, Watson, Andrew Taylor and Ruth Evans (University Park: Pennsylvania State University Press, 1999), pp. 331–52.

[8] On the exemption of saints' lives from the ban, see Nicholas Watson, 'Censorship and Cultural Change in Late-Medieval England: Vernacular Theology, the Oxford Translation Debate, and Arundel's Constitutions of 1409', *Speculum* 70 (1995), pp. 822–64.

[9] Bruce C. Brasington, 'Non imitanda set veneranda: The Dilemma of Sacred Precedent in Twelfth-Century Canon Law', *Viator* 23 (1992), pp. 135–52. Karen A. Winstead notes the increasing tendency in later-medieval lives to make virgin martyrs 'charismatic heroines' and to 'accentuate . . . the differences between the saint and ordinary people' rather than emphasising, as earlier lives do, the martyr's status as one of the faithful; *Virgin Martyrs: Legends of Sainthood in Late Medieval England* (Ithaca NY: Cornell University Press, 1997), p. 65.

[10] Wendy R. Larson, 'Who Is the Master of This Narrative? Maternal Patronage of the Cult of St Margaret', *Gendering the Master Narrative: Women and Power in the Middle Ages*, ed. Mary C.

Certain kinds of *vitae* are particularly focused on such 'formal' power, its assertion and its relationship to authority. These include both lives where the saint is fiercely opposed to the ruling power, such as the lives of the virgin martyrs of the early Church, and those where the saint him- or herself holds a significant degree of earthly power, royal or otherwise. A consideration of the deployment of power and authority in these lives gives a sense of where the outlines, and fault lines, lie. Virgin martyr lives, for example, which show earthly power and spiritual authority in direct conflict, were extremely popular throughout the Middle English period.[11] Their appeal owes much to their beautiful, virtuous and intelligent heroines, but most of the lives gain their dramatic impetus from the heroine's fierce conflict with a man who represents earthly power in its pagan form, and who tries to conquer the virgin and make her conform to his view of the world.

The power disparity between the pagan judge or tormentor (sometimes both at once) and his supposed victim is always very evident to the pagan, who sees himself in a position of complete strength and cannot understand the refusal of the young girl before him to bow to his wishes. A typical interaction appears late in Chaucer's *Second Nun's Tale*, when St Cecilia, after converting considerable numbers of important citizens, is finally dragged before the tyrant Almachius to answer for her deeds. After a little verbal sparring, in which Almachius characterises Cecilia's answers to his questions as 'rude', he asks, pompously but somewhat pathetically, 'Ne takestow noon heede [Have you no regard]/ Of my power?' Cecilia has her reply ready:

> 'Youre myght', quod she, 'ful litel is to dreede,
> For every mortal mannes power nys
> But lyke a bladdre ful of wynd, ywys.
> For with a nedles poynt, whan it is blowe,
> May al the boost of it be leyd ful lowe.'[12]

Both the tone and the insulting simile of the bladder full of wind make it aggressively clear that Cecilia does not, in fact, take any heed whatsoever of Almachius's supposed power, and that she maintains an emphatic distinction between (mere) earthly force and heaven-sent authority. Her reference to 'mortal *mannes* power', moreover, needles Almachius on another point that frequently enrages the pagan authorities in virgin martyr legends: that he is being insulted and disregarded by a mere girl, a fact designed to drive home the power inversion these texts inevitably stage.[13] Earthly power, in this context, almost always means the power to coerce by fear or force; the saint shows the utter impotence of such power in the face of God's much greater, and more generous, ability to

---

Erler and Maryanne Kowaleski (Ithaca NY: Cornell University Press, 2003), pp. 94–104, p. 95.
11 See Winstead, *Virgin Martyrs*.
12 *The Riverside Chaucer*, gen. ed. Larry D. Benson (Boston: Houghton Mifflin, 1987), p. 268, lines 432, 435–41.
13 See Anke Bernau's discussion of the gender dynamics of virgin martyr legends in her contribution to this volume, pp. 116–18 below.

inspire and convert, an ability that spectacularly transfers itself to women preacher saints such as Cecilia.

The life of Cecilia, like that of Katherine of Alexandria, is somewhat unusual among virgin martyr legends in that the threat to the protagonist is primarily spiritual and not physical.[14] While many of the virgin martyrs are threatened with marriage to a pagan or, more commonly, rape, and undergo extensive tortures and dismemberment, these two saints fight their battles almost entirely on intellectual grounds. They are tested first, and at length, by verbal disputation and by the killing of their followers, and only later by the tortures attempted on themselves, which do not for the most part have a sexual aspect. While the saint's gender is always a concern, the tyrants here initially avoid physical coercion or threats against the virgin's apparent bodily vulnerability in favour of an attempt to persuade; in other words, they want very much to win by means of authority, rather than power.[15] The preference is stated explicitly in the *South English Legendary* life of Katherine of Alexandria. When the fifty philosophers who have been called to dispute with her balk at debating with a mere girl, the emperor replies that they shouldn't be over-confident and adds, 'ich wole bet [I would prefer] þat ȝe hire ouercome · mid resouns a somme wise/ Þan we hire mid strenȝþe makede · to do sacrefise.'[16] In the end, of course, the pagan opponent is always forced to fall back on his earthly powers. The saint, backed by God, is far better supplied than her opponent with argument and authority, and so he must exercise his will by means of force – thus, as the emperor implicitly recognises, ceding the moral high ground.

Even in lives intended to focus attention on the power of weakness by emphasising the gap in earthly status between pagan ruler and recalcitrant female Christian, however, hagiographers tended to stack the deck a bit more in favour of their heroines than they claimed. While the pagan tormentors have the power of the state behind them, as well as (often) the authority of the virgin's family and the reluctant support of the public, which usually urges the martyr to give in, they tend to face opponents who are far from unprotected, and not only through their relationship to God. They are nearly always of noble birth; always extraordinarily beautiful; excellent public speakers, when called upon; and exceptionally strong-willed. Even without the trumping support of God and the important and authoritative power conferred by virginity, they have considerable sources of strength.[17]

This is all the more clear if we look at the life of another kind of female saint, Elizabeth of Hungary – notably, a 'modern' saint rather than one from the early Church, and one whose context was thus more recognisable and her actions,

---

[14] Although Cecilia is married, she converts her husband on their wedding night – her entry into what we might call active sainthood – and both remain virgins.

[15] In cases where physical vulnerability is seemingly at issue, the threat never finally materialises; the saint is invariably protected from sexual violation, although she may undergo numerous other kinds of tortures.

[16] *SEL*, p. 536, lines 81–2.

[17] On the complexity of power and authority in virgin martyr lives, see Lynn Staley's discussion of Chaucer's *Second Nun's Tale*, *Powers of the Holy*, pp. 198–213, and Winstead, *Virgin Martyrs*.

potentially, more imitable by audiences of her legend. Although high-born and married to a powerful man, Elizabeth lacks any other source of earthly power (she is not a virgin, not outstandingly learned, and so forth) and never expresses herself outspokenly, instead conveying her holiness through penance, unquestioning obedience and charity.[18] In the account of her life by Osbern Bokenham this happily married wife and mother is able to exercise some earthly influence, as when she urges her husband to go on crusade to the Holy Land. In her relationship with her confessor Conrad, however, whom most *vitae* depict as the primary authority figure in her life, she demonstrates utter meekness in the face of his demands and punishments, even when these take the form of beating her or separating her from her children and friends. Her obedience is given as a token of the same kind of reversal that the lives of the virgin martyrs present, but in a different context: Bokenham emphasises the wonder that she 'þat stood in swyche lyberte' should be 'subiect' to one as poor as Conrad, but mitigates Conrad's low earthly position by pointing out that 'of kunnyng/ And of doctryne ful excellent was he,/ And ful perfyth eke was of good lyuyng'.[19] In a sense, the earthly reversal that afflicts the pagan tormentors of the virgin martyrs is here expressed through the person of the noble Elizabeth, with Conrad taking the role of the socially inferior but spiritually superior exponent of the faith. All this is a far cry from the pointed debates, mass conversions, spectacular rescues and exploding torture devices that characterise many virgin martyr legends, and shows the complexity of power relations in a tradition that values power so ambivalently.

Even so, however, these legends of holy women present a relatively clear dichotomy between spiritual authority and earthly power in which the latter comes off very badly. They simply do so in a way that conveys that, often, even spiritual authority benefits from an admixture of earthly resources. This is not only because of the strength-in-weakness motif or the fact that voluntary renunciation was a compelling display of faith in a period when so many suffered want involuntarily; it also conveys the sense that '[p]ower was dangerous to the spirit but somehow it was close to God'.[20] That closeness and the complex interdependence of earthly and heavenly power hinted at by virgin martyr legends are still more evident in the lives of saintly rulers, a group of significant size in medieval hagiography.

A fourteenth-century *vita* of King Edward the Confessor, one of the most popular of English saints, addresses the conjunction of earthly and heavenly authority combined in its subject with careful emphasis on which role takes precedence. Early in the life, a bishop living in difficult times before Edward's reign has a vision of St Peter, 'and with hym a semely yong man richely arayed in the clothyng of a kyng, whom Seinte Peter did consecrate and anoynte'.[21] The

---

[18] Obedience could, of course, be a way of expressing the different value assigned to different authority figures; that Elizabeth is obedient above all to her confessor rather than her husband conveys the relative devaluation of male secular authority. See the discussion by Bernau, p. 111 below.
[19] Bokenham, *Legendys*, lines 9810, 9813, 9814–16.
[20] Weinstein and Bell, *Saints and Society*, p. 195.
[21] *Supplementary Lives*, p. 5.

future King Edward is thus both legitimated by and shown as subject to the eternal authorisation of heavenly forces. Shortly after this vision, he himself is depicted in the text confessing his entire reliance on God: 'Lo gode Lorde, I haue none helpe but the only'– a frequent observation by or about saints, and one that serves here to emphasise Edward's link to a saintly community rather than his earthly rank, and also his subjection, in spite of his earthly power, to God and the Church.[22] For the clerics who authored much medieval hagiography, this message has a clear earthly benefit; it exalts their social role above those even of monarchs, and asserts their right to jurisdiction over those rulers.

At the same time, of course, a ruler such as Edward still exercised considerable power on earth. A nice instance of the confluence of earthly and heavenly roles comes when, well into his reign, he challenges his powerful but untrustworthy father-in-law Godwin, whom he suspects of having murdered Alred, Edward's brother, and who has in his view 'mysvsid [abused] the kyngis power'.[23] When Godwin claims innocence of the charge of betraying Alred, and asks that the bread he is eating may choke him if it is so, Edward blesses the bread, which duly chokes the 'dogge and traytoure' Godwin.[24] The episode neatly conflates the elimination of a political threat and of a wicked man, showing Edward defending his kingship by means of his holiness. With regard to the common people, Edward invariably takes the role of protector in both his earthly and his saintly personae, performing healing miracles on the bodies of his subjects and on his divided nation, eliminating taxation and supporting the Church, but the threat to his kingship and political control calls forth another side of his sacred power.

In addition to the play of power and authority in the figure of Edward himself, his *vita* – like those of other saintly rulers – is ideally placed to intervene in larger questions. In Edward's case, the opportunity is all the more valuable and important because he is the next to last of the Anglo-Saxon kings, and his life comments on the troubled succession and the Norman Conquest that followed close upon his death. On his deathbed, Edward has a striking vision that he leaves to his subjects as a kind of last will and testament. He sees the trouble that will come upon his realm, in which

> [p]reestis haue offendid, for thaye mynister the holy sacramentis with vnclene þoughtis and pollute hondis . . . and as for princis and gentyls thaye ben founde fals and vntrewe and felowis to feendis and thevys and rubbers of the cuntre which haue no drede to God ne to his wurship. . . . And the prelatis also kepe not rightwysnes.[25]

The emphasis on the failings of religious men as well as secular rulers is a reminder that the authority of the Church was not absolute; a holy king was in an ideal position to keep the potential corruption of the powerful late-medieval Church in check. More striking, though, is the mysterious message that follows,

---

[22] *Supplementary Lives*, p. 6.
[23] *Supplementary Lives*, p. 20.
[24] *Supplementary Lives*, p. 21.
[25] *Supplementary Lives*, pp. 24–5.

in which Edward is told of a 'grene tre' that will be cut from its root but eventually return to it and bring forth remedy, an image that ends the vision.[26] The writer of the life proceeds with an extensive discussion and interpretation of this vision. The 'grene tre' is the realm of England that descended from Alfred to his true successor, Edward. It is cut from its root when the realm is divided and translated to a different line in the persons of Harold Godwinson, followed by William the Conqueror and his son William Rufus, and returns to that root when Henry I 'came into this reame not with mannys strength [i.e. by force] but by very true love of his comyns' and subsequently married Maude, daughter of Edward's niece, uniting the Norman and English lines and instituting a dynasty.[27]

The intrusion of this elaborate political prophecy into Edward's death scene – his last words immediately follow its explication – sufficiently indicates its importance to the writer. It serves a number of functions. First, it critiques both the 'usurper' Harold, son of the despised Godwin, and the conqueror William, while nonetheless allowing for the legitimacy of the current rulership descended from both and lending visionary authority to their line. In the description of 'Harry the furste' and his arrival in England, moreover, it associates royal legitimacy and authority not with earthly power – 'mannys strenght' – but with divine favour on the one hand and, on the other, the will of the people ('very true love of his comyns'). In doing so, it co-opts the powerless as supporters of the powerful, turning the subjugation of the commons into an ability to legitimate their rulers, once again showing the complex interplay of actual and perceived power and the ability of authority to exploit the various means at its disposal.

If the life of Edward works to show how even virtuous earthly power is subject to God, and the lives of the virgin martyrs how vicious earthly power loses all force in the face of divine favour, the life of another English saint shows a still more tangled interaction. This is the story of Thomas Becket, whose complex secular and sacred career – as royal chancellor, unyielding archbishop and, ultimately, martyr – offered tremendous scope for an exploration of secular and sacred power. As archbishop, Becket represented the interests of the earthly Church, and his battles with Henry II, the patron and friend who became his bitter enemy, show starkly the ways in which sacred power had to rely on, as well as oppose, secular lordship. We see this, for example, in the way that each man characterises the struggle between them. Becket's insistence on the Church's earthly rights (centrally, the right to try its clergy in its own courts rather than in royal ones) leads Henry to lament that '3if he grantede sein Thomas · at þulke tyme is wille/ Is poer inis owe lond · nere neuere eft worþ a wille' [If at that time he granted St Thomas his will, his [Henry's] power in his own land would no longer be worth anything].[28] Henry very clearly recognises, that is, the central problem: while Becket claims only to want to 'saue oure ri3te', that is, the Church's privileges, such a move effectively gives him power of veto

---

[26] *Supplementary Lives*, p. 25.
[27] *Supplementary Lives*, p. 26.
[28] SEL, p. 641, lines 946–7.

over any political move Henry might make. Becket makes the same argument from the other direction, of course, saying that he is only protecting the Church as its leader ought to do. For Henry to yield is, in a worldly sense, impossible, and the life, though it does not favour Henry, makes his perspective clear enough to show that the conflict is not one of purely evil secular power against heroic saintly virtue.

If the life of Edward shows how closely the discourses of hagiography could become intertwined with those of royal legitimacy, however, the life of Thomas Becket shows how hagiography could equally be exploited in the struggle for earthly power between the Church and the emerging state. Becket himself is presented as an adept at exploiting the motifs of both secular and sacred power to his own advantage, becoming in a sense a hagiographer within the story. He repeatedly, for instance, makes use of the imagery of knighthood, which both recalls his earthly debts to Henry and claims their supersession by a Christian ideal of knighthood almost as old as Christianity.[29] As Becket's conflict with Henry deepens and his own earthly supporters begin to desert him, he fills their place with a new kind of knight:

> Sein Thomas nom [gathered] bi þe wey · pouere men inowe
> And ladde wiþ him to is in · and to þe mete hom sette
> And seruede hom is owe body · and mete inou ham vette
>   [served them himself and gave them sufficient food]
> Þis beoþ he sede Godes kniȝtes · oþer men me habbeþ forsake.[30]

Becket here masterfully turns weakness into power. By replacing wealthy, influential secular supporters with poor men as 'Godes kniȝtes' he recalls the lessons that the last shall be first and gives a kind of moral resonance to his own resistance against earthly greatness; by serving those poor men with 'is owe body' he pointedly recalls Christ's service to his followers, invoking the ultimate moral authority for his actions and participating in a tradition of charity that gave Christianity – and Christian sainthood – much of its moral force. Becket further exploits the language and imagery of knighthood when he goes, with only the 'armure' of his vestments, 'for Holy Churche to fiȝte' against Henry: the language simultaneously conveys the weakness of vestments as earthly armour and the spiritual authority with which they (literally) invest him.[31]

The power that Becket upholds and asserts – the power of God and the authority and autonomy of the Church that derived from it – is rejected by the king during the lifetime of the saint. It is only with Becket's martyrdom, the ultimate expression of his earthly weakness and the king's earthly power, that the archbishop's spiritual authority fully comes into its own. A ruler may claim, like Almachius in Chaucer's life of St Cecilia, that he has 'bothe power and auctoritee/ To maken folk to dyen or to lyven', and may feel that this, indeed,

---

[29] The idea of saints as knights of Christ is one with a long history that the prologue to one version of the *South English Legendary*, the so-called 'Banna Sanctorum', itself reinforces; *SEL*, pp. 1–3, lines 15–68.
[30] *SEL*, p. 639, lines 884–9.
[31] *SEL*, p. 641, lines 953–63.

marks the height of his control over the world around him.³² But as Cecilia immediately points out, the tyrant's power is only the power to kill, and even that is granted by God, while the power to give life, as many miracles attest, belongs to God alone. This is one, though only one, of the ways in which martyrdom turns apparent weakness into an almost irresistible strength.³³ By igniting, in effect, the latent power of the saint's spiritual authority, it fatally undermines the force of the saint's death as an expression of control.³⁴ In the case of Thomas Becket, his martyrdom does indeed give victory. Henry's first act is to disavow the deed, and the penance set him by the pope's envoys for having incited it includes renouncing the statutes that were the basis of his dispute with the archbishop.³⁵ Becket's death leads directly to Henry's submission to the Church. But the crowning moment of reversal comes when Henry, doing elaborate penance at Becket's tomb years after his death, is rescued by the saint from the political enemies who now beset him.³⁶ The secular and the ecclesiastical ruler are once more in alignment, as Becket's death has made him Henry's most powerful friend.

If martyrdom is a tightly wound expression of the power reversals inherent in the conflict between saints and their earthly oppressors, however, it also points to a deeper question of control. In the early Church, the period that created and bequeathed the concept of martyrdom and its idealised hagiographical form to the Middle Ages, martyrdom was seen as a triumph over both death and death-dealing power.³⁷ It became an expression of Christian identity and resistance, and as such was embraced and even trained for; careful physical and psychological preparation for torture made asceticism into a tool by which the early martyrs could turn the tables on their tormentors.³⁸ 'The more the torturers inflicted pain, the more they provided the martyrs with the means to their goal of salvation': here we see precisely the mechanism whereby earthly weakness becomes spiritual strength.³⁹ Moreover, asceticism shows that triumph over another begins with command over the self, with the Christian's rule over his or her own body. While martyrdom is the limit case of this self-rule, the phenomenon is visible throughout saints' lives. A saint represents a particularisation and

---

32 *Riverside Chaucer*, p. 268, lines 471–2.
33 It also, of course, assimilates the martyr to Christ, a point repeatedly made explicit in the life of Becket; see, for example, *SEL*, p. 672, lines 1897–900; p. 680, lines 2145–52; p. 681, lines 2171–8.
34 The ability of martyrdom to reverse political fortunes and turn a shameful death into a spiritual victory is also apparent in the popular cults that developed around Simon de Montfort and Edward II after each was 'martyred' for political reasons (though neither was ultimately canonised). See Mary-Ann Stouck, 'Saints and Rebels: Hagiography and Opposition to the King in Late Fourteenth-Century England', *Medievalia et Humanistica* n. s. 24 (1997), pp. 75–94, and Thomas J. Heffernan, 'Dangerous Sympathies: Political Commentary in the *South English Legendary*', *The South English Legendary: A Critical Assessment*, ed. Klaus P. Jankofsky (Tübingen: Francke Verlag, 1992), pp. 1–17.
35 *SEL*, p. 685, lines 2277–303.
36 *SEL*, pp. 687–8, lines 2365–400.
37 Peter Brown, *The Cult of the Saints: Its Rise and Function in Latin Christianity* (Chicago: University of Chicago Press, 1981), pp. 74–80.
38 Maureen A. Tilley, 'The Ascetic Body and the (Un)Making of the World of the Martyr', *Journal of the American Academy of Religion* 59.3 (1991), pp. 467–79.
39 Tilley, 'Ascetic Body', p. 473.

personalisation of God's force or *potentia*; as in the Incarnation of Christ, though of course not as completely or powerfully, the heavenly is made manifest on earth through an individual.[40] While that individual's particularities may not be a major focus of attention, his or her body often is, becoming the site where God asserts his control over the ultimate expression of earthly power, the power to cause death. Thus, even setting aside the ultimate sacrifice of martyrdom, one of the basic and most important expressions of power and authority in the saint's life – the one on which, in many cases, the rest of his or her authority rests – is power or 'mastery' over his or her own body and bodily desires.[41]

This important link is clear in all the lives discussed above. Becket, before his conversion, is a worldly and powerful chancellor, but his election as archbishop provokes a new attitude. Putting on a hair shirt, he determines to master his flesh,

> For him þoȝte he miȝte wel · of oþer habbe maistrie
> ȝif he hadde of is owe fleiss [his own flesh] · al out þe seygnurye [control]
> ȝif is soule is maister were · and is fleiss is hyne [servant]
> Him þoȝte he miȝte is dignete · bringe to gode fine [bring his dignity to a good end].[42]

Later he is accused of taking this 'mastery' too far, when the French king says to him, 'Gret maister wostou [you would] alonde [in this land] beo . to muche were þi poer'; here the control over himself that Becket seeks as a way to maintain his 'dignete' becomes associated – for reasons made evident in the previous discussion – with a desire for worldly power rather than simply spiritual excellence.[43]

A similar conjunction appears in the life of Katherine of Alexandria as told in the *South English Legendary*. Here the saint uses a formulation very like Becket's to rebuke the emperor. He criticises her for being so sure of herself in the face of considerable contrary opinion, and she replies that her words are worth as much as his:

> As god mai þe resoun beo · of me as of þe [my reasoning may be as good as yours]
> For emperour me saiþ þu ert · & echman is also
> Þat mai hote & his men mote · nede his heste do [who can command, and his men must do as he bids]
> Of bodi & soule þu ert ymaked · as þu miȝt þe silf iseo
> Mid riȝte þi soule maister is · & þi bodi hire hyne [her servant] schal beo
> If þanne þi bodi maister is · & þi soule his hyne
> Aȝe cunde [against nature] þanne hit is & þu worst · þerfore in helle pyne [suffer the pains of hell].[44]

---

[40] Brown, *Cult of the Saints*, pp. 55–8, pp. 60–3, p. 88.
[41] See Bernau, pp. 109–10, 115 below, for strikingly literal examples of this bodily mastery in the lives of St Paul Hermit and St Christine; her discussion of masculine sanctity, pp. 112–15, is also relevant here.
[42] *SEL*, p. 619, lines 261–4.
[43] *SEL*, p. 664, line 1653.
[44] *SEL*, p. 535, lines 56–62.

A basic lesson of Christianity – that the soul should rule the body – is both here and in Becket's *vita* explicitly linked to the issue of earthly power, and used to suggest that the saint with power over him or herself is the equal of any king or emperor. A proper understanding of microcosmic hierarchy translates into power in the larger world; like Becket's, Katherine's 'maistrie' over herself translates into mastery over others, as when the philosophers, entirely defeated by her arguments, '[n]ecoupe [could not] hi answerie no3t o word · ac 3yue hire þe maistrie'.[45]

Even the life of Elizabeth of Hungary, which, as noted above, is far less centred on power than the other lives considered here, makes a similar connection between self-control and saintliness – and, more particularly, the ability to act in and on the world, however modestly. Bokenham writes that

> Thow wyth þe brydyl of abstynence
> She hyr-self refreyned, as herd haue ye
> Yet to pore men swych affluence
> Of almesse she rehersyd & swych lyberalte,
> that she noon suffryd wych she myht se
> In-to myserye or myschef for to falle;
> Wherfore thorgh-oute al þat cuntre
> 'Modyr of pore men' folk dede hyr calle.[46]

Here the connection is slightly different: rather than being enabled to rule others by virtue of her self-rule, the saint is enabled to help others – and, not incidentally, to give her earthly motherhood (a possible weakness in the case for sainthood) a spiritual dimension. Her charity is her major means of self-expression and activity in the world, and Bokenham implies that it is deeply linked with her asceticism.[47]

The life of Edward presents a particularly interesting instance of how bodily self-control intersects with worldly power. While Edward is neither a martyr nor especially known for ascetic practices, he was commemorated in early lives for his virginity. This, one of the commonest forms of self-control and probably the one that most effectively garnered moral authority, especially for women, could nevertheless cause problems when exercised by a king. The life itself makes this clear:

> dyuers of this londe grucchid [complained] ayenste hym because he had no frute [descendant] to reigne after hym, and som said he had take a wyfe ayenst his wylle by compulcion of a fals stok, and [for] that he wolde bryng forthe no mo tyraundis he wolde not knowe his wyfe by generacion.[48]

---

[45] *SEL*, p. 537, line 130.
[46] Bokenham, *Legendys*, lines 9945–52.
[47] On the late-medieval admiration of heroic charity as a way to express saintly humility and prowess at the same time, see Weinstein and Bell, *Saints and Society*, pp. 157–8, pp. 232–3, and P. H. Cullum, 'Gendering Charity in Medieval Hagiography', *Gender and Holiness: Men, Women and Saints in Late Medieval Europe*, ed. Samantha J. E. Riches and Sarah Salih (London: Routledge, 2002), pp. 135–51.
[48] *Supplementary Lives*, p. 10.

As Katherine J. Lewis has recently observed, claims of chaste marriage could be very useful in situations where a king had failed to produce an heir, substituting for earthly failure a spiritual triumph that increased saintly authority to compensate for the loss of earthly descendants. In this case, Edward's posthumous reputation for virginity may have not only strengthened his own claims to sanctity, but made him available as a model for a later childless king, Richard II.[49] In this instance as in others, self-control had the capacity to transmute weakness into strength.[50]

Despite the frequent challenges to earthly authority – including that of the earthly Church – that saints' lives often depicted, then, a crucial part of their message could be used to defuse the implications of such challenges. As Jocelyn Wogan-Browne observes, 'the language of ascesis . . . writes . . . personal body disciplines as heroic charisma and strength in the service of God's superior kingdom and authority'.[51] While such a connection enabled the subjects of hagiography to perform heroic deeds in the world, it also gave an outlet for spiritual energies on the part of lay readers that could help to avoid social upheaval. Kings and bishops might use hagiographic models to strengthen their hands and justify political action (or heal political breaches); readers of less exalted standing could be assured that they took a saintly path by containing themselves and directing their energies toward self-discipline.[52]

This is a story often told about late-medieval hagiography: that despite the models it provided for outspoken resistance to the powerful, it was seemingly regarded in late-medieval England as an innocuous genre, suitable for the spiritual enrichment and guidance of the laity. Such a lack of anxiety suggests that attempts to contain the potential energies of saintly authority – by promoting admiration instead of imitation, or by diverting audiences' attention to the saint's self-control rather than his or her earthly disruptiveness – were, on the whole, successful. I would like to conclude here, however, by considering for a moment some lives that address not formal but informal power, whose role in Middle English hagiography and its reception may complicate our sense of the ways in which saints and their readers could influence the world around them.

---

[49] Katherine J. Lewis, 'Becoming a Virgin King: Richard II and Edward the Confessor', *Gender and Holiness*, ed. Riches and Salih, pp. 86–100.

[50] The case of Edmund of East Anglia is in some ways analogous: Edmund's refusal to save himself, like Edward's and Richard's childlessness, leaves his people without a leader, but the steadfastness that was seen as the core of martyrdom revalues this as a spiritual victory for the ruler. That these two nonetheless became the 'royal saints of English kingship' suggests the efficacy of the hagiographic topoi applied to them; Mitchell, 'Richard II', p. 120.

[51] Wogan-Browne, *Saints' Lives and Women's Literary Culture*, p. 179.

[52] For kings who turned to saints for legitimacy in times of crisis, see not only Richard II; Mitchell, 'Richard II'; Nigel Saul, 'Richard II's Ideas of Kingship', *Regal Image of Richard II and the Wilton Diptych*, ed. Gordon, Monnas and Elam, pp. 27–32; but also Henry V, son of Richard's deposer; Nancy Bradley Warren, 'Kings, Saints, and Nuns: Gender, Religion, and Authority in the Reign of Henry V', *Viator* 30 (1999), pp. 307–22; Neil Beckett, 'St Bridget, Henry V, and Syon Abbey', *Studies in St Bridget and the Brigittine Order* 2, ed. James Hogg, Analecta Cartusiana 35.19 (Salzburg: Institut für Anglistik und Amerikanistik Universität, Salzburg 1993, pp. 125–50. For a parallel case involving a pious noblewoman, see Anne Dutton, 'Piety, Politics, and Persona: MS Harley 4012 and Anne Harling', *Prestige, Authority and Power in Late Medieval Manuscripts and Texts*, ed. Felicity Riddy (York: York Medieval Press, 2000), pp. 133–46.

The influence of readers, or rather of audience, is one that lies behind all hagiography, insofar as saints almost invariably came to be sainted thanks to the popular will. While formal, papal canonisation was securely in place throughout most of the Middle English period, it was nonetheless crucial that a cult have a spontaneous local following.[53] The composition of saints' lives presents a corollary of this foundational truth: it is clear that the audience for which a given life was written would have shaped the hagiographer's choices. Modern scholars of the *South English Legendary* and the *Gilte Legende* point out that the move from Latin to English is not a mechanical exercise, but allows the translator to take his audience into account and inflect the story for their benefit.[54] In a sense, then, the cultural authority of these lives had as its necessary origin popular admiration of and response to the saint, and its mode of transmission was equally determined, particularly in the later Middle Ages, by a consideration of audience.

This reciprocal relationship between hagiography and the community of the faithful is evident in certain late-medieval *vitae* that show a marked interest in informal power and authority. The rise to prominence of the so-called Holy Kinship, the human extended family of Jesus, is one instance that highlights new developments in the conception of the saint.[55] We see its effects particularly through the history of the lives of St Anne, the mother of Mary, in Middle English hagiography. Largely overlooked as an independent saint before the fifteenth century, she rises to much greater prominence in that period, appearing in three stanzaic lives and in Bokenham's *Legendys of Hooly Wummen*, as well as taking a prominent role in the N-Town cycle play, and forming part of the *Gilte Legende* and Caxton's *Golden Legend*, where she appears in the story of the feast of the Nativity of the Virgin, rather than as an independent figure.[56] She is also a presence in Chaucer's writings; though he never wrote her legend, he invokes her in both the *Prioress's Tale* and the *Second Nun's Tale*.[57]

The Middle English collections accurately reflect a larger phenomenon in late-medieval Europe. The greatly increased devotion to St Anne and the elaboration of the idea of the Holy Kinship in this period show that a female saint whose earthly life was almost diametrically opposed to that of the virgin

---

53 André Vauchez, *Sainthood in the Later Middle Ages*, trans. Jean Birrell (Cambridge: Cambridge University Press, 1997), pp. 11–57.
54 Sister Mary Jeremy Finnegan, 'An Involved Narrator: The Redactor of the *Gilte Legende* MS B.M. Add. 35298', *Studies in Medieval Culture* 4.3 (1974), pp. 467–71; O. S. Pickering, 'The Outspoken *South English Legendary* Poet', *Late-Medieval Religious Texts and Their Transmission: Essays in Honour of A. I. Doyle*, ed. A. J. Minnis (Cambridge: Brewer, 1994), pp. 21–37; Klaus Jankofsky, 'National Characteristics in the Portrayal of English Saints in the South English Legendary', *Images of Sainthood in Medieval Europe*, ed. Renate Blumenfeld-Kosinski and Timea Szell (Ithaca NY: Cornell University Press, 1991), pp. 81–93.
55 For some other, more troubled intersections of sanctity and family life, see Bernau, pp. 108–10 below.
56 Manfred Görlach offers a helpful table of which saints appear in which Middle English collections, although he fails to note Anne's presence in Bokenham's text; Görlach, *Studies in Middle English Saints' Legends* (Heidelberg: Universitätsverlag C. Winter, 1998), pp. 12–13.
57 Ann Astell, 'Chaucer's "St. Anne Trinity": Devotion, Dynasty, Dogma, and Debate', *Studies in Philology* 94.4 (1997), pp. 395–416, discusses the different ways in which the saint functions in the two texts.

martyrs could validate forms of power and influence (kin and maternal) more accessible to lay readers.[58] Anne's inherent authority as the mother of the mother of the Saviour was dwelt on at considerable length; indeed, this role comprises almost the entirety of her legend in most Middle English versions. It also spread outward to inflect the lives of some of the other members of this 'large and powerful kinship', which included St John the Baptist as well as the apostles John the Evangelist, James the Less, Simon and Jude.[59] A fifteenth-century life of John the Evangelist, for example, begins with an account of the saint's affiliation with the kin group that derives from Anne. After a brief overview of the trinubium – Anne's three marriages and their offspring – it points out that this makes John the Evangelist

> nevew to oure lady and cosyn germayne to oure lorde Ihesu Crist. . . . And in this is greet praysynge and wurshep of Saint Iohn, that he was and is so nyȝe kyn to oure lord Ihesu Crist and to oure lady.[60]

Such attention to family, which persists throughout this life, is a distinctively late-medieval feature of its interests and clearly intended to increase John's prestige and thus, presumably, his power and desirability as an intercessor.

Bokenham's life is equally emphatic about Anne's foundational role as a kind of icon of kinship. In emphasising her 'nobyl & royal kynrede' he has to work against his sources to some extent, since, like the *Legenda aurea*, *Gilte Legende* and *Golden Legend* accounts, his begins with a discussion of the descent of Joachim and Joseph.[61] His prologue, however, focuses on the kindred under discussion as that of the Virgin Mary, and like the *Legenda aurea* he makes a brief apology for the fact that '[t]he custome of scripture not vsyth, lo,/ Of wymmen to wryte the genealogye', forcing him to provide an account of Joachim's line rather than Anne's.[62] Once past the treacherous waters of biblical genealogy, he is free to focus warmly on the familial aspects of Anne's own life. Her love for Joachim is given considerably more play than is typical in saints' lives, where marital affection is often regarded as a temptation to be withstood rather than as a good in itself, and their joint desire for a child and its happy outcome made Anne the patron saint of barren women.[63] Bokenham reinforces the centrality of familial affection, and expands it outward to his readership, in the final prayer where he invokes her aid for the work's dedicatees:

> Prouide, lady, eek þat Ion denstone
> & kateryne his wyf, if it plese þe grace

---

[58] See *Interpreting Cultural Symbols: Saint Anne in Late Medieval Society*, ed. Kathleen Ashley and Pamela Sheingorn (Athens GA: University of Georgia Press, 1990).
[59] *Middle English Legends of Women Saints*, ed. Sherry L. Reames with Martha G. Blalock and Wendy R. Larson (Kalamazoo: Medieval Institute Publications, 2003), p. 251. For images and discussion of the Holy Kinship, see *Interpreting Cultural Symbols*, ed. Ashley and Sheingorn, especially the introduction and Sheingorn, 'Appropriating the Holy Kinship: Gender and Family History', pp. 169–98.
[60] Cambridge, St John's College, MS N.17, ff. 24r–v.
[61] Bokenham, *Legendys*, line 1513.
[62] Bokenham, *Legendys*, lines 1527–8.
[63] On Anne's love for Joachim, see e.g. Bokenham, *Legendys*, lines 1742–8.

> Of god aboue, thorgh þi merytes a sone
> Of her body mow haue or they hens pace.⁶⁴

Anne's fruitfulness thus extends beyond her own family, to bless and help others who may be in similar situations.

To the thread of kinship highlighted in Anne's life is added another, also relevant to the lives of many of her readers. As popular as, if not more popular than, the images of the Holy Kinship that attend her story is that of Anne as Mary's teacher, a guise in which she appears extensively in art-historical sources.⁶⁵ The image of the mother instructing her daughter was one that must have resonated deeply with lay patrons of the time, given the extent to which they fostered its replication; it both reflected and validated one of the primary authoritative roles women held in medieval culture, as their children's first teachers.

In a sense, the lives of Anne and the devotion to the Holy Kinship in late-medieval England point to a conception of power and authority that, unlike those discussed earlier, focuses less on conflicts between individuals and more on networks of affiliation and support that were, of course, an important kind of power in their own right – and one that underlay much of hagiography to begin with. Thomas Becket and Edward the Confessor employ hagiographic topoi to ally themselves with a saintly community; the cults of St Anne and her extended family bring that community of saints into an almost coterminous relationship with earthly networks, by imagining a woman saint as a powerful helper to mothers or by envisaging Jesus' earthly environment as a kin-based one like that of a late-medieval layperson. Such associations were only strengthened by the influence lay readers exercised on the translation of Latin hagiography into the vernacular and on the copying of saints' lives.⁶⁶ Insofar as the power of sanctity actually arose from cooperation between communal agreement and individual heroics, such lives reflect an important aspect of the earthly mechanics of the cult of saints. As Augustine asked, 'How could that City [of God] have made its first start, how could it have advanced along its course, how could it attain its appointed goal, if the life of the saints were not social?'⁶⁷ Lives that emphasise social and kin bonds thus point to an existing and powerful element of hagiographic tradition, making it available in new ways for a devout, literate laity.

---

64 Bokenham, *Legendys*, lines 2092–5. See the discussion of Bokenham's 'hagiography of kinship' in Gail McMurray Gibson, 'Saint Anne and the Religion of Childbed: Some East Anglian Texts and Talismans', *Interpreting Cultural Symbols*, ed. Ashley and Sheingorn, pp. 95–110, p. 104.

65 See Pamela Sheingorn, '"The Wise Mother": The Image of St Anne Teaching the Virgin Mary', *Gesta* 32 (1993), pp. 69–80.

66 For one example of such influence, see George R. Keiser, 'Patronage and Piety in Fifteenth-Century England: Margaret, Duchess of Clarence, Symon Wynter and Beinecke MS 317', *Yale University Library Gazette* 60 (1985), pp. 32–46.

67 Augustine, *City of God*, trans. Henry Bettenson (Harmondsworth: Penguin, 1984), bk 19, ch. 5, quoted in David Aers, 'Faith, Ethics, and Community: Reflections on Reading Late Medieval English Writing', *Journal of Medieval and Early Modern Studies* 28.2 (1998), pp. 341–69, p. 345. An important aspect of many heroically confrontational lives, of course, is the saint's conversion of those around him or her; both Katherine and Cecilia provide themselves with extensive Christian 'families' before their deaths. The narratives, however, derive their force more from conflict than from these networks.

By contrast with the 'exceptional power' that enabled certain extraordinary late-medieval women to 'act and to criticize in ways that were not open to ordinary women', or the martyrdom that set the saint forever apart from the run of everyday mortals, the power that a saint such as Anne represented was so unexceptional, so ordinary, as to be almost invisible, particularly to modern audiences.[68] Nonetheless, the fact that her cult, and the stories of her extended family, became so popular in late Middle English hagiography should remind us again of the inexhaustible variety of medieval hagiography and its presentation of the saints' virtues and abilities. The life of St Anne is not about 'maistrie' but about love, less about control over oneself or others than about fruitfulness and generation. It thus offers a distinctive way of thinking about power and authority in the later Middle Ages, pointing us toward the power of family in an affective sense as well as a political one and reminding us of the shifting grounds of legitimacy in a period of political upheaval and the growth of lay sanctity.

---

[68] Elizabeth Petroff, 'Medieval Women Visionaries: Seven Stages to Power', *Frontiers* 3.1 (1978), pp. 34–45, p. 34.

4

Violence, Community and the Materialisation of Belief

ROBERT MILLS

Saints' lives afford ample opportunities for the representation of violence. Legends of martyrs who are stripped, beaten, burned and beheaded find their place alongside tales of saints who beat their demonic adversaries to a pulp, saints who self-harm, even saints who commit murder. The deaths of the wicked in hagiography are sometimes comparable in ghastliness to the sufferings of their saintly counterparts, while collectively writings about saints may be couched in the language of a militant, aggressively didactic Church. This chapter focuses on a particular configuration of violence in Middle English hagiography: its coupling with ideology. While it is clear that representations of brutality and bloodshed may be enjoyed in and of themselves, even in the context of religious piety, I wish to consider here how violence – and the representation of violated bodies – gets deployed as a means of materialising specific institutions, ideas and beliefs.

In exploring the relationship between violated bodies and beliefs, the main texts under consideration will be those assembled in the collection known as the *South English Legendary*. The collection's modern title is somewhat misleading in that the work to which it refers was a diffuse and open text, relentlessly modified and adapted to suit the locations in which it was copied and the historical circumstances in which it was disseminated. Related legends are extant in at least sixty manuscripts, an index of the work's popularity and capacity for adaptation, but no two manuscripts are alike in contents and emphasis. *SEL* manuscripts range in date from the end of the thirteenth century to the beginning of the fifteenth, with a date of c. 1270 assigned to the earliest (lost) version of the collection.[1] For the purposes of my argument here, the interest lies in the extent to which the shifting, protean qualities of *SEL* resonate with the various trajectories of violence contained within. The legends most frequently abstracted from a collection such as *SEL* by modern critics concern the sufferings of virgin martyrs,

---

[1] On the textual history of *SEL*, see Manfred Görlach, *The Textual Tradition of the South English Legendary*, Leeds Texts and Monographs, n. s. 6 (Leeds: School of English, University of Leeds, 1974). The problems raised by the work's title are discussed in Thomas R. Liszka, 'The *South English Legendaries*', *The North Sea World in the Middle Ages: Studies in the Cultural History of North-Western Europe*, ed. Liszka and Lorna E. M. Walker (Dublin: Four Courts Press, 2001), pp. 243–80. For an extended literary analysis of *SEL*, see Anne B. Thompson, *Everyday Saints and the Art of Narrative in the* South English Legendary (Aldershot: Ashgate, 2003).

women who died protecting their chastity.² This process of abstraction is not without medieval precedent: compilations such as the Katherine Group and Osbern Bokenham's *Legendys of Hooly Wummen* testify to the particular ability of female saints, virgin martyrs especially, to capture the imaginations of audiences in late medieval England.³ One of the issues over which much ink has been spilt in recent criticism is the encoding in these legends of narratives about rape; a related problem concerns the extent to which the violence enacted on virgin martyrs is pornographic.⁴ These are topics to which I shall return in due course, but this chapter will also foreground the relationship between the virgin martyr, held up as the paradigmatic breeding ground for expressions of sacred violence, and other narratives of bodily violation in hagiography compilations. To what extent is one violent moment or motif mapped onto another in the semiotic system of hagiography? How might the virgin martyr of *SEL* provide a model and interpretive framework for other manifestations of hagiographic violence, and how might this contribute to our understanding of the ideological messages that the compilation as a whole was designed to convey?

Sublime bodies

At the outset, it is important to recognise the formulaic nature of *SEL*'s language and imagery with respect to the violence directed against the martyr's body. Judges and tormentors are consistently associated with the epithet 'luþer', referring to their evil natures, while the tortures they impose on their victims often follow analogous trajectories. The work's Latin martyrs (that is to say, those early Christian saints with corresponding Latin *passiones*) generally undergo a

---

2   See, for instance, the legends included in *Chaste Passions: Medieval English Virgin Martyr Legends*, ed. and trans. Karen A. Winstead (Ithaca NY: Cornell University Press, 2000), pp. 27–43. For other discussions of virgin martyr hagiography, many of which discuss *SEL*, see notes 3 and 4.

3   For general commentaries on Middle English virgin martyr legends, which include investigations of violence, see Sheila Delany, *Impolitic Bodies: Poetry, Saints and Society in Fifteenth-Century England: The Work of Osbern Bokenham* (Oxford: Oxford University Press, 1998); Thomas J. Heffernan, *Sacred Biography: Saints and their Biographers in the Middle Ages* (Oxford: Oxford University Press, 1988), pp. 266–99; Sarah Salih, *Versions of Virginity in Late Medieval England* (Cambridge: Brewer, 2001), pp. 41–106; Karen A. Winstead, *Virgin Martyrs: Legends of Sainthood in Late Medieval England* (Ithaca NY: Cornell University Press, 1997); Jocelyn Wogan-Browne, *Saints' Lives and Women's Literary Culture: Virginity and its Authorizations* (Oxford: Oxford University Press, 2001), pp. 91–122.

4   Catherine Innes-Parker, 'Sexual Violence and the Female Reader: Symbolic "Rape" in the Saints' Lives of the Katherine Group', *Women's Studies* 24 (1995), pp. 205–17; Katherine J. Lewis, ' "Let me suffre": Reading the Torture of St Margaret of Antioch in Late Medieval England', *Medieval Women: Texts and Contexts in Late Medieval Britain: Essays for Felicity Riddy*, ed. Jocelyn Wogan-Browne, Rosalynn Voaden, Arlyn Diamond, Ann Hutchison, Carol Meale and Lesley Johnson (Turnhout: Brepols, 2000), pp. 69–82; Corinne Saunders, *Rape and Ravishment in the Literature of Medieval England* (Cambridge: Brewer, 2001), pp. 120–51; Jocelyn Wogan-Browne, 'The Virgin's Tale', *Feminist Readings in Middle English Literature: The Wife of Bath and All Her Sect*, ed. Ruth Evans and Lesley Johnson (London: Routledge, 1994), pp. 165–94. See also Kathryn Gravdal, *Ravishing Maidens: Writing Rape in Medieval French Literature and Law* (Philadelphia: University of Pennsylvania Press, 1991), pp. 21–41, commenting on Old French hagiography.

basic catalogue of torments: most are stripped and publically beaten, their flesh drawn until blood flows and bones are exposed, before being burned in a fire from which they emerge unharmed; the proceedings are commonly interrupted by a spell in prison and, after more torments, the saints die from their wounds or suffer a final death blow to the neck (usually decapitation); often the martyrs' bodies are subjected to further post-mortem humiliations, albeit temporarily, in the form of attempts to deny them Christian burial. There are variations to this basic script, most notably in terms of quantity and duration: the *SEL* narrator says of Vincent 'I ne hurde neuer martir non · þat hadde more torment', while we are told that Christine was subjected to an ordeal that continued for a good two years.[5] Certain modes of torment occur less frequently in addition to or as substitutes for the usual scenes of beating and burning: Sebastian's penetration with arrows and Katherine's wheel are among the most memorable of the punishments imposed, a notoriety which is reinforced by their frequent reproduction in iconography. Yet these tortures are themselves 'recycled' in other legends.[6] Sebastian's sagittation is mirrored in the story of the Anglo-Saxon King Edmund who, like his Roman forebear, is shot with arrows until he resembles a hedgehog. (Indeed, the narrator explicitly draws attention to the parallel, commenting that Edmund was penetrated with arrows 'as ful as an illespyl [hedgehog] is · of pikes [spikes] al aboute . . . as þe holi man imartred was · þe holi seint Bastian', 513.47–51.) But the arrow motif also occurs in the legend of Christopher, with the twist that, though more than two hundred soldiers try to shoot the saint, their missiles hang about him in mid-air; one of the arrows ends up blinding the pagan king. Likewise, the razor-laden wheels brought forth with the intention of tearing Katherine's flesh find their match in the torture instrument used to violate Juliana, except that in Juliana's case the consequences are rather more severe: whereas Katherine's wheels are destroyed by an angel from heaven before they can do the saint any harm, Juliana's wheel cuts into her flesh and deep into her bones, so that 'marrou sprang out alaboute' (67.147).

In considering the repetitious quality of hagiographic violence, it is clear that gender plays a role in the distribution of certain methods of torture. Many critics have noted the attention paid to female breasts in virgin martyr legends, notably in the context of their removal: famously this is the fate of Agatha but also, in *SEL*, of Christine and of the Empress in the Katherine legend.[7] Fewer have remarked on the frequency with which allusions to cooking occur in the torments of male martyrs.[8] In *SEL*, Vincent, George, Quiriac, Christopher,

---

[5] *SEL*, p. 31, line 181: further page and line references will be given in parentheses.
[6] On the 'borrowing' of torture motifs from one legend to another, see Samantha J. E. Riches, 'St George as a Male Virgin Martyr', *Gender and Holiness: Men, Women and Saints in Late Medieval Europe*, ed. Riches and Sarah Salih (London: Routledge, 2002), pp. 65–85, p. 77.
[7] Martha Easton, 'Saint Agatha and the Sanctification of Sexual Violence', *Studies in Iconography* 16 (1994), pp. 83–119; Gravdal, *Ravishing Maidens*, p. 24; Heffernan, *Sacred Biography*, p. 283; Salih, *Versions of Virginity*, pp. 85–7, 94; Marilyn Yalom, *A History of the Breast* (London: Pandora, 1998), pp. 32–6.
[8] Robert Mills, ' "Whatever You Do is a Delight to Me!": Masculinity, Masochism, and Queer Play in Representations of Male Martyrdom', *Exemplaria* 13.1 (2001), pp. 1–37, p. 11; Jocelyn Wogan-Browne and Glyn S. Burgess, 'Introduction', *Virgin Lives and Holy Deaths: Two Exemplary Biographies for Anglo-Norman Women* (London: Dent, 1996), pp. xl–xli.

Lawrence, Denis and Quentin are subjected to an assortment of culinary processes: all are pounded like steak and roasted on a fire or gridiron, sizzling in their own body fat; some are baked in ovens or have their wounds rubbed with oil or salt; occasionally, after death, their corpses are thrown to wild beasts who, hungry though they are, develop a miraculous distaste for martyred flesh. Vincent's legend contains some of the most developed gastronomic imagery in *SEL*: responding to attempts to burn him to dust, the saint goes into the fire, we are told, 'as gladlich as to feste' (27.76). Frustrated by the saint's survival, the judge takes Vincent up on his imagery of feasting by attempting to transform him literally into food: he orders plates of iron to be used to sear his flesh, causing his fat to run 'as þei it friinge [frying] were' (28.92); he is then cast into another fire and salt cast in his wounds, at which point the saint jokes 'þis is a murie feste' (28.103). The judge eventually decides that he will be better off tormenting the saint's dead body and, after Vincent finally gives up the ghost, he arranges for the carcass to be thrown into a field, to be devoured by wild beasts and birds. Unsurprisingly, however, this final attempt to transform the saint into edible flesh falls flat: when a wolf tries to carry off Vincent's body, a flock of ravens successfully wards off the predator.

The transformation of the saint's flesh into food might usefully be interpreted in the light of its parallels with Christ's incarnation and ultimately, through the imagery of sacrifice, with the Eucharist. But it also highlights the potential for gender trouble in the representation of martyrs. In the course of reconfiguring the male saint's body as meat, the violence of martyrdom aligns him with modes of fleshly passivity; this produces a subject position at odds with his previous status as wielder of earthly power and responsibility (Vincent, like Lawrence, is a deacon, and Sebastian a military commander).[9] The legends of female saints, conversely, produce their own disruptive effects in the context of torture: while male martyrs, in the process of being tormented, might be divested of certain signifiers of earthly masculinity, the battles female virgin martyrs undergo to protect their chastity potentially associate them with privileges that, in late medieval culture, were commonly gendered male. The response of all martyrs to their tortures is to preach and pray, and to jeer at their tormentors, but the language of female saints in *SEL* is arguably more aggressive than their male counterparts, accentuating the degree to which they are stepping out of line. Saints such as Agatha, Christine and Juliana may be 'nice girls' – young women with privileged upbringings – but their conversations with enemies are frequently peppered with acts of verbal aggression.[10] Karen Winstead renders the 'vnwreste bouk' with which the saint taunts Duke Quincian in the legend of

---

[9] Mills, 'Whatever You Do'; Riches, 'St George'.
[10] On the speech of virgin martyrs, see Gail Ashton, *The Generation of Identity in Late Medieval Hagiography: Speaking the Saint* (London: Routledge, 2000); Maud Burnett McInerney, 'Rhetoric, Power, and Integrity in the Passion of the Virgin Martyr', *Menacing Virgins: Representing Virginity in the Middle Ages and Renaissance*, ed. Kathleen Coyne Kelly and Marina Leslie (London: Associated University Presses, 1999), pp. 50–70; Robert Mills, 'Can the Virgin Martyr Speak?', *Medieval Virginities*, ed. Anke Bernau, Ruth Evans and Sarah Salih (Cardiff: University of Wales Press, 2003), pp. 187–213.

Agatha 'asshole!' in modern American-English translation, which seems perfectly apt in this context.¹¹

Female saints are also potentially virilised through their ability to enact, as well as suffer, violence. Margaret's subjugation of the demon who confronts her in prison is especially striking in this context:

> Heo nom him bu is luþer pol [She took him by his evil head] · and harde him to gronde caste,
> And hure ri3t fot [right foot] sette anon · up is necke bihinde faste.
> ...
> Faste heo bond þis foule wi3t [stinking demon] · and scorgede him wel sore.
> Grislich he 3al [He screamed horribly] and ofte sede · 'Hende maide þin ore [Have mercy, gracious virgin],
> Alas þat ich here com · mi mi3te me is bynome [my power has been sapped].
> Alas þat a tendre maide · me ssel þus ouercome'. (297–8.177–86)

The beating received by the demon at the hands of Margaret parallels the beatings more commonly visited on saints, hinting at the reversals hagiography potentially engineers. Although a saint's own capacity for violence is typically displaced onto the agency of God (acts of divine intervention are the most common cause of death for the pagan tormentors), these instances of female figures taking the upper hand in physical battles against their aggressors have provided much grist to the mill in the rehabilitation of virgin martyr legends in recent feminist criticism.¹²

The violence *of* the virgin martyr hints at a wider context for martyrdom legends such as those collected in *SEL*. In the Prologue to Corpus Christi College Cambridge MS 145, the manuscript considered by modern editors to be the most complete early version of *SEL*, the narrator begins with the relatively innocuous image of God as a gardener and Christ as a seed from which the 'nywe frut' of Christendom has sprung (1.3). The tone soon becomes more sinister, however, when we learn that the ground on which the seed is sown is hard and must be germinated with Christ's blood; this, in turn, is supplemented by the blood of Christian martyrs. Then the imagery shifts again: the martyrs produce this nourishment in their roles as 'our Louerdes kny3tes . . . þat schadde hare blod for Cristendom' (1.19–20); Christ becomes a king, doing battle 'to holde up is ri3te' (2.23), while the martyrs are described as his 'rerewarde [rearguard]' (3.53). Initially, in this opening moment, the martyrs' torments appear to have been domesticated – turned into irrigation for the garden. But it is clear from the lines

---

11 Winstead, *Chaste Passions*, p. 30.
12 Nikki Stiller, *Eve's Orphans: Mothers and Daughters in Medieval English Literature* (London: Greenwood, 1980), pp. 19–20; Winstead, *Virgin Martyrs*, pp. 76, 90–2; Wogan-Browne, 'Virgin's Tale', pp. 178–9. For an argument that, despite their displays of physical prowess, virgin martyrs remain 'fundamentally weak', see Elizabeth Robertson, 'The Corporeality of Female Sanctity in *The Life of St Margaret*', *Images of Sainthood in Medieval Europe*, ed. Renate Blumenfeld-Kosinski and Timea Szell (Ithaca NY: Cornell University Press, 1991), pp. 268–87.

that follow that they have also been appropriated in the service of a militant Church, doing battle against the evils of the world. The imagery is partly designed to generate interest in an audience more familiar with a diet of epic and romance: while admitting that 'men wilneþ [desire] muche to hure telle [hear tell] · of bataille of kynge/ And of kniȝtes þat hardy were', the narrator sneers that much of this is 'lesynge' [falsehood] (3.59–60). In contrast, readers are encouraged to turn their attention to battles

> ... þat nis no lesinge [falsehood]
> Of apostles & martirs · þat hardy kniȝtes were,
> Þat studeuast [steadfast] were in bataille · & ne fleide noȝt for fere,
> Þat soffrede þat luþer men · al quik hare lymes totere [suffered evil men to tear their living bodies]. (3.62–5)

These lines subtly rework the imagery of the Prologue one last time, for now the saints who perform military service to defend Christendom against attack are also depicted explicitly as embattled but unwavering victims, subject to the violence of 'luþer men'. In this way, the *SEL* Prologue neatly incorporates what is perhaps medieval hagiography's most persistent ideological manoeuvre: the representation of Christendom as both inviolate and constantly under threat.

In this context, it may be helpful to invoke what Sarah Kay has termed the 'sublime body' of the Christian martyr. Kay's argument, which is developed in relation to Anglo-Norman hagiography, concerns the construction of the martyr's torments as a space between two deaths – a space that allows for the invention of fantasies of incessant violence that exceed the limits of the possible.[13] Martyrdom legends turn on the conviction that acts of violence proliferate long after they should – acts such as Sebastian's sagittation or Vincent's roasting, which one might reasonably expect to bring about the victim's death. The martyrs' bodies are thus located in a universe beyond the frontier of natural death – the death 'they seek and might, symbolically and naturalistically, have been allowed' – with the result that the saints remain 'suspended in a miraculous state of indestructibility'.[14] (While the second death in Kay's model finds its analogy in the final beheading scene, which ostensibly silences the saint's voice, even this act of violence does not necessarily 'work' – martyrdom legends frequently end with requests that the saints in heaven intercede on the readers' behalf.) The space between two deaths in turn allows the martyr to take on ideological significance, as an indestructible support for belief. Hence, in *SEL*, saints are frequently represented emerging from their torments whole, as is the case with Sebastian, whose 'holy bodi' is discovered by the Christian woman Irene 'hol & sond · wiþoute ech maner wonde' [whole and

---

[13] Sarah Kay, 'The Sublime Body of the Martyr: Violence in Early Romance Saints' Lives', *Violence in Medieval Society*, ed. Richard W. Kaeuper (Woodbridge: Boydell, 2000), pp. 3–20; Sarah Kay, *Courtly Contradictions: The Emergence of the Literary Object in the Twelfth Century* (Stanford: Stanford University Press, 2001), pp. 216–31. Kay borrows the phrase 'sublime body' from Slavoj Žižek, who draws in turn on Lacan: see Žižek, *The Sublime Object of Ideology* (London: Verso, 1989), pp. 134–5.
[14] Kay, *Courtly Contradictions*, pp. 224, 232.

sound, without any sort of wound] (18.55) – a play on wholeness and holiness that highlights the saint's capacity for corporeal sublimation.

Belief, and its materialisation in the context of the suffering body, is also usefully explored in Elaine Scarry's *The Body in Pain*, which describes pain's appropriation in a process Scarry terms 'analogical substantiation'. This phenomenon entails making the body's pain signify in ways that attach it to referents other than the human body, abstractions and cultural constructs such as religion or sovereignty or nation.

> That is, the felt-characteristics of pain – one of which is its compelling vibrancy or its incontestable reality or simply its 'certainty' – can be appropriated away from the body and presented as the attributes of something else (something which by itself lacks those attributes, something which does not in itself appear vibrant, real, or certain).[15]

In evoking these ideas my point is that the martyr's sublime body, an object taken beyond the limits of sentience, constructs a framework for the substantiation – the making alive – of an abstract institution such as the Church. Violence, for this reason, is integral to the construction of Christian community, as the *SEL* Prologue explicitly announces in its evocation of Christendom as a battleground bespattered with the blood of martyrs. 'Wel aȝte we louie Cristendom' (3.57), the narrator announces, as if Christendom itself is a body to be protected, cared for and desired. Finding itself reflected in the pained but invincible bodies of saints, the Christian *corpus* reaffirms its ideological hegemony.[16] Violence must be constantly encountered and continually endured in these contexts, because the suffering it produces lends an aura of realness to the cultural fiction being invoked. How otherwise could one 'love' an abstraction such as the Church?

The concept of the sublime body permits particular insights into narratives about female virgin martyrs, where rape – or more precisely the threat of rape – is clearly at issue. Kathleen Coyne Kelly rightly draws attention to the unrepresentability of rape in hagiography, while at the same time exploring the role of sexual coercion in these legends as a prospect both fantasised and ultimately withheld.[17] In MS Corpus Christi 145, there are at least ten women who fall into this category: Agnes, Agatha and Lucy are forced into brothels; efforts are made to compel Juliana, Margaret and Ursula to marry; Anastasia is wedded against her will, though she manages to escape when her husband tries to consummate the marriage; direct attempts at rape are carried out on Margaret, Lucy, Anastasia's three maids and Agnes. In each case the evil seducers are thwarted and, in the end, the rape or sexual assault is never followed through. A

---

15 Elaine Scarry, *The Body in Pain: The Making and Unmaking of the World* (Oxford: Oxford University Press, 1985), pp. 13–14.
16 For an insightful discussion of the relationship between virginity and violence in the manufacture of this *corpus*, see Anke Bernau, 'A Christian *Corpus*: Virginity, Violence, and Knowledge in the Life of St Katherine of Alexandria', *St Katherine of Alexandria: Texts and Contexts in Western Medieval Europe*, ed. Jacqueline Jenkins and Katherine J. Lewis (Turnhout: Brepols, 2003), pp. 109–30.
17 Kathleen Coyne Kelly, *Performing Virginity and Testing Chastity in the Middle Ages* (London: Routledge, 2000), pp. 40–62. See also Bernau in this volume.

raped virgin is a semiotic impossibility in hagiography, after all, since violation of the virgin's body would radically detract from its potential for sublimation as ideology. Be that as it may, some critics have maintained that sexual violence is displaced onto the scenes of torture, which, with their focus on scenes of penetration and female nakedness, possess a latent erotic content.[18] Male martyrs get penetrated too, of course, and it is possible that their own torments occasionally possess a sexual resonance, when read from a certain angle: Lawrence, George and Quentin are all stripped naked before being beaten in *SEL*, a humiliation that transforms their bodies into bare – albeit bloodied – flesh.[19] Yet, in their exposure to the threat of rape, female virgin martyrs clearly possess a particularly vibrant symbolic potency, as stand-ins – and substantiating supports – for the 'body' of the Christian Church. Impermeable, but repeatedly threatened with assault, their sublime bodies become an outstanding resource for the ideological materialisation of Christendom.

Abject anti-bodies

So far this chapter has focused on the construction, through scenes of violence, of the martyr's sublime body – an entity able to be subjected to unimaginable wounding and dissolution, while at same time remaining suspended in a state of impregnability. I would now like to shift attention to the ways in which this body provides support for additional, more particularised ideological agendas. Partly because of the rich intertexual webs it spins, *SEL* affords insights into the historically situated nature of the meanings communicated by hagiographic violence. Representations of violence in *SEL*, as we shall see, provide platforms for working through anxieties about religion, race and nation; they allow hagiographers subtly to negotiate and reconfigure relations of gender, class and language within a particular cultural context, but in so doing create a forum for the expression of virulent misogyny, xenophobia and anti-Semitic sentiment. This seems to be the case especially in hagiography telling the stories of saints who lived in the period after the early Christian persecutions: in *SEL*, for example, this category includes a large number of lives devoted to 'English' or Anglo-Saxon saints. It is evident, nonetheless, that the narrative conventions of Latin martyrdom legends – including virgin martyr legends – find themselves played out once more in these other, more 'local' versions of sanctity. A consideration of these interactions also highlights the role, in saints' lives, of bodies and identities which readers are ultimately asked to reject – historically specific figures fantasised by hagiographers as the opposite of sanctity. The inclusion of sacred enemies helps circumscribe the claims of the Church to universal legiti-

---

[18] Gravdal, *Ravishing Maidens*, p. 24; Heffernan, *Sacred Biography*, pp. 273–6. Christine, who is not threatened directly with sexual coercion due to her father's jealous efforts to shield her from other men, is nonetheless subjected to a variety of sexualised torments, including being covered with snakes which lick and kiss her and play with her breasts: *SEL* life of Christine, lines 298–304.

[19] Kay, *Courtly Contradictions*, p. 226; Mills, 'Whatever You Do', pp. 7, 13–14; Riches, 'St George', p. 72.

macy, by demonstrating the abundant threats to which it is subjected in particular times and places. At the same time the violent ends these figures meet serve to underscore their corporeal destructibility and distance from the sublime. A particularly memorable case of non-saintly abjection occurs in the life of Hilary, which represents a debate between the saint and evil Pope Leo. Hilary makes such an incisive critique of the pope's arguments that he takes his adversary up shit creek – literally! Having announced his predicament to Hilary, the narrator explains, Leo

> wende forþ anon · his neode bistod hym faste [his business was
>   pressing].
> He lyuerede hym so at warderobe · þat is gottes out he caste
> [He relieved himself in such a way at the privy that he cast out his
>   guts].
> Al hit wende out by one way · amty his wombe was
> [It all went out by one way, his stomach was empty],
> And he fel doun ded anon · þer was a grislich cas [grisly episode].
>   (7.67–70)

The enemies of saints in episodes such as this are assigned bodies that come apart at the seams – in Leo's case, by virtue of a disastrous visit to the papal privy. The production of the sublime body of the saint partially relies, in other words, on the incorporation of a continually shifting cast of abject 'anti-bodies', whose function is to act as foils to the invincibility of their saintly antagonists.

The cultural resonance of these antitypes is often related to historical circumstances. It should be recalled that *SEL* was originally conceived only a few decades after the Fourth Lateran Council in 1215. In addition to reorganising the clergy, Lateran IV essentially offered a definition of what it meant to be a member of the Christian community in Western Europe. Among the most famous of the Lateran decrees was the directive that all faithful confess, perform penance and receive communion at least once a year. The torrent of religious writing produced in the thirteenth century for the instruction of lay people, among which *SEL* is included, has been viewed as a deliberate response to this decree.[20] But the canons of 1215 were also designed to defend the Catholic faith against its perceived enemies: the decrees open with measures designed to extirpate heresy and end with a series of prohibitions specifically aimed at limiting Jewish contact with Christians.[21] Heretics do not have a significant role in *SEL*, although the tormentors of Latin martyrs are consistently cast as idol-worshipping pagans, many of whom swear by the God 'Mahon' [Mohammed]. In the later Middle Ages, Islam was sometimes regarded as a heretical movement, a 'fraudulent new version' of Christianity, and the anachronistic portrayal of Muslims as the tormentors of early Christians in *SEL* no doubt served to connect the era of crusades with ongoing efforts to materialise the Church as an

---

[20] Thompson, *Everyday Saints*, p. 26.
[21] For a summary of the role of Lateran IV in defining Christian community, see R. I. Moore, *The Formation of a Persecuting Society: Power and Deviance in Western Europe, 950–1250* (Oxford: Blackwell, 1987), pp. 6–11.

invincible yet endangered 'body'.²² Heretics also feature explicitly in the account of the life of Peter the Dominican, a preaching friar from Verona who was himself born 'of misbileuede men' (162.2) but who realised the errors of his ways in his youth. The adult Peter is sent by the Pope to Lombardy to deal with an outbreak of 'strong heresie' (162.10), but a group of misbelievers plot to do him in: cast in the role of martyr, the saint is escorted into a wood and stabbed, his brain cleft in two by a heretical executioner.

Given the tendency to collapse distinctions between pagans, heretics and Muslims in hagiography, it is not surprising that saints' lives also present Jews as agents of torture in certain contexts. In fact Jewish communities in England in the twelfth and thirteenth centuries chiefly *suffered* violence. Crusading fervour in the reign of Richard I provided the circumstances for the burning of at least thirty London Jews in 1189 and the mass suicide of York's Jewry in 1190; the hanging of nineteen Jews in Lincoln in 1255, after the discovery of a boy's body in a well, was one of several allegations of ritual child murder directed against England's Jewish communities during this period.²³ Despite the reality of English Jewish experience, *SEL*, which was originally compiled twenty years before the official expulsion of all Jews from England in 1290, contributes to the misrepresentation of Jews as perpetrators rather than victims of violence. Although the legendary's anti-Semitism has been largely overlooked by critics, *SEL* manuscripts feature several texts that present Jews as violators. Most often Jews are portrayed as enemies of Christ (and therefore implicitly of Christians): Margaret decries 'þe luþer Giwes · þat God slowe on þe rode' [the evil Jews who killed God on the cross] (294.84), hinting at links between Christ's and her own tormentors, while direct comparisons are made between Thomas Becket's death and the treatment exacted on the Lord by the Jews. But in one instance Jews are explicitly depicted as agents of martyrdom: the life of Barnabas culminates in an account of how the saint is dragged by Jews to their synagogue, thrown into a great fire and burned to death. What is more in other texts the fantasy of the Jewish tormentor surfaces in the miracle stories appended to certain legends. Several miracles attributed to Nicholas feature Jews, including the story of a man who, despite his Jewish identity, shows a particular devotion to the saint. The man decides to make an image of Nicholas to worship in his house and one day, before going away on business, entrusts his 'god' to the saint ('god' appears to be a pun on the concept on goods as property, goodness as a moral quality and possibly the idea of god in the sense of deity). While he is away, thieves break in and steal the Jew's 'god'; the man returns home and reprimands the statue, asking it to 'ʒolde' [yield] his 'godhede' [goodness] (564.437). He then proceeds to subject the statue to a vigorous beating:

---

[22] Susan Schibanoff, 'Worlds Apart: Orientalism, Antifeminism and Heresy in Chaucer's *Man of Law's Tale*', *Exemplaria* 8 (1996), pp. 59–96, p. 70. On the presentation of Muslims as pagans, see Bernau, 'Christian *Corpus*', p. 125. The other representatives of pagan worship in *SEL* are, of course, Vikings: the legends of Edmund, Oswald and Alphege all chronicle encounters between English saints and Danish tormentors.

[23] Moore, *Formation*, pp. 31, 36.

> Harde scourgen he nom [He took hard scourges] · & þis ymage beot
> [beat] faste
> Þat grete pieces wende awei [fell away] · He furde [acted] as he were
> wod [mad]
> & euere he bad þe seli treo [humble wooden image] · ȝulde hom his
> god [yield to him his goods/goodness].   (564.438–40)

The description here clearly parallels the beatings of martyrs, which likewise cause pieces of flesh to fall away from the saints' bodies: in the life of George 'þe peces folle to gronde' (157.35), while in Margaret we are told 'Bi peces þat fleiss fel adoun' (296.122). Moreover, while the Jew is engaged in beating the image, Nicholas himself appears to the thieves in a vision, 'al towonded & al todrawe' [all wounded and torn apart] (564.442) and 'wiþ sides blodrede' [with blood-red sides] (564.448), thereby evoking an indexical link between statue and saint. The thieves, terrified, return the Jew's 'god' and the Jew promptly converts to Christianity. The miracle seems partly designed to convey a message about the appropriate use of images, but it also casts the Jewish man in the role of persecutor, albeit temporarily: the restoration of the Jew's goodness goes hand in hand with his recognition of saintly suffering.

While there are no references in *SEL* manuscripts to the myth of Jewish host desecration, a narrative that was first recorded in 1290 and that advanced the notion that Jews procured and subsequently tortured the Eucharist, there is an anti-Semitic narrative included in the repertoire of miracles inserted after the *SEL* life of Theophilus that possesses clear Eucharistic associations and that in turn gestures towards the fates of martyrs. The story of the Jewish Boy, commonly transmitted in Marian collections, was a special favourite of twelfth-century monastic writers; the version in *SEL* is the earliest translation in English.[24] One Easter, so the story goes, a boy of Jewish parentage decides to accompany his Christian playmates to church. While there he is especially drawn to the figure of the Virgin Mary in a crucifixion tableau and, like his companions, he subsequently receives Christ's flesh and blood in Communion. The boy's worried parents, who have been looking all over for him, are initially pleased when their son returns. After hearing where he has been, however, the boy's father proceeds to cast him into the oven. Hearing the mother's lament, 'folk' from round about go to the oven and find the boy sitting there, playing casually with the fire; the child explains how the woman he saw in church beside the cross protected him from the fire with her veil. The bystanders subsequently take the father and cast him in the oven instead; unlike the boy, he burns to dust. Jews in this tale are characterised as archetypes of cruelty: while the evil father is punished for enacting violence against his son, the earthly mother and the boy eventually convert to Christianity. As such, the initial Jewishness of mother and son is overridden by their qualities of maternal helplessness and childish innocence. In the *SEL* version the boy is described only as a 'Giwes child', not as a Jew *per se*, and the boy's final declaration highlights his ultimate

---

[24] For an overview of the Jewish Boy tradition, see Miri Rubin, *Gentile Tales: The Narrative Assault on Late Medieval Jews* (New Haven: Yale University Press, 1999), pp. 7–28.

distance from Jewish identity: 'Ich biluue on hure sone · þat þe Giwes honge on þe treo' (229.236). The boy's placement in the oven in this tale draws parallels with the sacrificial 'cooking' of male martyrs. His sublimation as an inviolate body is effected by a process of culinary conversion that deliberately mimics the transubstantiation of bread into Christ's body in the Eucharist. Ovens are places of danger but also sites of transformation and sources of food; like the prisons, towers and brothels in which female virgin martyrs are commonly enclosed, the oven into which the boy is pushed is reinvented as a womb-like space of containment which transmits the saving grace of Christ. The disjunction between paternal violence and childish innocence also strongly resonates with virgin martyr legends: in both instances, the sacred figure is represented as youthful while an adult aggressor commits an act of child abuse; the disjunction between sublime body and abject anti-body is reinforced by the brutal punishment of the patriarchal tormentor.[25]

In certain versions of *SEL*, indeed, the intersections between virgin martyr hagiography and the story of the Jewish Boy extend further, to encompass a still more particularised set of meanings. One text not included in the standard EETS edition of *SEL* but which appears in BL MS Egerton 1993 (dated to c. 1335–50) is the legend of Mildred, an abbess from the Anglo-Saxon period.[26] Mildred's life contains a number of conventions familiar from virgin martyr hagiography. The narrative begins by describing how the saint's mother sends her, as a young noblewoman, to a nunnery 'biȝende þe see' (65). 'So god and queinte and vair [fair] heo was', we are told, '& of portire so hende' [so gracious in demeanour] (69), that a knight of 'gret power' (71) falls in love with her. After Mildred refuses the knight's advances, he recruits the abbess of the house to aid him in his sexual conquest; the 'luþer abbesse' proceeds to shut the girl in an oven to no effect. At this point the narrator seizes on the opportunity to connect Mildred's sublime body with her virginal identity, asserting: 'Clene a þing is maidenhod no fuir ne mai brenne' [virginity is a pure thing no fire may burn] (101); he also draws attention explicitly to the Eucharistic overtones of the oven motif, commenting how 'as me bakeþ a kake/ Me þinkeþ þer was a swete lof to oure Lords bord [Lord's supper] ibake' (89–90). Next the nasty abbess drags Mildred from the oven by the hair and subjects her to a violent beating. Although her flesh is torn from top to toe, Mildred exclaims in a prayer to God that she would rather die than consent to foul deeds; finally the saint sends word to her mother (along with tresses of hair torn from her head by the abbess), which effects her rescue and return to England. The story concludes by describing how Mildred becomes a nun in her mother's own house and eventually an abbess herself – setting a much better example, the narrator remarks, than 'þe oþer biȝende see' (147).

---

[25] For connections between other anti-Semitic narratives and English virgin martyr lives, see Ruth Evans, 'The Jew, the Host and the Virgin Martyr', *Medieval Virginities*, ed. Bernau, Evans and Salih, pp. 167–86; Wogan-Browne, *Saints' Lives*, pp. 118–22.
[26] Text in Paul Acker, 'Saint Mildred in the *South English Legendary*', *The South English Legendary: A Critical Assessment*, ed. Klaus P. Jankofsky (Tübingen: Francke Verlag, 1992), pp. 140–53, pp. 145–9.

The Mildred legend possesses striking similarities with the virgin martyr narrative, with its motifs of sexual coercion and virginal defiance and its scenes of beating and burning. The tale of the Jewish Boy likewise presents an obvious intertext for the scenes of baking, the rescuing mother figure and the confrontation between youth and age. But there are also significant differences in the trajectory of the story: unlike the virgin martyr, Mildred does not ultimately die from her sufferings (instead, like the Jewish child, this is an early chapter in her life); in contrast to both virgin martyr and Jewish Boy narratives, the agent of torture is gendered female. The association of women with evil is especially apparent in *SEL*'s Anglo-Saxon lives, where tales of wicked sisters and stepmothers provide an excuse for narratorial asides that are pretty overtly misogynistic. The young king Edward the Elder is murdered by his stepmother, a 'luþer womman' (111.34), while out hunting in a wood in Dorset: she loves her own son Æthelred better and plans to make him king in Edward's place, for, we are told, 'stepmoder is selde [rarely] god' (110.10). Similarly, the legend of Kenelm relates how the saint succeeds his father to the throne of Mercia at the age of seven and the saint's sister Quenride plots to have her brother murdered. Kenelm's guardian Askbert carries out the dirty deed but it is Quenride for whom the narrator reserves his most powerful criticism: 'For me seiþ þer nis no felonie [villainy] þat womman ne can þenche [think]' (283.110). These anti-feminist asides are balanced by representations elsewhere in *SEL* of women who are exemplary in spite of their non-saintly status. The wife of Julian the Hospitaller, who mistakenly murders his parents while they are asleep in his bed (thinking they are his wife in bed with a lover), acts as a paragon of marital commitment in the wake of her husband's violent deed; the *Southern Passion*, a lengthy meditation on the sufferings of Christ included in many *SEL* manuscripts, uses women's loyalty to Christ during the Passion as an excuse for making an impassioned plea *against* conventional misogyny.[27] Consequently, while certain *SEL* texts cast the tormentors of saints in a feminine guise and attribute their actions to the evils associated with women, overall *SEL* embodies a multiplicity of viewpoints regarding the gendering of violence. The Mildred story is unique among *SEL* texts in imagining a female agent of physical violence; in this way, it demonstrates the potential drawbacks of abstracting individual texts from a hagiography compilation and making one saint's life stand for many.[28] Torture scenes in virgin martyr hagiography may well have possessed the capacity to produce modes of 'religious pornography' in certain contexts, a reader taking delight in the systematic exposure and penetration of the female saint's body by identifying with the position of tormentor; but the abject anti-body in the life of Mildred – the wicked abbess who takes it on herself to destroy the body of her young charge – is gendered in a way that allows no simple transfer between

---

[27] For a discussion of the *SEL* narrator's ambivalent attitude to women, see Thompson, *Everyday Saints*, pp. 139–71. The most complete text of the *Southern Passion* 'Defence of Women' appears in O. S. Pickering, 'The "Defence of Women" from the *Southern Passion*: A New Edition', *South English Legendary*, ed. Jankofsky, pp. 154–76.

[28] The murderess in the life of Kenelm is unsuccessful in her attempts to poison her brother and she dispatches Askbert to deal the final death blow.

subject positions within and beyond the text. The knight–suitor may have functioned as a point of identification for certain (impious) readers of the legend looking for sexual titillation, but it is the abbess who is the ultimate embodiment of sin, in her position as a representative of institutional power.

Power, and its mismanagement, is a theme that appears more generally in other legends collected in *SEL* manuscripts; the ascription of violence in these texts is specifically related to the work's linguistic context. We have seen, in the Mildred narrative, how torments are displaced to a location outside England: the abbey is situated in a 'strange londe' (65) across the sea, implicitly France, enabling the text to set up an exemplary contrast between two good (English) abbesses and a bad (foreign) abbess. This is in keeping with *SEL*'s 'anti-Norman' sentiments, which have often been remarked upon by critics.[29] Just as the tormentors of *SEL*'s Latin martyrs might be represented, anachronistically, as Muslims, they also had things in common, linguistically, with the kings and aristocrats of thirteenth-century England: the wicked protagonists in many of these legends address their saintly interlocutors with phrases such as 'bel ami', 'beu frere' and 'beu sire'. The use of such language places the tormentors within an Anglo-Norman milieu and hints at another context for the legendary's circulation. *SEL* is the first large-scale anthology of writings in Middle English; most religious writing produced in this period was in Latin and the bulk of vernacular texts circulated during the thirteenth century were in Anglo-Norman. It is also clear that writing in English in the late thirteenth and early fourteenth centuries was a political decision: while *SEL* contains no explicit petitions on behalf of the English language such as those found in the Prologue to Robert Mannyng's *Chronicle* of 1338, the *SEL* Prologue has little positive to say about the world of courtly romance.[30] Moreover, certain legends incorporated into *SEL* manuscripts allow political sympathies to bubble dramatically to the surface. The life of Wulfstan, bishop of Worcester between 1062 and 1095, includes an account of the battle of Hastings in which the Norman invader is labelled 'William Bastard' (10.63); the legend subsequently includes a fictionalised episode in which William and Archbishop Lanfranc attempt to force his resignation as bishop, in terms reminiscent of martyrdom hagiography. William has already, through Hastings, been linked with the spilling of 'so many mannes blod' (11.88), a

---

[29] Jill Frederick, 'The *South English Legendary*: Anglo-Saxon Saints and National Identity', *Literary Appropriations of the Anglo-Saxons from the Thirteenth to the Twentieth Century*, ed. Donald Scragg and Carole Weinberg (Cambridge: Cambridge University Press, 2000), pp. 57–73; Renee Hamelinck, 'St Kenelm and the Legends of the English Saints in the *South English Legendary*', *Companion to Early Middle English Literature*, ed. N. H. G. E. Veldhoen and H. Aertsen (Amsterdam: Free University Press, 1988), pp. 21–30; Klaus P. Jankofsky, 'National Characteristics in the Portrayal of English Saints in the *South English Legendary*', *Images of Sainthood*, ed. Blumenfeld-Kosinski and Szell, pp. 98–93, p. 85; Thompson, *Everyday Saints*, pp. 46–50.

[30] On the politics of writing in English in this period, see Thorlac Turville-Petre, *England the Nation: Language, Literature and National Identity, 1290–1340* (Oxford: Clarendon, 1996); Thompson, *Everyday Saints*, pp. 26–46. For an argument that the Katherine Group life of Juliana possesses a comparable ideological remit in the promotion of Anglo-Saxon ethnic identity, see Gayle Margherita, *The Romance of Origins: Language and Sexual Difference in Middle English Literature* (Philadelphia: University of Pennsylvania Press, 1994), pp. 43–61, and see also Lewis in this volume on hagiographic representation of the national past.

description that alludes to the atrocities of pagan tormentors, but it is also striking that Wulfstan is led into court 'as a þeof touore a Iustice' [like a thief before a judge] (12.108); in addition Wulfstan maintains a balance between speaking against the king 'baldelich' (11.95) and performing actions 'wel mildelich' (12.115, 130), thus displaying characteristics reminiscent of the attitudes of martyrs. Although William eventually concedes defeat, after Wulfstan has performed a dramatic miracle in which he thrusts his crosier into the tomb of Edward the Confessor (Edward was the Anglo-Saxon king who originally made him bishop), the conflict between sovereign power and saintly humility in the life of Wulfstan may have created an outlet for xenophobic sentiments on the part of the text's redactors. Certainly this is the case in Bodleian Library MS Laud 108, the earliest surviving *SEL* manuscript: in a passage excised from later versions of the collection, the narrator declares that when Edward the Confessor died 'Gret reuþe [pity] it was to al engelond, so weilawei þe stounde [accursed be the hour]/ For straunge men þere comen sethþe [after] and brou3ten enguelond to grounde'.[31]

If *SEL* weaves a complex web of associations between foreignness and violence, images with clear contemporary relevance to the collection's original creators and audiences, the work equally inscribes concepts of nation, language and religion with differences of class. Class proves less divisive in virgin martyr legends where both tormentors and saints are equally highborn, but several *SEL* legends are also populated by a cast of 'simple folk' who invariably take the saint's side.[32] We have already seen in the story of the Jewish Boy how 'folk' in the neighbourhood take action against the boy's father by casting him into the oven, and the followers of Thomas Becket are sometimes depicted as poor or simple people. In addition, the Anastasia legend includes an account of how the servants of the pagan judge, thinking he is an ugly devil, proceed to spit on their master and to beat him with 'duntes grete' [great blows] (587.45); in fact the judge's demonic appearance arises from his sexual liaison with the dirty pots and pans he mistakes for Anastasia's maids. The class conflict occasionally receives more specific inflections, too, as in the legend of Dominic contained in MS Laud 108, which incorporates a complimentary statement about the father of Simon de Montfort – a thinly veiled allusion to the son himself.[33] De Montfort was a popular hero who led a baronial revolt against Henry III; epitomising resistance to monarchical power, he was himself venerated as a saint-like figure in the aftermath of his death in the battle of Evesham in 1265. The sympathetic reference to de Montfort in certain versions of *SEL* is in keeping with the anti-Norman sentiments expressed elsewhere in the collection, since it points towards tensions between the monarchy and high nobility, characterised as foreign, and the broad ranks of the English baronage.[34] These references suggest,

---

[31] *The Early South-English Legendary*, ed. Carl Horstmann, EETS os 87 (London: Trübner, 1887), p. 72, lines 59–60.
[32] Thompson, *Everyday Saints*, pp. 50, 55–7, 177–8.
[33] *Early South-English Legendary*, ed. Horstmann, p. 279, lines 40–4.
[34] Thomas J. Heffernan, 'Dangerous Sympathies: Political Commentary in the *South English Legendary*', *South English Legendary*, ed. Jankofsky, pp. 1–17.

collectively, that the conflicts encountered in representations of hagiographic violence register a complex interplay between notions of class, language and nation in thirteenth- and fourteenth-century England.

Conclusion

This chapter has not dealt explicitly with one manifestation of sacred violence that plays a significant role in certain modes of hagiography: violence turned against the self. *SEL* includes occasional instances of the phenomenon, for example the scene where Benedict, responding to a visit by a demonic temptress, strips himself naked like a martyr and rolls around in thorns. Martyrdom, in this scene, provides a script for monastic discipline and a model for penance: the narrator comments that Benedict amends his sins through pain, 'as we ssolde oure mid riȝte' [as we should rightly do ourselves] (122.25), a message especially appropriate to lay readers in the wake of Lateran IV. At the same time, hagiographers were careful not to promote more extreme modes of self-violation to ordinary lay folk. One of the miracle stories included in the life of James of Compostela concerns a young pilgrim who is confronted by a devil disguised as James. The devil tells the man he must do penance for the lechery he has committed, by cutting off the member with which he has sinned; 'þe sunne ichelle þe forȝiue [I shall forgive you the sin]', the devil exclaims, 'ȝif þou wost beo imartrid · & þisulue martri [martyr thyself] for mi loue' (338.336–8). The pilgrim does as the devil suggests and dies of his injuries, but the real James intervenes and intercedes with the Virgin Mary on the pilgrim's behalf. Mary brings the man back to life, although he has to make do henceforth with a little hole 'wanne he wolde pisse' (340.382) instead of the genitals he removed. This story expresses a concern that the boundaries between the legitimate sacrifice of martyrs and gratuitous self-harm might be blurred. The most memorable model of sanctity in a collection such as *SEL* is martyrdom, but the miracle of the castrated pilgrim suggests that radical self-mutilation was not necessarily an acceptable method of bodily sublimation for ordinary Christians.

Instead it was the body of the exceptional Christian that was most frequently invoked in hagiography as a prop for ideology. Violence was a crucial component in the delineation of saintly identity and ultimately helped construct, through a process of analogical substantiation, the inviolable 'body' of the Church. At the same time, this chapter has demonstrated that symbolic binaries, and the violent struggles they produce, map onto one another in saints' lives; and that the forms in which this process manifests itself – the abject anti-bodies that loom large in the imaginations of hagiographers – often bear the traces of historical specificity. The precise identity of the 'victim' in a given text cannot always be established in advance, since the scapegoat for different Christian audiences shifted according to circumstance – from subjugated demon to evil stepmother, from child-abusing Jew to Anglo-Norman monarch, from 'Islamic' pagan to incontinent pope. In this respect, an overview of a 'collection' (in the loose *SEL* sense) permits different insights into the uses and abuses of violence in hagiography than that provided by studies limited to one or two individual saints, since it foregrounds the symbolic exchanges that transpire between different models of sanctity (say between virgin martyr narratives and the story of an Anglo-Saxon abbess, or between a roasted male martyr and the oven-baked Jewish boy). The characterisation of certain saints' lives as pious pornography may be appropriate to the extent that violent scenes in Middle English hagiography have the capacity to elicit sexual responses; but critical readings also need to pay attention to the full range of inter- and extra-textual meanings attached to sacred violence. Violence and hagiography form a productive partnership with one another because violence provides the representational support for a complex symbolic system – and it is in this sense that suffering, as the *SEL* Prologue narrator puts it, bears 'frut'.

5

Gender and Sexuality

ANKE BERNAU

As holy examples of Christian perfection, saints were frequently treated or promoted as patterns for ideal behaviour – either for male or female religious, but also for lay audiences in late medieval England. It is not surprising that this 'ideal' was also gendered, as it was believed that men and women should occupy different positions and perform different roles within society, no matter how much or little this view accorded with the complexities of lived reality.[1] They were constructed as different (and *differently*) by a range of discourses, from medical to romance texts, as well as by hagiography.[2] While many of the authors or translators of saints' lives in late medieval England still tended to be male as well as clerical, this chapter will show that the way in which gender and sexuality are represented is far from monolithic.

Hagiography deals with the lives of holy individuals representing a wide range of gendered lay and religious positions: male and female virgins, widows, wives, husbands, eunuchs, transvestites, queens, kings, hermits, bishops, popes, monks, nuns and so on. Sexuality is equally multiple: husbands and wives are either living within chaste marriages or have numerous children; virgins are either sexually aroused and must fight temptation or have already overcome fleshly desires; eunuchs raise the question as to whether their seeming absence of sexual desire is a spiritual accomplishment or a by-product of their physical state; prostitutes copulate extravagantly until they repent, often also extravagantly.

---

[1] See *Gender and Holiness: Men, Women and Saints in Late Medieval Europe*, ed. Samantha J. E. Riches and Sarah Salih (London: Routledge, 2002).

[2] There is a vast amount of literature on this. In addition to works cited below, see, for instance, *Medieval Theology and the Natural Body*, ed. Peter Biller and A. J. Minnis (York: York Medieval Press, 1997); *Woman Defamed and Woman Defended: An Anthology of Medieval Texts*, ed. Alcuin Blamires with Karen Pratt and C. W. Marx (Oxford: Clarendon Press, 1992); Caroline Walker Bynum, *Fragmentation and Redemption: Essays on Gender and the Human Body in Medieval Religion* (New York: Zone Books, 1991); *Becoming Male in the Middle Ages*, ed. Jeffrey Jerome Cohen and Bonnie Wheeler (New York: Garland, 1997); Ruth Mazo Karras, *From Boys to Men: Formations of Masculinity in Late Medieval Europe* (Philadelphia: University of Pennsylvania Press, 2003); Thomas Laqueur, *Making Sex: Body and Gender from the Greeks to Freud* (Cambridge MA: Harvard University Press, 1992); *Constructing Medieval Sexuality*, ed. Karma Lochrie, Peggy McCracken and James A. Schultz (Minneapolis: University of Minnesota Press, 1997); *Gendered Voices: Medieval Saints and Their Interpreters*, ed. Catherine M. Mooney (Philadelphia: University of Pennsylvania Press, 1999); *Framing Medieval Bodies*, ed. Miri Rubin and Sarah Kay (Manchester: Manchester University Press, 1994).

The work of feminist, gender and queer theorists in the past two to three decades has shown that gender and sexuality must be understood as cultural and historical constructions, rather than natural, stable, self-explanatory categories.³ They are shifting, mutable terms, whose definitions are dependent on numerous factors, such as who is writing and when, what genre is being written in, what tropes are being used, which audience is being addressed, and so on: such factors are addressed in other chapters of this *Companion*. While gender and sexuality are not synonymous or interchangeable terms, they are nonetheless fundamentally interconnected. Simon Gaunt states that they 'are not the same thing, but nor can they be theorized separately. Like gender, sex is not ahistorical; the value and meaning given to sexual acts and desires evolves according to historical circumstance.'⁴ As this chapter will show, hagiography is a good place to look for both the ideals of and tensions within medieval representations of gender and sexuality.

To begin with, there are generic considerations that govern the type of saint under consideration: the main structural difference is that between the *vita* and the *passio*. The *vita* describes the life of a saint, while the *passio* tells of the passion – the martyrdom – of a saint; not all saints are martyrs and this distinction has a profound impact on the ways in which sanctity is performed and achieved.⁵ At the same time what underlies and to some extent unites all of these distinct manifestations is the protagonist's zealous Christian faith. As the saints are ideal exemplars of heroic Christianity, one can expect certain traits or ideals of behaviour that will be shared by all, regardless of gender, sexuality, manner of life or death and so on. In fact, one major theme that informs the representation of gender and sexuality within hagiography is the transformative and unifying potential of the Christian faith:

> For as the body is one, and hath many members; and all the members of the body, whereas they are many, yet are one body: So also is Christ.
> For in one Spirit were we all baptized into one body.⁶

Terms such as 'body' and 'spirit' were deeply gendered, women being aligned with the former and men with the latter. The paradigmatic body, representing the 'norm', was also male, as both religious and medical treatises explained that the male was the superior creation. Women, it was thought, were not only more prone to sin but were also physically inferior to men, lacking the heat that was believed to be crucial for nature to manifest itself in its most perfect form. This meant that the binary of male–female was viewed as asymmetrical. Women were urged by religious writers to achieve a more masculine identity through spirituality and chastity – traits which were thought to turn them away from

---

3 See, for instance, Judith Butler, *Gender Trouble: Feminism and the Subversion of Identity* (New York: Routledge, 1990) and *Bodies That Matter: On the Discursive Limits of 'Sex'* (New York: Routledge, 1993); Mark D. Jordan, *The Invention of Sodomy in Christian Theology* (Chicago: University of Chicago Press, 1997).
4 Simon Gaunt, *Gender and Genre in Medieval French Literature* (Cambridge: Cambridge University Press, 1995), p. 14.
5 See Gaunt, *Gender and Genre*, p. 186.
6 1 Corinthians 12:12–13

their more carnal natures – while men were never exhorted by the same writers to become more like *women*, even though they might be encouraged to follow the example of a specific saintly *woman*. This is an idea expressed succinctly by St Jerome, who states that the woman 'who becomes more a servant of Christ than of the secular sphere . . . ceases to be a woman (*mulier*) and is called a man (*vir*)', since, he argues, 'we all aspire to the condition of perfect manhood'.[7] In her comprehensive study of medieval medical and scientific traditions, Joan Cadden points out that that the 'feminine' and the 'masculine' were associated with behavioural traits, which either sex could assume. She concludes that therefore 'manly', for instance, 'stands for a set of qualities derived from the notion of an ideal natural man, but applicable to women as well'.[8] This is an important recognition, which will inform the reading of gender and sexuality of all the saints' lives drawn on here: the tension between a belief, on the one hand, that men and women are fundamentally different – even opposites – and, on the other, the understanding that certain gendered traits and characteristics could be achieved and performed by either, thus contesting the notion of a clear opposition.

From the twelfth century onwards, sexuality became increasingly categorised as different aspects of sexual behaviour were regulated by a range of religious and legal authorities.[9] The demand that individuals be assimilated into heterosexual duality – alongside a more general concern with the division of society into clearly defined and bounded categories – was particularly prevalent in the eleventh to thirteenth centuries.[10] After marriage became a sacrament in the twelfth century, the Church was increasingly involved in a complex regulatory process which sought to emphasise the necessity of marriage upon the laity whilst no longer tolerating clerical marriages or concubinage. This was part of a sustained attempt to construct religious identities as different and separate from worldly identities, with an increased emphasis on the importance of sexual purity for both male and female religious.[11] Marriage was for the less pure and therefore, while the Church actively encouraged marriage for the laity, its clerical writers often depicted it as a state of strife and misery. While many clerical treatises on marriage from this period seem to be directed very clearly at men or women who are in or are thinking about embarking on a religious life, saints' lives were read by a wider audience.[12] As Gaunt points out, vernacular hagiog-

---

[7] St Jerome, 'Commentatorium in Epistolam ad Ephesios'; translation from John Oppel, 'Saint Jerome and the History of Sex', *Viator* 24 (1993), pp. 1–22, p. 21.

[8] Joan Cadden, *Meanings of Sex Difference in the Middle Ages: Medicine, Science, and Culture* (Cambridge: Cambridge University Press, 1993), p. 205.

[9] See Anke Bernau, 'Virginal Effects: Text and Identity in *Ancrene Wisse*', *Gender and Holiness*, ed. Riches and Salih, pp. 36–48; esp. pp. 37–8.

[10] See James A. Brundage, *Law, Sex, and Christian Society in Medieval Europe* (Chicago: University of Chicago Press, 1987), p. 3 and Dyan Elliott, *Spiritual Marriage: Sexual Abstinence in Medieval Wedlock* (Princeton: Princeton University Press, 1993).

[11] See Sarah Beckwith, 'Passionate Regulation: Enclosure, Ascesis, and the Feminist Imaginary', *South Atlantic Quarterly* 93.4 (1994), pp. 803–24, p. 807; Bernau, 'Virginal Effects', p. 37; Jane Tibbetts Schulenburg, 'Strict Active Enclosure and its Effects on the Female Monastic Experience (ca. 500–1100)', *Medieval Religious Women I: Distant Echoes*, ed. John A. Nichols and Lillian Thomas Shank (Kalamazoo: Cistercian Publications, 1984), pp. 51–86, p. 78.

[12] See, for instance, *Holy Maidenhood, Anchoritic Spirituality: Ancrene Wisse and Associated*

raphy, unlike Latin hagiography, was not just produced within clerical circles for clerical audiences. He concludes that vernacular hagiography therefore cannot be read simply as an expression of either clerical *or* lay values, but as a complex blend of the two.[13] In addition, marriage was increasingly used by religious writers such as Bernard of Clairvaux (1090–1153) as a metaphor, to describe the passionate union of the faithful soul with Christ.

In collections of saints' lives such as the immensely popular *Golden Legend*, translated from Latin into English by William Caxton in the fifteenth century, it is more common to find the motif of idealised Christian marriage in the background, only occasionally drawn upon. Most of the saints themselves are not married, but in some instances they come from exemplary parents. St Nicholas, for instance, is said to have been 'born of rich and holy kin', who, after bringing him into the world, 'lived in continence and led an heavenly life'.[14] That desiring sex within marriage apart from the purpose of procreation is sinful was a view expressed from the Church Fathers onwards. In his 'On Marriage and Concupiscence' Augustine of Hippo, citing St Paul, explains that 'chastity in the married state is God's gift', chastity here referring not to marital fidelity but to sexual abstinence within the marital relationship itself.[15] Sex within marriage was acceptable only if its purpose was procreation; otherwise it was bestial, practised only for 'the gratification of lust'.[16]

Ideal marriage is most ideally represented by the Blessed Virgin Mary's parents, Anne and Joachim. In his version of the life, Osbern Bokenham, an Augustinian friar, tells us that both Anne and Joachim are virtuous and therefore well matched. Before Anne becomes pregnant with Mary, 'Twenty wynter þey lyued wyth-out issw,/ In chast maryage and not vycyous.'[17] Their chastity in turn provides the perfect, unblemished source for Mary's purity and chastity. Another example of chaste marriage is found in the life of St Cecilia, who can be understood as a sign of perfect chastity in three ways: she is and remains a virgin herself; she convinces her husband Valerian on their wedding night that they should live in a state of married chastity; she converts him to Christianity and so renders their marriage 'chaste' in body *and* in soul. St Alexis, another saint who convinces his betrothed to live in a chaste marriage on their wedding night, signals his stance towards marriage by his name: 'Alexis is as much as to say as going out of the law of marriage for to keep virginity for God's sake' (6.205). While there are some examples of married saints, marriage is not usually

---

Works, trans. Anne Savage and Nicholas Watson, with a preface by Benedicta Ward (New York: Paulist Press, 1991), pp. 223–43, p. 236; John Lydgate, 'Payne and Sorowe of Evyll Maryage', ed. Eve Salisbury (TEAMS online, http://www.lib.rochester.edu/camelot/teams/psfrm.htm), esp. lines 11–14.

[13] Gaunt, *Gender and Genre*, pp. 181–2.

[14] *Golden Legend*, trans. Caxton, vol. 2, p. 110. Further volume and page references to this edition will be given in brackets in the text.

[15] St Augustine, 'On Marriage and Concupiscence', bk 1, ch. 3, in *Medieval Sourcebook: St Augustine: From 'On Marriage and Concupiscence'* [http://www.fordham.edu/halsall/source/aug-marr.html]. October 1998. For the full text, see the Christian Classics Ethereal Library online.

[16] St Augustine, 'On Marriage', bk 1, ch. 5, *Medieval Sourcebook*.

[17] Bokenham, *Legendys*, lines 1659–60.

represented as co-existing easily with a holy life. So while Cecilia and Alexis may have married and have convinced their spouses to live in holy chastity, both Cecilia and her husband Valerian are martyred before long, and Alexis leaves his wife the morning after the wedding. In other instances, the marriage of a saint is acknowledged, but passed over or placed at a comfortable distance (6.213–16). At other times, the successful achievement of saintly – or even merely clerical – purity is shown to be affected detrimentally by marriage, for example in the life of St Remigius (Remy). Here Remigius's celibate, single status is contrasted with the married state of Genebaldus. While the latter has 'left his wife for to enter into religion', they begin to see each other again, and end up having sex numerous times. Eventually Genebaldus throws himself upon Remigius's mercy, renouncing his position as bishop (2.212).[18]

Marriage is not the only framework within which gendered and sexual identities are played out. The family context, primary in shaping the lives of all of its members in a range of hierarchical relationships, is also an arena in which sanctity and gender are performed and achieved.[19] Pious parents are sometimes shown to play an active role in placing the saint on his or her path towards holiness. St Pernelle (Petronilla), the daughter of St Peter the Apostle, is a beautiful virgin. Her father causes her to suffer from a fever and aches continuously and, when asked why, replies 'For it is expedient to her to be sick.' Her beauty is perceived to be a threat to her virginity, and her father's punishment portrayed – and understood by both him and Petronilla – as a salutary means of keeping her chastity safe (3.187). In the case of St Marina, one of several cross-dressing female saints, it is her widowed father who causes her to don men's clothes so that she can enter the monastery with him. St Quirine is a rarer example; he is an infant martyr. His mother, Juliet, is tortured for refusing to worship idols. Her three-year-old son witnesses this and begins to cry. When the pagan provost tries to comfort him, the child pushes him away, crying out as if to say 'And I am also Christian.' The provost responds by hurling the child down the steps, so that 'the tender brain fell abroad out of his head upon the steps'. Juliet is said to be 'therof right glad', giving 'thankings unto God' that her child has gone to heaven before her (3.225). Here, parents and children unite in faith, demonstrating what is presented as idealised gendered and familial relations.

Nonetheless, Christianity is more frequently shown to disrupt or redefine the definition of 'family' and therefore also to renegotiate the roles for men and women posited in that framework. St Alexis, mentioned above, might have come from pious and chaste Christian parents, and might have convinced his wife to live chastely, but this does not mean that these relationships are not dramatically transformed by his decision to dedicate his life to God. After living in Syria for seventeen years, he returns to Rome and is taken into his parents' home unrecognised, living there as an impoverished pilgrim. When he dies and his parents are told who he is, the life recounts in vivid detail the family's grief, with his mother's lament pinpointing the lack they all perceive in him: 'Thou

---

[18] After being shut in a tiny cell for seven years, he is forgiven and reinstated.
[19] For more on kinship, see Claire M. Waters, 'Power and Authority' in this volume, pp. 83–6.

sawest thy father, and me thy sorrowful mother so oft weep for thee, and wouldst never make to us *semblance of son*' (6.211: my emphasis). Performing the usual duties in a recognisable fashion would have made Alexis achieve the 'semblance of a son'; the fact that he doesn't means that all that those around him see is the pilgrim he has chosen to become. This is also exemplified by the life of St Sebastian, in which two noble brothers, Marcellianus and Marcus, are encouraged by the saint to strive for martyrdom. Their wives, clutching their small infants, cry out to them: 'Say ye now that be our dear husbands, in what ward leave ye us and your children! . . . [I]n what manner may ye be so hardened, so *out of nature*, and so cruel?' (2.233; my emphasis). In these examples, the traditional – here referred to as 'natural' – obligations of men as sons, husbands and fathers are shown to be swept aside by the more insistent demands of their religious calling, which justifies their actions as well as redefining what 'natural' masculinity entails. All of the relationships which characterise secular, heterosexual masculinity are displaced; a whole community is being put aside. Sebastian warns them, 'lose ye not the everlasting life for the blandishing words of women', and the pleas of family and friends are put down to blind ignorance: 'if they knew what is that other life . . . without doubt they would haste them for to go with you' (2.235). Sebastian reminds the parents of Marcellianus and Marcus that their sons will prepare a better life for them in the hereafter, demonstrating that they are still fulfilling the duties of sons and husbands, but in what is a more – the only – meaningful context.

Appropriating tropes and motifs taken from the secular sphere – as well as from the romance genre – allows the writers of hagiography to recontextualise them in what is represented as their 'real' meaning: a 'true' knight is a soldier of Christ, focusing on the afterlife. The same transformation is found in lives of female saints. When St Pauline (Paula) turns herself completely towards God after her husband's death, she leaves her five children to follow Paulinus, patriarch of Antioch, and Epiphanius, bishop of Cyprus, to Jerusalem: 'for the amorous desire that she had to Jesu Christ surmounted the love that she had to her children' (3.2). The word 'amorous' here highlights how differently love or desire signifies in a Christian framework: had she left her children for any worldly 'amorous desire' it would have signalled utter depravity, while here it demonstrates her superior faith. Christianity bestows a different primary gender role on her – that of Christ's lover – and her role as mother must give way before it. Christianity claims for itself the right to define relationships, as is made explicit in the life of St John the Almoner, when the saint tells his nephew that 'very affinity is not only of the flesh and blood, but it is known by the strength of virtue' (2.275).

Some lives are even more direct in their negative representation of secular family ties, showing them to be *actively* destructive. In the life of St Andrew, a young man comes to the saint, telling him that his mother has tried to commit incest with him. His refusal causes her to accuse him of attempted rape to the authorities; if found guilty, he faces death. A more gruesome example of this can also be found in the life of St Christine. When Christine refuses to worship her father's idols, he has her imprisoned and then publicly tortured. In his version Bokenham tells his audience that, in an act of contemptuous defiance, Christine takes a gobbet of her flesh and throws it into her father's face 'as she had lyst to iape [play]'.[20] In the *Golden Legend*'s version, she challenges her father to eat her flesh, which he has begotten (4.95). The saint is repudiating her flesh and her kinship in the most literal and dramatic way possible, drawing on the potent symbolic nexus of cannibalism/ blood relation/ eucharistic imagery in the process. This act denies the father's ownership of his daughter's body – or, rather, restricts his possession of her strictly to the physical sphere. Her Christian faith makes her a member of the body of Christ, which was believed to be enacted literally in celebrations of the Eucharist. That trope of consumption is played off against the devouring that Urban represents: while the latter destroys, the former purifies and makes anew. The way in which Bokenham's version lingers on the saint's budding sexuality and her father's desire to keep her hidden from potential suitors also suggests the possibility of incestuous desire on the father's part.[21]

It is important to point out that these examples do not propose that the gender hierarchies of a patriarchal system no longer apply, just that such terms as 'father', 'wife', 'child' and 'family' signify differently. While in the lives of female saints, Christianity is shown to facilitate their change from obedient daughters and wives to outspoken heroines of the faith, this is understood to be justifiable within a very specific context, because their obedience is now owed to the supreme patriarch: God the Father. In the case of rebellious wives, the husbands in question are usually pagan and at times the implication is that the women therefore are not required to be obedient to them. This to some extent contains the subversive potential of female disobedience, even rendering it humorous. When, in the life of St Thomas the Apostle, the king of India's wife converts, thereafter refusing to sleep with her husband, it is not difficult to detect a certain *schadenfreude* here, as the refusal to sleep with the king entails consequences for the wider secular realm (2.146). At the same time, it is emphasised that the queen is utterly obedient and humble towards Thomas; male Christian holy authority has *replaced* the pagan husband's authority. In other, similar, cases such as in John Capgrave's *Life of St Katharine of Alexandria* (c. 1445), the converted, rebellious wife of the pagan oppressor is martyred, therefore confining the disobedience to a limited if heroic moment.[22] In fact, the very sense that what is happening here is dramatic evidence of the transformative power of Christianity also shows that patriarchal gender hierarchies are still in place; these women are, as saints and martyrs, after all *exceptional*. The pagan husbands are emasculated as their wives turn towards a superior masculine power; it is noticeable that the various heathen tyrants and administrators are depicted in ways which belie their masculinity: they rant, they are out of control, they are ultimately helpless. Within those relationships, it is the Christian wife who becomes more 'masculine' than her husband; *within* a Christian context, however, she is located in a paradigm where masculine Chris-

---

[20] Bokenham, *Legendys*, line 2469.
[21] The hint of incest, however, is not discernable in the *Golden Legend*'s version.
[22] John Capgrave, *The Life of St Katharine of Alexandria*, ed. Carl Horstmann, with a foreword by F. J. Furnivall, EETS os 100 (London: Kegan Paul, Trench, Trübner, 1893).

tian authority is superior. Gendering therefore also depends on other categories, such as race, religion and class. As Gaunt notes, a secular patriarchy is being challenged and shown to be overcome by a spiritual one.[23]

The example of a contemporary medieval female saint who wished to maintain her virginity – Elizabeth of Hungary (d. 1231), 'the kyngys doughtyr [of] vngarye [Hungary],/ & wyf to Langrauye, pryince of turyngye [Thuringia]' – is instructive in thinking through the effect that historical context has on the depiction of gender.[24] In Bokenham's words, Elizabeth is 'By hyr [fadyr] constreynyd to entryn . . . / The state wych longyth to weddit men' and agrees reluctantly to do 'hyr fadrys wyl'.[25] Obedience to her father is emphasised and obedience to male authority remains a central theme in this *vita*, particularly in the saint's relationship with her spiritual advisor, Master Conrad, who is of far lower social status than she. When she visits a nunnery without consulting him, his rage is so great that

> he hyr so sore eek dede betyn be
> That thre wokys aftyr both morwe & eue
> The merkys of hyr wundys men myht se.[26]

Here, the demands of her worldly status meet religious ideals; the requirements of the lay sphere are clearly not synonymous with those of the religious. The implication in this *vita* is that, while secular masculine authority cannot be repudiated in the absolute manner that a pagan setting allows, it is nonetheless inferior – and therefore ideally subordinate – to a religious masculine authority. Furthermore, the emphasis on obedience in this life is extended and made relevant to both women *and* men in a passage where Bokenham contrasts Elizabeth's exemplary behaviour with that of contemporary religious:

> What wumman koude now obeyin to
> Swych a comaundement wythoute offence
> As dede þis myroure of pacyence, lo!
> Vnneth ony nunne yt mekely wold do;
> And, to seyn pleyn treuthe, I trowe yt nolde here
> Wyth-owtyn murmur & grucchyng also
> Neythyr prest ner munk, chanoun ner frere.[27]

Thus, while there are clearly gendered aspects to this *vita*, there are other instances when gender differences are erased in discussions of qualities that are perceived to be desirable in both, such as obedience.[28]

A type of *vita* in which gender and sexuality most obviously play a defining role is that which relates the repentance of a once sexually promiscuous woman. The most well known of such examples is the life of Mary Magdalene. Bokenham

---

[23] Gaunt, *Gender and Genre*, p. 196.
[24] Bokenham, *Legendys*, lines 9463–4.
[25] Bokenham, *Legendys*, lines 9669–70, line 9676.
[26] Bokenham, *Legendys*, lines 10334–6.
[27] Bokenham, *Legendys*, lines 9834–40.
[28] For a reading of Elizabeth that focuses on her social status, see Waters in this volume, pp. 74–5.

describes how she combines 'Youthe, abundaunce, & eek beute' and yet 'for lak of deu dylygence' these very qualities show themselves – as they so frequently do in such narratives – as 'Mynystrys ... vn-to insolence,/ And of alle vycys þe bryngers yn'.[29] Similarly, Mary of Egypt explains to the priest Zozimus in the *Golden Legend* that, from the age of twelve, she was a 'public' woman in Alexandria for seventeen years, 'abandoned [her body] to lechery and refused no man' (3.107). In both of these examples, extensive repentance follows on their recognition of their sinfulness. This is also the case with the beautiful courtesan, Thaïs, who is taken by the abbot Pafuntius [sic] to 'a monastery of virgins, and there he closed her in a cell, and sealed the door with lead' (5.242). This motif of the sexually dissolute sinner is one that is told mainly about women and is perhaps best expressed in the explanation of Thaïs's name:

> Thais is said of taphos, that is to say death, for she was the cause of the death of many that died for her in sin. Or she is said of thalos, that is to say delight, for she was delicious to men, and accomplished all worldly delights, or she is said of thalamo, that is will or affection of marriage, for at the last she had will to be married to God by great penance. (5.240–1)

Death, sensual delight and marriage are all tropes shown to be intricately bound up with Thaïs's gender and sexuality. Here, overcoming carnal, feminine nature through 'great penance' is shown to be heroic enough to merit sanctity, even while there are also moments where the representation of the women's gender is blurred. Mary Magdalene is so reformed and full of grace that she is explicitly referred to as a 'preacher', a role that lay men and *all* women were explicitly forbidden to perform in late medieval England, and the life concludes by referring to her as '[t]hys holy *apostelesse*', an even more exceptional epithet.[30] After forty-seven years spent in the desert, Mary of Egypt is so transformed that she is now a role model for the priest, Zozimus, who goes to the desert to find 'some holy fathers' – it emerges that she is, in fact, the 'holy father' he has looked for (3.106). The penance these women perform offers them some access to roles that were gendered masculine. Age and self-renunciation play a large role in this process; the further away they are not just in spiritual but also in temporal terms from their sexualised youth, the less they are defined by the negative qualities associated with femininity. Such examples tend not to be found in the lives of holy men; even when they are shown to struggle with sexual temptation, the trope of the extreme 'sexual sinner' is decidedly gendered, in keeping with beliefs surrounding female sexuality and carnality.

While previous work on gender and hagiography has tended to focus on the representations of female saints, particularly female virgin martyrs, more recent work in the field has seen an emerging interest in the question of how male sanc-

---

[29] Bokenham, *Legendys*, lines 5397–400.
[30] Bokenham, *Legendys*, l. 6301. For more on women's preaching, see Alcuin Blamires, *The Case for Women in Medieval Culture* (Oxford: Clarendon Press, 1997) and Claire M. Waters, *Angels and Earthly Creatures: Preaching, Performance, and Gender in the Later Middle Ages* (Philadelphia: University of Pennsylvania Press, 2003).

tity is constructed in these narratives.[31] To treat 'male saints' as a heading designating a particular group of holy men, or a particular *kind* of masculine sanctity is impossible, just as there is no simple category of 'female saints'. Even a relatively brief overview of, for instance, the *Golden Legend*, will reveal the sheer variety of how male saints are represented. There are virgins, eunuchs, fathers, hermits, apostles, bishops, popes, clerics, knights, kings and so on. What this demonstrates is that the representation of gender in these narratives is frequently related to other categories, such as class or profession, the latter of which is not as prominent in the lives of female saints.

One recurring theme is that of the male saint as a teacher, a preacher – someone who has authority and acts publicly, such as St Silvester (2.197). St George's name crystallises what was viewed as a specifically Christian 'perfect masculinity', for it signifies that 'He was a pilgrim in the sight of the world, and he was cut and detrenched by the crown of martyrdom, and he was a good councillor in preaching' (3.126). In the lives of male saints it may appear initially as though gender is not foregrounded in the self-conscious way it is in those of female saints, but if this is so, it is only because masculinity was understood as 'the norm' and the naturally more spiritual gender. Men could – indeed *should* – act publicly, vocally, spiritually, i.e. like men. Learning and education – especially in religious matters – are emphasised in a number of male saints' lives in ways that are rarely found in the lives of female saints. This learnedness is intimately connected with other types of virtues, which demonstrate the saint's suitability for acting as a public role model to others, stressing their authority. After highlighting his extensive education and remarkable courage, the life of the apostle Matthias tells us that his exemplary nature could be seen in the fact that '[h]e did that which he preached' (3.59). The emphasis here on *action* and *practice* is based on the assumption that men can live their spirituality in ways either not available to women at all (as bishops, popes, saintly kings), or only in a limited fashion, as a sign of a particular woman's exceptional status (as martyrs, teachers, advisors, role models). The contrast here is not so much between the 'carnal' man (in the sexual sense) and the 'spiritual' man, but between the 'secular' man and the 'spiritual' man, where 'worldly' is often, though not exclusively, aligned with 'carnal'. That perfect masculinity is claimed by and for Christianity, is shown explicitly in the life of Thomas Becket. After the English king, Henry II, has made him archbishop, he 'became a holy man, suddenly changed into a new man, doing great penance ... And under his habit he ware the habit of a monk, and so was he under within forth a monk, and outward a clerk' (2.184–5). Evidence of this new *inner* perfection is made visible in externalised actions, in performances of humility and self-mortification. He is not the same as he was; being 'a holy man' means living a completely different

---

[31] For a range of varied readings of virgin martyrs see, for instance, Gail Ashton, *The Generation of Identity in Late Medieval Hagiography: Speaking the Saint* (London: Routledge, 2000); Kathleen Coyne Kelly, *Performing Virginity and Testing Chastity in the Middle Ages* (London: Routledge, 2000); Sarah Salih, *Versions of Virginity in Late Medieval England* (Cambridge: Brewer, 2001); Jocelyn Wogan-Browne, *Saints' Lives and Women's Literary Culture c. 1150–1300: Virginity and Its Authorizations* (Oxford: Oxford University Press, 2001).

kind of masculinity, which is underlined by the break in his previously close relationship with the king. It is noticeable that masculinity in these lives is frequently established in the relationships men have with each other, rather than primarily with regard to their relationships with women. Thus, Becket's new identity is lived out in the tension between seeming a 'clerk' but being a 'monk' underneath.[32] In contrast, female saints tend to be represented through the ways in which they relate to various men in their lives, be they lovers, husbands, fathers, suitors, tyrants or clerics.

Nonetheless, sexuality and its relationship to gender are also recurring themes in the lives of male saints, even if they do not always present the focal point of the narrative. Virginity, for instance, is mentioned numerous times as the condition in which some of the male saints live, even if it is not as pervasive or indeed as emphasised as it is in the lives of female virgin saints.[33] While many of the narrative tropes in the lives of male virgin saints are similar to those in the lives of female virgin martyrs – pagan parents, heathen communities, singular in their holiness – the latter are not usually or routinely referred to as brilliant preachers and leaders of men. Instead, it is mainly their physical beauty and spiritual purity that are focused on, even while they might also be exceptionally eloquent in their defiance.

Virginity is also a state that male saints convince other people – frequently women – to maintain. On his travels to India, St Thomas the Apostle extols a newly-wed couple to maintain the 'sureness of your flesh, the which is queen of all virtues' (2.141). Saints Nereus and Achilleus, both of whom are 'gelded', convert the young wife Domicella, Emperor Domitian's niece, by impressing upon her the importance of virginity. Their own 'sexless' state can be read as analogous to virginity and they use the familiar contrast between the lives of virgins and the lives of wives to persuade her: '[T]hey praised it much in showing that it was . . . *of nature born with creature human*. And the woman that is married is subject to man, and is beaten with staves and fists' (3.179). She promptly converts, taking the veil to her husband's impotent fury. Here virginity is not only represented as innate in human beings – as the most natural state of all – but is also an identity that can only be claimed by Christians. This allows the writer to suggest that being human also means being Christian. In this sense, virginity can be read as a gender and sexual identity that erases differences within Christianity, requiring certain traits of all men and women who choose to commit themselves to it. At the same time, however, this levelling movement is counteracted by the divergent ways in which virginity is related to men and women in the *vitae*.

In the lives of male saints virginity (or chastity) is a virtue mentioned alongside others the saint possesses, rather than providing the central narrative thrust. When it does appear as central, it tends to do so as chastity under attack; the male saint as struggling with sexual temptation, which is rarely the case in the narratives of female virgin saints. In the life of St Benet, or Benedict, the saint

---

[32] For more on the construction of Thomas Becket's authority see Waters in this volume, pp. 77–80.

is assaulted by desire after he has chosen the life of a hermit: 'And after that came to him a great temptation of the flesh, by the which the devil tempted him in showing him a woman, and he burnt sore' (3.82). Sexual temptation is a recurring theme, and in its depiction it is likened – sometimes explicitly – to forms of torture. This is made clear in the life of St Paul Hermit, who sees two Christian men being tortured. The first one is coated with honey and left in the burning sun to be stung to death by wasps because 'he abode firmly in his faith'. While the reason for the second man's punishment is not stated as clearly, the emphasis on his youth highlights not only the cruelty of the pagan judge, but also his susceptibility to sexual temptation. This is confirmed by the nature of his torture, which involves being tied down on a bed strewn with sweet-smelling flowers and herbs:

> After, [the judge] made an harlot, a ribald, come to him alone for to touch his members and his body, to move to lechery. Finally, when the voluptuosity of his flesh surmounted him, and he might not defend himself ne his members, he bit off a piece of his tongue and spit it in her visage. (2.205)

Here, the man's dramatic and successful resistance to sexual desire is represented as worthy of 'laud and victory' in a manner reminiscent of the lives of the female saints discussed above. While on one level the biting off of the tongue is a motif that is similar to St Christine's careless attitude to her flesh, the difference is that the male saint depicted here inflicts injury on himself because he feels intense sexual arousal, a motif only rarely found in the lives of female virgin martyrs.[34] Biting out his tongue in order to master his unruly flesh provides an interesting parallel between the tongue and penis, highlighting some of the underlying attitudes to male sanctity. As men were believed to be by nature more reasonable than women, the issue of self-control, the role played by the will, is also central to what it meant to be male and to be holy. Reason and will triumph over carnality in a climactic moment (displacing the sexual climax this scenario was building up to), rather than a drawn-out process of complete self-transformation that Thaïs or Mary of Egypt go through. It is also worth noting that while the women overcome a carnality which has been shown to destroy others, the young man in the life of St Paul Hermit is being tempted by a woman rather than being the tempter himself.

The tensions and inconsistencies inherent in categories of gender and sexuality arguably find their most complex expression in the lives of virgin saints. The condition of womanhood was divided into three estates placed on a hierarchical scale in medieval thought: virginity ranked highest, widowhood came second and the role of wife last. As *Holy Maidenhood* explains: '[Y]ou can understand by the degrees of their happiness which one surpasses the others and by how much. For marriage brings forth her fruit thirtyfold in heaven, widowhood

---

[33] See, for example, the life of St John the Evangelist, *Golden Legend*, trans. Caxton, vol. 2, pp. 161–76, esp. p. 161.
[34] An exception to this is found in the life of St Justina, *Golden Legend*, trans. Caxton, vol. 5, pp. 166–72.

sixtyfold; maidenhood, with a hundredfold, outdoes them both.'[35] This hierarchy shows that women were always defined according to a certain state of sexuality which, in this explicitly heterosexist model, meant in relation to men. The state viewed as most removed from an expression of sexuality – virginity – was praised as the most ideal. While we have seen examples of married and widowed saints, the category of female virgin saint – and really usually female virgin *martyr* – provides the largest number of narratives about female sanctity.[36] In Bokenham's *Legendys*, ten out of the thirteen lives contained in the collection are about virgin martyrs; the other three are, respectively, the lives of Anne, the mother of the Virgin Mary; the repentant whore Mary Magdalene; and Elizabeth of Hungary, none of whom are martyrs. So virginity does seem disproportionately important for women, and has a disconcertingly close relationship with death and torture in hagiography.

The repeated formula according to which these narratives are structured presents the audience with a young, exceptionally beautiful maiden, who is usually of noble birth. The maiden wishes to keep herself chaste for Christ, but is pursued by a powerful suitor whose advances she spurns. Proclaiming her faith and frequently challenging male authorities in public, she is imprisoned, tortured and eventually killed. Bokenham's life of St Faith opens by telling us that

> Thys mayd born was of nobyllest blood
> Of al þat cyte as touchyng nature;
> And thow she fayre were, she also was good,
> And in al hir werkys both clene & pure,
> Of contenaunce sad and of chere demure.[37]

St Agnes, next in the collection, is young, but 'in hir soule she had suffycyent age'.[38] Their purity is one of body *and* of soul, for true virginity cannot reside in the body alone. In addition to these stereotypically feminine virtues, they are also sometimes depicted as possessing some that are more usually associated with masculinity, such as wisdom, outspoken intelligence and steadfastness. One such motif is that of the 'soldier of Christ', found, for example, in the life of St Valentine in the *Golden Legend*; what is said here is also applicable to any of the female martyrs: 'the knight is said valiant that fleeth not, and smiteth and defendeth valiantly and overcometh much puissantly' (3.43). In the legend of Ursula and the eleven thousand virgins, the queen of Sicily, Gerasina, tells her daughters and the other virgins who have joined her that they are 'knights of her company' and they all 'swear [to] this new chivalry' (6.63). Learning is put at the forefront of Capgrave's life of Katherine of Alexandria, when he portrays her as a young queen, defending her choice of virginity in front of the lords and

---

[35] *Holy Maidenhood*, p. 233. As Savage and Watson note: 'The "three states" are a medieval commonplace'; *Anchoritic Spirituality*, p. 414, n. 31.
[36] See Bynum, *Fragmentation and Redemption*, p. 379, n. 81.
[37] Bokenham, *Legendys*, lines 3608–12.
[38] Bokenham, *Legendys*, line 4114.

learned clerks who want her to marry for the sake of political stability.[39] All versions of her life emphasise Katherine's wisdom, education and eloquence. This topos of outspoken – even rude – speech is a common one in the legends of female virgin martyrs.[40] Here we see very young women challenging kings, prefects, clerks – all of them men occupying worldly positions of prestige and power. Yet this power turns to naught in the face of the virgins' faith, purity and, at times, literally unstoppable speech.

While virginity was believed to be 'masculinising' in its effects, these representations replace an earthly with a heavenly passion. The virgin does not owe obedience to an earthly husband, but is nonetheless sexualised as the *sponsa Christi*, the bride of Christ.[41] These young women are kept within a heteronormative paradigm in that the earthly husband is replaced by a heavenly one; biological offspring with spiritual. At the same time, using the same terms for the virgin's relationship with Christ (or a male angel) as those used for women's relationships with men allows the saint's life to highlight the differences between the two. As St Agnes says about Christ: 'fulle oftyn in armys he halsyd [embraced] hath me/ Wyth-out blemyssyng of myn uirgynyte'.[42] On her wedding night, St Cecilia begins telling her spouse Valerian about her love for Christ by saying that 'An aungel of god a louere haue I,/ Wych my body kepyth wyth greth jelusy.'[43] The twist here is that this heavenly lover is available to men as well as women. As Cecilia explains: 'yf þat he se/ Þat þou me louyst in perfyth clennesse . . . Than shal he þe louyn as wel as me.'[44] Christ himself is a figure both masculinised and feminised in the later medieval period: on the one hand, he is the supreme bridegroom, on the other he represents both nurture and passivity in his willing sacrifice.

It is in their suffering that female virgin martyrs find most eloquence and show most hardiness. These accounts are troubling, not just for the graphic detail they offer, but also for what has been perceived as their sexualised nature. In some cases, the retaliation of the rebuffed suitors is explicitly sexual: saints are either placed in brothels, or locked in rooms with brutal men whose mission it is to rape them (they never succeed). Yet even in those lives where the torture

---

[39] Capgrave, *St Katharine*, bk 2, esp. lines 22–3. See Karen A. Winstead, 'Piety, Politics, and Social Commitment in Capgrave's *Life of St. Katherine*', *Medievalia et Humanistica* 17 (1991), pp. 59–80. See also Sheila Delany, *Impolitic Bodies: The Work of Osbern Bokenham: Poetry, Saints, and Society in Fifteenth-Century England* (Oxford: Oxford University Press, 1998) and Donald Weinstein and Rudolph M. Bell, *Saints and Society: The Two Worlds of Western Christendom, 1000–1700* (Chicago: University of Chicago Press, 1982).

[40] On the incommensurability of this topos of rude speech in relation to medieval culture's ideal of humble and silent femininity, as well as on women preaching more generally, see Blamires, *Case for Women*; Maud Burnett McInerney, *Eloquent Virgins: From Thecla to Joan of Arc* (New York: Palgrave Macmillan, 2003) and Merry E. Wiesner, 'Women's Defense of Their Public Role', *Women in the Middle Ages and the Renaissance*, ed. Mary Beth Rose (New York: Syracuse University Press, 1986), pp. 1–27.

[41] The *sponsa Christi* motif was also used by male religious to describe their souls' relationship to Christ; see Salisbury, 'Introduction', in *The Trials and Joys of Marriage*, (http://www.lib.rochester.edu/camelot/teams/salintro.htm). This is not, however, as common in the hagiographical material.

[42] Bokenham, *Legendys*, lines 4174–5.

[43] Bokenham, *Legendys*, lines 7501–2.

[44] Bokenham, *Legendys*, lines 7510–14.

inflicted is not overtly named as rape, it nonetheless always draws the audience's gaze to the virgin's physical beauty and nobility, for instance by referring to her torn breasts or beautiful, bleeding skin. Many critics have read these kinds of torture as a form of displaced rape, a penetration of the virgin body that does not cast doubt on her sexual intactness. As Kathleen Coyne Kelly points out, the virgin has to remain a virgin in order for the hagiographical narrative and the truths that it and she represent to remain inviolate as well: 'The raped virgin is a paradox, an oxymoron that would cause the whole system of stable, fixed signs to collapse.'[45]

The debate over whether or not the female virgin martyr can be read either as an image of heroic empowerment or one of horrific, sadistic subjection is not resolved, but recent studies have provided a different approach to this impasse, focusing instead on the inherently performative nature of virginity.[46] Because virginity is not a gender identity that can be determined visually (although medieval writers did attempt to provide a list of visible signs of virginity) it is a condition that requires a continuous enactment of characteristics which can then be said to make manifest that person's virginal status. Since virginity is perceived to be a spiritual as well as bodily condition, the body becomes privileged as the site upon which the inner qualities (such as modesty and humility) are externalised as guarantors of the virgin's authenticity. This performative nature of virginity radically undercuts the notion of gender as somehow self-evident and unchanging in that it shows precisely how this gendered identity – and therefore, by implication, all gender identities – requires a repetition of behavioural acts that signal 'virginity' (or 'femininity' or 'masculinity'). The possibility of disruption to that performance always remains a real possibility, posing a serious challenge to the idea that gender is stable.

In contrast, until very recently, there has not been much scholarship on male virginity in hagiography. John H. Arnold has recently expanded on Kelly's study of male virginity by identifying four 'basic narrative patterns, two of which relate to the powers and actions of the self, and two of which focus on outside intervention'.[47] The first pattern is represented by lives such as that of Benedict, where the saint uses bodily chastisement to overcome sexual temptation. Arnold sees this as 'a dramatization and extension of male monastic identity and its attempts to discipline the body'. The second pattern, represented for instance by the life of St Alexis, focuses on the role of the will in ruling the self. The third pattern is exemplified by narratives in which the saint is granted a vision that shows the temptation he is facing for what it really is; Arnold here cites the lives of St Anthony and St Josaphat as examples. The fourth pattern shows God intervening in more physical ways; for instance by angels protecting the saint and hindering the agent of harm. These insights have led critics such as

---

[45] Kelly, *Performing Virginity*, p. 61; see also Mills in this volume.
[46] See Kelly, *Performing Virginity*; Salih, *Versions of Virginity*.
[47] John H. Arnold, 'The Labour of Continence: Masculinity and Clerical Virginity', *Medieval Virginities*, ed. Anke Bernau, Ruth Evans and Sarah Salih (Cardiff: University of Wales Press, 2003), pp. 102–18, pp. 103–4. For Kathleen Coyne Kelly's discussion of male virginity, see Kelly, *Performing Virginity*, pp. 91–118.

Samantha J. E. Riches to question the assumptions made by others, that 'an emphasis on gender and sexuality is a distinguishing feature of the legends of female martyrs, when compared to their male counterparts', asking instead 'Can this conception not equally be applied to at least some male martyrs?'[48] The examples cited above show that it can.

Arnold concludes that while 'female virginity [in hagiography] is fantasized as an extraordinary ontology . . . male chastity dramatized a form of male agency'.[49] Yet there are narratives in which even this opposition is problematised: those of the cross-dressing saints. Here, women are shown to take on a male disguise, usually at a time in their life that coincides with the threshold of sexual maturity, and either join monasteries with their fathers (see example discussed above), or on their own, in order to be able to live a life dedicated to Christ.[50] While these lives were clearly popular, it is noticeable that it is always women who cross-dress, not men. The reasons for this are to be found in the asymmetrical perception of gender addressed earlier. Female cross-dressing was seen as somehow comprehensible, part of an attempt to achieve a more perfect gender identity, while male cross-dressers were seen to be participating in a reversal of the natural order, demonstrating a perverse desire for the irrational and carnal.[51]

The few instances of men cross-dressing as women support this view. In the life of St Jerome, for instance, it is related that those jealous and resentful of his criticism of the clergy's excessive lifestyle left women's clothes by his bed so that he might put them on and become the object of ridicule, stripped of his authority. In contrast, the lives of saints who cross-dress emphasise the aptness of especially religious male clothing for these women, which matches the women's virile spirits: they are performing externally what is understood as an inner masculinity. The fact that most of them are virgins further underlines this immasculation. In the life of Margaret/Pelagien, for instance, s/he writes down her/his life for the monks among whom s/he has lived when s/he realises s/he is about to die: 'I, of noble lineage, was called Margaret in the world, but for I

---

[48] Samantha J. E. Riches, 'St George as Male Virgin Martyr', *Gender and Holiness*, pp. 65–85, pp. 67–8. See also Karen A. Winstead, *Virgin Martyrs: Legends of Sainthood in Late Medieval England* (Ithaca NY: Cornell University Press, 1997) and Ashton, *Generation of Identity*. Scholars who have discussed hagiography and masculinity are Katherine J. Lewis, 'Becoming a Virgin King: Richard II and Edward the Confessor', *Gender and Holiness*, ed. Riches and Salih, pp. 86–100; Joanna Huntington, 'Edward the Celibate, Edward the Saint: Virginity in the Construction of Edward the Confessor', *Medieval Virginities*, ed. Bernau, Evans and Salih, pp. 119–39; Robert Mills, ' "Whatever You Do is a Delight to Me!": Masculinity, Masochism and Queer Play in Representations of Male Martyrdom', *Exemplaria* 13 (2001), pp. 1–37.

[49] Arnold, 'Labour of Continence', p. 112.

[50] See Anke Bernau, 'The Translation of Purity in the Lives of St Eugenia and St Euphrosyne', *Studies in Anglo-Saxon England*, ed. Kathryn Powell and Donald Scragg, special issue of *the Bulletin of the John Rylands University Library of Manchester* 86 (forthcoming), pp. 11–37.

[51] See John Anson, 'The Female Transvestite in Early Monasticism: The Development of a Motif', *Viator* 5 (1974), pp. 1–32; Vern Bullough, *Sexual Variance in Society and History* (Chicago: University of Chicago Press, 1976), pp. 365, 393; Lynda L. Coon, *Sacred Fictions: Holy Women and Hagiography in Late Antiquity* (Philadelphia: University of Pennsylvania Press, 1997), p. 43; Valerie R. Hotchkiss, *Clothes Make the Man: Female Cross-Dressing in Medieval Europe* (New York: Garland, 1996).

would eschew the temptations of the world, I called myself Pelagien. *I am a man*' (5.240; my emphasis). These saints, while reverting to what is arguably shown to be their 'true' feminine gender identity in death, persistently speak and live their identity as masculine. The success of their adopted identity is highlighted by the trope of 'misguided sexuality', which often plays a central role in these lives. Here, the saints become objects of desire both for the brothers among whom they live and, more frequently, for women outside the monastic community. This allows the lives to contrast the religious woman – immasculated by her faith – to her more feminine and (therefore) sexual counterpart in the world, while also offering intriguing moments of (unwitting) same-sex desire. The representation of young women rising to positions of authority in monastic communities – in some cases even becoming abbots – highlights also the potent agency of such an identity, which does not so much *erase* or level gender roles, but shows how they are translated and redefined when moved from one arena to another. The ongoing oscillation between the names and pronouns used to refer to the saint – sometimes we have a 'she' who is called Margaret (or Marine, or Eugenia), sometimes a 'he' who is called Pelagien (or 'brother Marine') – undercuts any clear separation of the ways in which masculinity and femininity signify.

What this chapter has suggested is that while in late medieval hagiography certain gendered modes of behaviour are thought to be more 'natural' to one sex than the other, they are also shown to be open to appropriation by others. There is a whole range of characteristics that are put forward as ideal for both: obedience, humility, chastity, courage, to name a few. Certain tropes, such as that of the *sponsa Christi*, clearly present an attempt to resignify worldly relationships within a religious framework, and while this is far more commonly used in the lives of female saints, at other times it appears to be available to men as well.[52] Characteristics that were thought to be feminine, such as passivity or weakness, were deliberately appropriated to signify conditions that male saints experience or might even strive for. Therefore, while on the one hand there are attempts to delineate gender differences – for instance in the life of Benedict, where certain sins (such as disobedience, rebelliousness) are portrayed as being more common in male religious, and others (gossiping) more common in female religious – on the other there are also gendered motifs and behaviours which are applied to both genders. At other times, references to gender difference are used to highlight the fact that courage and bravery are more astonishing in a woman and that this should therefore spur on male Christians, for instance when St Sebastian cries out, '[W]hy live we so long? Women go tofore us to the crown of martyrdom' (2.241–2). The representation of gender and sexuality is also contingent upon other categories, such as religious affiliation, class and race. Christian women behave in ways that are more 'masculine' than pagan men, and the latter are often also characterised by a moral weakness and carnality that is more frequently associated with femininity. What becomes clear here is that while

---

[52] Other scholars have discussed how motifs such as charity, for instance, are also gendered in saints' lives: see P. H. Cullum, 'Gendering Charity in Medieval Hagiography', *Gender and Holiness*, ed. Riches and Salih, pp. 135–51.

saints are unified by their zealous faith, gendered and sexualised tropes are to some extent free-floating. They resonate and signify very differently, both intra- and inter-textually. At the same time, there is always the implication that the Christian faith possesses the authority to transform, translate and resignify identity in general while also providing a unifying paradigm. Kelly's point, that '[i]t is simply not possible to generalize about the representation and function of the . . . saint', can be extended to saints' lives more generally.[53] A man is different from a woman, but a prostitute is also different from a female virgin and a mother, just as she is different from a monk, who is also different to a king.

---

[53] Kelly, *Performing Virginity*, p. 51.

6

History, Historiography and Re-writing the Past

KATHERINE J. LEWIS

This chapter has two distinct but related aims: to explore some of the ways in which Middle English hagiography can be employed as a source by historians, and also to demonstrate that hagiography itself functioned as a form of historiography in late medieval England. For some time now, historians have been well aware of the value of saints' cults as a tool to further our understanding of medieval society and its inhabitants. The materials of saints' cults and the dynamics of rituals associated with them can illuminate many characteristics of the settings in which they operated; not just religious and devotional matters but also aspects of political power, socio-cultural ideologies, personal prestige and communal identity, to give only a few examples.[1] The work of Donald Weinstein and Rudolph M. Bell has been particularly influential in this respect, with their exploration of the ways in which 'the pursuit as well as the perception of holiness mirrored social values and concerns' in this period.[2] However, it is notable that, despite this, historians of later medieval England rarely make use of Middle English hagiography as a source for their investigations. It has largely been left to literary scholars to demonstrate the ways in which these texts can be examined not only for what they tell us about a particular genre, but for the information which they contain about attitudes, ideals and practices as well.[3] For example, Gail McMurray Gibson has explored the ways in which the Middle English accounts of a particular saint's life, in this case St Anne's, could be appropriated to serve a variety of purposes and agendas, and the collection in which her essay appears suggests that the responses of devotees to these narratives may not have been those expected or intended by their authors.[4] Similarly

---

I would like to thank the editor of this volume for her extremely helpful comments on an earlier draft of this essay.

[1] E.g. *Saints and their Cults: Studies in Religious Sociology, Folklore and History*, ed. Stephen Wilson (Cambridge: Cambridge University Press, 1983), especially Wilson's introduction; André Vauchez, *Sainthood in the Later Middle Ages*, trans. Jean Birrell (Cambridge: Cambridge University Press, 1997).

[2] Donald Weinstein and Rudolph M. Bell, *Saints and Society: The Two Worlds of Latin Christendom, 1000–1700* (Chicago: University of Chicago Press, 1982), p. 6 and passim.

[3] The fact that I make frequent use of Middle English hagiography in my own research has apparently led several people to assume that I am a literary scholar, when in fact I am an historian (albeit one with an interdisciplinary doctoral degree in Medieval Studies, rather than in history per se).

[4] Gail McMurray Gibson, 'The Religion of Childbed: Some East Anglian Texts and Talismans',

Karen A. Winstead's study of Middle English virgin martyr legends investigates 'the cultural work they performed', focusing in particular on variations and developments in the representation of saints such as Katherine of Alexandria and Margaret of Antioch, in order to uncover the extent to which these were informed by gender ideologies and therefore sought to respond to the changing status of women in fourteenth- and fifteenth-century England.[5] Saints' lives were absolutely staple and extremely popular reading matter for medieval English people, as well as being, arguably, one of the few literary forms to which we know that everyone would have been exposed, in the form of sermons. The analysis of Middle English hagiography can therefore provide us with an invaluable insight into their beliefs and pre-occupations, so the apparent reluctance of some historians to make use of it warrants further consideration.

Of course part of this reluctance derives from much wider perceptions of the uneasy relationship that has long been held to exist between History (as an academic discipline) and hagiography. Felice Lifshitz has described the ways in which the very identity of this definition of History as the 'scientific' pursuit of truth about the past came into being in the nineteenth century in conscious opposition to hagiography, with its 'superstitious' emphasis on the ineffable, the unverifiable and the miraculous.[6] Thomas Heffernan argues that the principal scholarly approach to hagiography has therefore been conditioned by 'the dominant positivist tradition' within historiography and that hagiography has become 'an epithet for the unreliable'.[7] Within an English historical tradition in particular this has been compounded by the legacy of the Reformation and the Enlightenment in which all manifestations of Roman Catholic belief were held to be evidence of little more than the stupidity and credulity of medieval people and their intrinsic inferiority to their rational and Protestant successors. For instance, the great eighteenth-century historian Edward Gibbon castigated William Caxton for having wasted the new technology of his printing presses 'to comply with the vicious tastes of his readers' and pandering to 'popular credulity with romances of fabulous knights and legends of more fabulous saints' rather than publishing classical literature, which Gibbon felt should have been his priority.[8] Indeed, another reason why hagiography has enjoyed such a poor reputation relates not only to the perceived unreliability of its contents, but also to its inherently 'low' status as a cultural production. Saints' lives have been (and still are) frequently condemned as badly written, trite, formulaic and unoriginal. Vernacular hagiography is very prone to such charges, which is also

---

Interpreting Cultural Symbols: Saint Anne in Late Medieval Society, ed. Kathleen Ashley and Pamela Sheingorn (Athens GA: University of Georgia Press, 1990), pp. 95–110.
5   Karen A. Winstead, *Virgin Martyrs: Legends of Sainthood in Late Medieval England* (Ithaca NY: Cornell University Press, 1997), p. 4 and passim.
6   Felice Lifshitz, 'Beyond Positivism and Genre: Hagiographical Texts as Historical Narrative', *Viator* 25 (1994), pp. 95–113, p. 110.
7   Thomas Heffernan, *Sacred Biography: Saints and their Biographers in the Middle Ages* (New York: Oxford University Press, 1992), pp. 38–71, p. 54.
8   Quoted by Nellie Slayton Aurner, *Caxton, Mirror of Fifteenth-Century Letters: A Study of the Literature of the First English Press* (New York: Russell and Russell, 1965), pp. 126–7; p. 201 for Disraeli's similar criticism of Caxton.

due to perceptions that it is merely a debased translation from a Latin original, aimed at people who were too dim to understand the language of intellect.

Latin hagiography is often deemed to be a more authentic and more verifiable form; written by educated clerics, generally to support a canonisation bid, its reliability was assessed, to some extent at least, in order to ascertain whether its subject was truly a saint or not. Indeed, the majority of work which has been undertaken on saints' cults in later medieval England employs Latin texts describing the lives and miracles of saints. Such works generally do not consider later translations of such material, despite the fact that both as narratives and physical objects they may contain unique clues to the dissemination and success of an individual saint's cult, as well as perceptions of its efficacy.[9] Moreover, vernacular saints' lives also deserve attention because, as Evelyn Birge Vitz points out, they were frequently rewritten or recast versions of a Latin original, aimed a particular audience, and responding to their needs, rather than simply slavish and inferior translations.[10] Jocelyn Wogan-Browne notes that 'What looks potentially dreary or appalling at the aerial-survey level of genre-history takes on life, multiplicity, and nuance at the level of particular texts in their context;' and there is, for example, much for the historian to draw from the increased popularity of and demand for vernacular saints' lives in later medieval England, especially among a female readership.[11] Not all saints' lives may have been as polished as Geoffrey Chaucer's life of St Cecilia but it could be argued that this has little to do with their value as potential sources.

Another notable feature of historically focused scholarship on saints in later medieval England has been the tendency to focus on 'real' saints: that is, empirical individuals who lived and died in the period, and whose lives and cults are therefore more quantifiable than those of the more legendary universal saints of the early Church. Self-evidently part of the emphasis here is due to an interest in texts that contain recreations of or direct comment upon events that happened in the time and place under investigation. On the other hand, it has to be said that there is very little Middle English hagiography relating to the cult of 'real' saints who actually lived in later medieval England. The majority were high-status men, such as Thomas of Lancaster, Edward II and Henry VI, whose violent deaths led to them being identified as martyrs and their burial places as shrines at which miracles were performed. There are also a few monastic/clerical examples of 'real' saints such as John of Bridlington and John Schorne.[12] One of the

---

[9] E.g. Ronald C. Finucane, *Miracles and Pilgrims: Popular Beliefs in Medieval England* (London: Dent, 1977) and Diana Webb, *Pilgrimage in Medieval England* (London: Hambledon Press, 2000) both provide excellent analyses of the cult of Thomas Becket, but without considering later vernacular accounts of his life and/or miracles.

[10] Evelyn Birge Vitz 'From the Oral to the Written in Medieval and Renaissance Saints' Lives', *Images of Sainthood in Medieval Europe*, ed. Renate Blumenfeld-Kosinski and Timea Szell (Ithaca NY: Cornell University Press, 1991), pp. 97–114.

[11] Jocelyn Wogan-Browne, *Saints' Lives and Women's Literary Culture c. 1150–1300: Virginity and its Authorizations* (Oxford: Oxford University Press, 2001), p. 5.

[12] There is an extant life of John of Bridlington (d. 1379), see Margaret Amassian, 'A Verse Life of John of Bridlington', *Neuphilologische Mitteilungen* 71 (1970), pp. 136–45, which is omitted from D'Evelyn and Foster, 'Saints' Legends': thanks to Matthew Holford for this reference. But apart from this, Gilbert of Sempringham (c. 1083–1189), Robert of Knaresborough

few Middle English hagiographic texts that does provide an account of an individual who lived in later medieval England is *The Book of Margery Kempe*, and this certainly has been used by many, historians and others, as a source for the period.[13] But, as noted at the outset, hagiographic texts can serve as evidence for more than contemporary events. Weinstein and Bell's study focuses on 'real' saints, despite stating that their interest lies 'not so much in whether the stories told of saints were true', but in the fact that 'they were told and retold'; their emphasis is on 'the perception of behaviour rather than the behaviour itself'.[14] By these standards there is no reason not to include the lives of legendary saints alongside the 'real' ones for the purposes of historical inquiry. Besides, the strict division which we may make between the two would have meant little to most medieval devotees, for whom Katherine of Alexandria was just as real and historically verifiable a figure as Catherine of Siena.[15]

Moreover, it should also be remembered that medieval people did not make an oppositional distinction between 'history' and 'hagiography' in the way that some later commentators have done. Several English authors, John Lydgate, John Capgrave and Osbern Bokenham for example, produced both saints' lives and historical narratives in the vernacular and neither they nor their audiences saw a contradiction or disjunction between the two.[16] Both historical writing and hagiography in the vernacular were very popular in later medieval England, and often appeared in the same manuscripts.[17] On a basic level both genres are concerned with retelling past events and ensuring that they conformed to known facts (such as dates, places, the testimony of witnesses and so on); that they contained plausible accounts that conformed to previously established archetypes; and, finally, that the narrative as a whole should have didactic significance.[18] The very first English historical text, Bede's *Historia*

(1160–1218) and Edmund Rich (c. 1175–1240) were apparently the most 'recent' English saints for whom there are surviving full-length Middle English lives. All four appear in brief in the *Kalendre*.

[13] E.g. most recently Anthony Goodman, *Margery Kempe and her World* (London: Longman, 2002). This is also the only Middle English hagiographical text that treats the life of a woman who lived in post-Conquest England.

[14] Weinstein and Bell, *Saints and Society*, p. 17.

[15] For an influential discussion of the constructed nature of all saints see Pierre Delooz, 'Towards a Sociological Study of Canonized Sainthood in the Catholic Church', Saints and Their Cults, ed. Wilson, pp. 189–216; notions of sainthood as 'real' or 'constructed' are better thought of as part of a continuum rather than as discrete and opposed.

[16] E.g. John Lydgate, *Troy Book*, ed. Robert R. Edwards (Kalamazoo: Medieval Institute Publications, 1998); John Capgrave, *The Chronicle of England*, ed. F. C. Hingeston (New York: Kraus Reprint, 1964); for Osbern Bokenham's translation of part of the *Polychronicon* see below.

[17] It should, perhaps, be noted, that within scholarship on chronicles, as on hagiography, there is still a tendency to focus on Latin narratives; Middle English chronicles have received far less attention, despite the enormous popularity of the *Brut* which survives in well over 150 manuscripts. Although see Mary-Rose McLaren, *The London Chronicles of the Fifteenth Century: A Revolution in English Writing* (Cambridge: Brewer, 2002).

[18] My approach here derives from Chris Given-Wilson's recent survey, *Chronicles: The Writing of History in Medieval England* (London: Hambledon and London, 2004), pp. 2–6, although he does not explicitly discuss hagiographic texts. The *Legenda aurea* life of Katherine of Alexandria provides an example of Jacobus de Voragine's frequent attempts to square hagiographic narratives with known facts about the past, as he points out that the identification of her persecutor as the Roman Emperor Maxentius was probably due to scribal error and that the

Ecclesiastica Gens Anglorum (c. 731), set out a moral agenda in the preface where Bede stated that in reading his book the audience should be inspired by the examples of good conduct set before them.[19] The idea that history should contain universal truths underpinned the approach that medieval chronicles took to the past.[20] Caxton made the same point in his preface to an edition of John Trevisa's translation of Ranulph Higden's *Polychronicon*:

> Historye is a perpetual conseruatryce of thoos thynges that haue be done before this presente tyme and also a cotydyan [daily] witnesse of bienfayttes [good deeds] of malefaytes [evil deeds] greate Actes and triumphal vyctoryes of al maner people. And also yf the terrible feyned Fables of Poetes haue moches styred and moeued men to pyte and conseruynge of Justyce How moche more is to be supposed that Historye assertryce of veryte [proclaimer of truth] and as moder of alle philosophye moeuynge our maners to virtue reformeth and reconcyleth ner hande alle thoos men which thurgh the Infyrmyte of oure mortal nature hath ledde the mooste parte of theyre lyf in Ocyosyte [idleness] and myspended theyr tyme. . . . Thenne syth historye is so precious & also proufyttable J haue delybered to wryte twoo bookes notable retenyng in them many noble historyes as the lyues myracles passyons and deth of dyuerse hooly sayntes whiche shal be comprysed by thayde [the aid] and suffraunce of almyghty god in one of them which is named legenda aurea that is the golden legend And that other book is named polycronycon in whiche bok ben comprised briefly many wonderful histories.[21]

The reference to the *Golden Legend* here is clearly a marketing ploy, but it also made generic sense for Caxton to make this connection between the two works. His preface to the *Golden Legend* contains a similar exhortation, absolutely standard to so many saints' lives:

> And that it proufytte to alle them that shal rede or here it redde and may encrease in them vertue and expelle vyce and synne that by the ensaumple of the holy sayntes amende theyr lyuyng here in theys shorte lyf that by their merytes they and I may come to euerlastyng lyf & blysse in heuen.[22]

It also describes his source materials as containing 'many hystoryes' of the saints.[23] This demonstrates his far from uncommon perception that 'history' was a discourse common both to a chronicle and to a hagiographic compendium. In addition, both forms of history had a moral, self-improving and truthful import which was entirely lacking from 'the terrible feyned Fables of Poetes'.

---

villain was in fact Maximinus as he was emperor in the East (including Alexandria) while Maxentius ruled only over the West; *Golden Legend*, trans. Ryan, vol. 2, p. 341.

[19] Bede, *The Ecclesiastical History of the English People*, trans. Bertram Colgrave, ed. Judith McClure and Roger Collins (Oxford: Oxford University Press, 1994), p. 3. A large proportion of Bede's English history is taken up with the lives and exploits of saints.

[20] Given-Wilson, *Chronicles*, pp. 2–3.

[21] Aurner, *Caxton*, pp. 290–1.

[22] Aurner, *Caxton*, p. 257.

[23] Aurner, *Caxton*, p. 257; compare for example the prologue to the collection of saints' lives sermons known as the *Speculum Sacerdotale* which exhorts the audience to imitate the saints; *Speculum Sacerdotale*, ed. Edward H. Weatherly, EETS os 200 (London: Oxford University Press, 1936), p. 1.

This edifying imperative had an important effect not just on the content of works such as the *Polychronicon*, but also on their form, which could be just as formulaic as hagiography on occasion. Using the example of battle descriptions Chris Given-Wilson notes the 'troubling sameness' in the accounts of battles drawn from different chronicles.[24] The explanation lies in the author's wish to give an accurate account of what happened at one specific battle and yet at the same time to use this event to draw out some wider implications as to the proper way of fighting battles more generally: 'A battle was not simply an event, it was also an exemplar, providing models to imitate or avoid, lessons to be contemplated.'[25] One battle could therefore stand in for all battles, just as Gregory of Tours famously observed that 'it is preferable to speak of the life of the fathers than lives, although there is a diversity of merit and virtue, in the world one life nourishes all bodies'.[26] In this way chronicles were just as likely as hagiography to be brought into the service of a moral or ideological agenda, and events described were often placed within a specifically Christian or Biblical framework.[27] Historians are well aware that this can have a profound effect on the strict accuracy of what is described within such texts. The writings of Thomas Walsingham on John of Gaunt should hardly be taken as the measured and straightforwardly factual account of an impartial observer, for instance. Yet despite this, historians do not, of course, entirely dismiss such texts out of hand; provided one attempts to ascertain the extent to which the author was describing events in terms of a variety of considerations and purposes, chronicles can provide a whole host of important information about later medieval English society.

It has already been noted that surviving Middle English hagiography does not directly describe people or events who actually lived in the later medieval period, but this does not mean that it was unaffected by contemporary issues. The same is true of narratives describing Britain's or England's legendary history and, in particular, the story of King Arthur. Thomas Malory's *Morte Darthur* does not attempt an accurate recreation of the reign of an early medieval king, any more than the Middle English accounts of virgin martyr saints seek to present a realistic portrayal of life for early Christian women. In both cases descriptions of the subject matter are informed far more obviously by considerations and issues contemporary to the composition of the texts.[28] Arguably

---

[24] Given-Wilson, *Chronicles*, p. 2.
[25] Given-Wilson, *Chronicles*, p. 2.
[26] Quoted in Heffernan, *Sacred Biography*, p. 7, from the preface of Gregory's *Life of the Fathers*.
[27] E.g. Antonia Gransden, *Historical Writing in England 2: c. 1307 to the Early Sixteenth Century* (London: Routledge and Kegan Paul, 1982), pp. 46–7, p. 129, p. 454.
[28] E.g. see Felicity Riddy, 'Contextualizing *Le Morte Darthur*: Empire and Civil War', *A Companion to Malory*, ed. Elizabeth Archibald and A. S. G. Edwards (Cambridge: Brewer, 1996), pp. 55–74 for discussion of the extent to which Malory's narrative was influenced by the English withdrawal from France in 1453 and the subsequent Wars of the Roses, meaning that the book should be interpreted within the context of both literary and historical representations of empire and civil war. Similarly Sheila Delany argues that Bokenham's *Legendys of Hooly Wummen* were informed and affected by political affiliations born of the Wars of the Roses; *Impolitic Bodies: Poetry, Saints and Society in Fifteenth-Century England: The Work of Osbern Bokenham* (New York: Oxford University Press, 1998).

legendary figures were particularly useful tools for authors in this respect for it was perhaps easier to manipulate the accounts of their lives with relative impunity, adding in or taking away certain elements in order to serve a particular purpose. For example, the Middle English life of Katherine of Alexandria developed a whole new section during the fifteenth century with the addition of a specifically English version of her youth and mystical marriage; an episode which, among several other possible motives, may have been intended to present her as a convincing model of lay piety to readers.[29] As noted at the outset, in this way the lives of saints provide an extremely useful means of exploring the contexts in which they were written, and understanding the audiences who read them. The composition of hagiography was influenced by a whole gamut of different motives, needs and claims, many of which are explored in more depth elsewhere in this collection. For the rest of this chapter I shall explore the ways in which these texts can be used to shed light on issues of national identity and the writing and rewriting of England's past.

The whole issue of later medieval English concepts of national identity remains relatively unexplored. Medievalists have certainly pointed out the fallacy of definitions of national consciousness which place its birth in the post-medieval period and have begun to apply postcolonial approaches to explore various formulations of nation and nationhood which held sway in the Middle Ages.[30] But a comprehensive analysis of such issues with specific reference to fourteenth- and fifteenth-century England remains to be written, despite its fruitfulness as a subject for such a study.[31] Patricia Clare Ingham, among others, has discussed the ways in which legendary British history was brought to bear on constructions of Englishness in this period and it is clear that representations of and ideas about the past played a key role in creating national character, for, as R. W. Southern notes, recall of the past aimed 'to give the community its identity in the present'.[32] There was an apparent resurgence of interest in the lives of Anglo-Saxon and early British saints in later medieval England which resulted in the production of new versions of several of their lives as an additional section within the 1438 *Gilte Legende*; in some cases the lives had only previously been available in English in the by then linguistically dated *South English Legendary*.[33] Caxton brought these to a wider audience by incorporating them into his 1483 publication of the *Golden Legend*. In addition

---

[29] Katherine J. Lewis, *The Cult of St Katherine of Alexandria in Later Medieval England* (Woodbridge: Boydell, 2000), pp. 194–215.
[30] E.g. *Concepts of National Identity in the Middle Ages*, ed. Simon Forde, Lesley Johnson and Alan V. Murray (Leeds: Leeds Studies in English, 1995); *The Postcolonial Middle Ages*, ed. Jeffrey Jerome Cohen (New York: Palgrave, 2001).
[31] The essays in *Imagining a Medieval English Nation*, ed. Kathy Lavezzo (Minneapolis: University of Minnesota Press, 2003) constitute the most recent work in this area.
[32] Patricia Clare Ingham, *Sovereign Fantasies: Arthurian Romances and the Making of Britain* (Philadelphia: University of Pennsylvania Press, 2001); R. W. Southern, 'Aspects of the European Tradition of Historical Writing: 4. The Sense of the Past', *Transactions of the Royal Historical Society* 5th ser. 23 (1973), pp. 242–63, p. 256.
[33] For the composition of the *Gilte Legende* see Manfred Görlach, *Studies in Middle English Saints' Legends* (Tübingen: Francke Verlag, 1998); for the additional lives, *Supplementary Lives*.

the lives of Anglo-Saxon saints such as Edmund of East Anglia, Edith, Ætheldreda, Cuthbert and Werburge were composed as independent Middle English texts.[34] The lives of saints Edward the Confessor, Dunstan, Oswald the bishop, Swithun and so on were very important repositories of information about the Anglo-Saxon past; for some who heard them as sermons perhaps one of the only forms of English historical narrative to which they would have been exposed.[35] The Middle English lives of later English saints such as Thomas Becket and Edmund Rich also explore nationalist themes, establishing both protagonists as champions and defenders of the nation, resisting royal power on behalf of the English people.[36] Lydgate's hagiography identified both St Alban and Edmund of East Anglia as the patrons and protectors of England.[37] But perhaps the most well known manifestation of English national identity in a saint's cult is provided by the appropriation of St George, whose legend has nothing to do with England, as the country's patron.[38] Caxton made a unique addition to his *Golden Legend* life of George to state that the saint 'is patrone of this royaume of englong and the crye of men of warre . . . let vs praye vnto hym that he be special protectour and defendour of thys royame'.[39]

Interest in native saints was, in part, a manifestation of devotion to figures whose shrines, in many cases, were important foci of pilgrimage and miracle-working, and also owed something to perceptions that a saint would be particularly inclined to answer the prayers of his or her fellow countrypeople. But, in the fifteenth century, a large part of the impetus derived from the fortunes of England in the international political arena. The Hundred Years War meant that there was a particular premium placed on establishing the singular and superior nature of English national identity in opposition to French.[40] Being able to demonstrate that England was an outstandingly holy nation with a long tradition of saintly inhabitants was an important element in the formation and maintenance of English national prestige and showed evidence of divine favour. English saints also provided the people with a tangible focus for pride in both past and present and a rallying point for their leaders, something of which Henry V was evidently very well aware. Christopher Allmand notes the active role which Henry played in promoting the cults of English and British saints by requesting that the feasts of Sts George and Dunstan be given greater promi-

---

[34] Further evidence for interest in native saints in this period is provided by the collection of English and British saints' lives known as the *Nova Legenda Angliae*, ed. Carl Hostmann (Oxford: Clarendon Press, 1901), later translated into abbreviated Middle English versions as *Kalendre*.
[35] E.g. Southwell Minster MS 7 contains versions of five *Gilte Legende* Anglo-Saxon saints' lives which were almost certainly used as sermons; they are bound with a copy of Mirk's *Festial*.
[36] Thorlac Turville-Petre, *England the Nation: Language, Literature and National Identity, 1290–1340* (Oxford: Oxford University Press, 1996), pp. 62–5.
[37] E.g. John Lydgate, *Saint Albon and Saint Amphibalus*, ed. George F. Reinecke (New York: Garland, 1985), p. 163, lines 761–77 where Alban and Edmund are mentioned together in this capacity.
[38] Samantha Riches, *St George: Hero, Martyr and Myth* (Stroud: Sutton, 2000).
[39] Aurner, *Caxton*, p. 260.
[40] Other important contextual factors here were provided, for example, by the machinations surrounding the Papal Schism, see J. P. Genet, 'English Nationalism: Thomas Polton at the Council of Constance', *Nottingham Medieval Studies* 38 (1984), pp. 60–78.

nence and raising the status of the feasts of Sts Winifred and Chad too.[41] Two other English saints, John of Beverley and the recently canonised John of Bridlington, were credited with having interceded to ensure English victory at Agincourt and during the triumphal procession in London to celebrate the king's return in 1415, the pageant depicted 'twelve kings of the English succession, martyrs and confessors . . . with sceptres in their hands, crowns upon their heads, their emblems of sanctity plain to see'.[42] Henry was said to have been born on September 16, the feast day of another English saint, Edith, and her Middle English life, written c. 1420 for the nuns of Wilton, presented King Edgar as a parallel to Henry V for his good rulership, piety and for his interest in monastic reform.[43] Indeed, as Wogan-Browne argues, this life presented the saint as a representative of England's holy nationhood, and was concerned with disseminating images of itself to those outside the convent as 'a national engine of intercession and the maintenance of order', in part by focusing on the miraculous revenge which Edith meted out to those who threatened the monastery's prerogatives.[44]

Henry V utilised devotion to native saints as one strand of a deliberate policy to inculcate feelings of national pride and common identity among his people, in order to support the ongoing war effort.[45] Interest in English saints went hand in hand with the rising profile of English as a language and the production of increasing amounts of both hagiography and history in the vernacular. It is therefore surprising that Middle English saints' lives have not received more attention as evidence of particular formulations of Englishness and as polemically informed versions of England's past.[46] If one compares the lives of the universal and British saints in the *Gilte Legende* to those of the English saints it is notable that only the latter contain significant amounts of contextual information about the geographic, historical, political and genealogical settings in which

[41] Christopher Allmand, *Henry V* (London: Methuen, 1992), p. 416.
[42] Allmand, *Henry V*, p. 415, quotation taken from the *Gesta Henrici Quinti*. The twelve king saints are not identified individually.
[43] For Henry's birthday, see Allmand, *Henry V*, p. 417 n. 63; Jocelyn Wogan-Browne, 'Outdoing the Daughters of Syon? Edith of Wilton and the Representation of Female Community in Fifteenth-Century England', *Medieval Women: Texts and Contexts in Late Medieval Britain: Essays for Felicity Riddy*, ed. Jocelyn Wogan-Browne, Rosalynn Voaden, Arlyn Diamond, Ann Hutchison, Carol Meale and Lesley Johnson (Turnhout: Brepols, 2000), pp. 393–409, p. 400.
[44] Wogan-Browne, 'Outdoing the Daughters of Syon?', pp. 400, 403. The same issue of monastic privileges also informs Lydgate's lives of Sts Edmund and Fremund, Sts Alban and Amphibalus and Henry Bradshaw's life of St Werburge, discussed below.
[45] Allmand, *Henry V*, pp. 404–25 for a wider discussion of concepts of nationhood and unity in Henry's reign. Saints continued to be used to support royal/nationalist propaganda in the next reign too; Lydgate used both Edward the Confessor and Louis IX to support Henry VI's claim to the English and French crowns, thus appropriating a representative of French national pride and identity to serve English political needs.
[46] At present, scholarship in this area has focused largely on the *South English Legendary*: Klaus Jankofsky, 'National Characteristics in the Portrayal of English Saints in the *South English Legendary*', *Images of Sainthood*, ed. Blumenfeld-Kosinski and Szell, pp. 81–93; Jill Frederick, 'The *South English Legendary*: Anglo-Saxon Saints' Lives and National Identity', *Literary Appropriations of the Anglo-Saxons*, ed. Donald Scragg and Carole Weinburg (Cambridge: Cambridge University Press, 2000), pp. 57–73. Catherine Sanok's forthcoming study will provide the first detailed consideration of representations of the past in later Middle English saints' lives. See also Woodcock in this volume.

the protagonists operated as well as genealogical connections between saints and royalty.[47] For example, the life of St Kenelm opens thus:

> In Englonde beth .iij. principal waters, that is Temyse, Severne and Humbyr. This kyng Kenelme was kyng of Wurcetterschyre, Warwykeschire, Gloucetterschire, and the bishop of Wurcetter was byshop of these .iij. [shyres] aforesaid, and also of Derbyschyre, Chesterchire, Schropschyre, Staffordschyre, Herfordshire, Notynghamshire, Northamptonshyre, Bokynghamshyre, Oxfordschire, Leycetterschire, Lyncolneschyre. Al this was callyd the Marche of Walys, and of al these contreys was Seint [Kenelme] kyng of, and that tyme was Wynchecombe [cheffe] cite of al these contreys and schires aforeseid. And that tyme were in Englonde .vj. kynges, and byfore that was Oswolde kyng of al Englonde, and aftir this same Oswolde is days was this departide in Seint Kenelmes days.[48]

The *Gilte Legende* lives between them cover the whole sweep of Anglo-Saxon history from the Conversion to the Norman Conquest, and the historical detail is reinforced by cross-referencing between the lives and by the appearance and reappearance of saints and kings in several different lives.[49] The cumulative picture that emerges is of a country and a people that are conspicuously holy and renowned for being so. Similarly, the Middle English life of St Ætheldreda, abbess of Ely, spends over a hundred lines setting the historical scene with reference to Hengist, Horsa, Cerdic, Penda, the Vikings, Æthelstan, Edmund of East Anglia and Edward the Elder before finally getting to the saint's immediate family and the saint herself in line 123.[50] The historical and geographic context was evidently felt to be crucial to the lives of English saints; a point underlined by Bokenham, who wrote a now lost legendary also containing the lives of many native saints, and who thought it best to produce a companion work to ensure that his readers would understand all of the background details:

> For as moche as in the engliche boke the whiche y haue compiled of legenda aurea and of other famous legendes at the instaunce of my specialle frendis and for edificacioun and comfort of alle tho the whiche shuld redene hit or here hit, is oftene-tyme in lyvis of seyntis, of seynt Cedde, seynt Felix, seynt Edwarde, seynt Oswalde and many other seyntis of Englond, mencyoun made of dyuers partis, plagis, regnis & contreis of this lande Englonde, the wiche but if they be declared, oyne fulle hard to knowene: Therefore, for the more clerere vndirsandynge of the seid thyngis and othur, y haue drawe owt in to engliche

---

[47] Frederick notes the same of the lives in the *South English Legendary*, 'Anglo-Saxon Saints' Lives and National Identity', p. 66. 'British' is used here specifically to refer to the people who inhabited the British Isles before the arrival of the Anglo-Saxons (examples of British saints in the *Gilte Legende* are Brendan, Winifred and Bride, or Brigid), whereas 'English' is used solely of saints descended from Anglo-Saxon migrants. 'Universal' saints refers to the apostles and early martyrs venerated across Europe in this period.
[48] *Supplementary Lives*, p. 207.
[49] For further discussion of the ideological operation of English history in these lives see Katherine J. Lewis, 'Anglo-Saxon Saints' Lives, History and National Identity in Late Medieval England', *History, Nationhood and the Question of National Identity*, ed. Helen Brocklehurst and Robert Phillips (Basingstoke: Palgrave, 2004), pp. 160–70.
[50] *Altenglische Legenden: Neue Folge*, ed. Carl Horstmann (Heilbronn: Henniger, 1881), pp. 282–5.

XV chapturs, the which Arnulphus Cistrensis in his policronica of this landis descripcioun writethe in the last end of his furst boke: the wych welle knowene ther-of in the seyd legende.[51]

Perhaps Caxton intended that his *Polychronicon* would also serve as a concordance to the native lives in the *Golden Legend*. A further detail which is generally included in English saints' lives is information about the location of their shrines and the miracles which continue to be performed at them to this day (as the texts generally observe). This underlines the sense that these saints still have a part to play in the lives of English people and the concerns of their nation, despite having lived so many centuries before.

I have argued elsewhere that the English past, as it appears in Middle English hagiography, is not simply retold but reformulated; the emphasis upon southern Anglo-Saxon saints in both the *Gilte Legende* and Caxton's *Golden Legend* continues the emphasis, which had been in existence since the tenth century, upon 'England' as a creation of the South.[52] These lives do not therefore simply reflect national identity; they also endeavour to mould it in certain ways as well. The imagined past which they offer to the audience is designed to make them feel part of an imagined community in the present, to adopt Benedict Anderson's influential term.[53] However, there are other hagiographic texts, surviving independently of legendary compilations, which allow us to see the ways in which such definitions of English national identity could be contested, and other versions offered in their place. For while Anglo-Saxon saints clearly served as representatives of national pride, they had originally lived in an England that was not a unified kingdom, but a political entity made up of several different realms, as the life of St Kenelm explains. The physical location of their shrines also encouraged perceptions of these saints and their cults as expressions of individual regional and institutional identity as well, thus demonstrating the potentially fragmented nature of the very idea of 'Englishness' in this period. The lives of English saints were brought to bear on contemporary political debates and controversies that privileged locality over nation.

Henry Bradshaw's life of the Anglo-Saxon royal abbess St Werburge, written between 1509 and 1513, provides an excellent illustration of this contention.[54] Bradshaw had already written a Middle English life of St Radegund at a crucial moment in the history of the Cambridge nunnery which bore her name, using the life as a means to reiterate the institution's autonomy and to reject the outside interference of Bishop Alcock, who sought to turn it into a college.[55]

---

[51] Bokenham, *Legendys*, pp. xvii–xviii.
[52] Lewis, 'Anglo-Saxon Saints' Lives', pp. 168–70; see Ingham, *Sovereign Fantasies*, pp. 193–204 for a similar argument about Caxton's edition of Malory serving the interests of a London elite and a new dynasty.
[53] Benedict Anderson, *Imagined Communities: Reflections on the Origin and Spread of Nationalism*, rev. edn (London: Verso, 1991).
[54] Henry Bradshaw, *The Life of St Werburge of Chester*, ed. Carl Horstmann, EETS os 88 (London: Trübner, 1887). References to the life will be by line number within the text. I am extremely grateful to Tim Thornton for drawing the political context of this life to my attention and for his insightful comments on an earlier draft of the following analysis.
[55] Tim Thornton, 'Opposition Drama and the Resolution of Disputes in Early Tudor England:

Bradshaw was a monk at the Abbey of St Werburge in Chester, which housed her shrine. Tim Thornton has explored the ways in which the life serves as propaganda responding to contemporary political quarrels revolving around the authority and autonomy of the abbey, both at the time when it was written and again when it was published.[56] The initial composition of the life arose from a dispute between the abbey and the city over the jurisdictional rights of the abbey's courts, culminating in an arbitration award of 7 August 1509 in favour of the city, which restricted the power of the abbey courts solely to its own precincts.[57] Abbot John Birchenshawe evidently did not accept this decision, and the life of St Werburge appears to have been written by Bradshaw as a direct response to this challenge to the abbey's rights.[58] Birchenshawe's determination to maintain his own rights and privileges, as well as those of the abbey, brought him into conflict with the bishop of Coventry and Lichfield and, as a result of this, with Cardinal Wolsey.[59] Significantly, it was when Birchenshawe's struggle against this formidable enemy was at its height that Bradshaw's life of St Werburge was printed with the abbey's sponsorship in 1521.[60] Birchenshawe evidently appreciated the text's value as a powerful means of expressing the independence and power of both abbey and abbot, through an account of the life and miracles of its patron saint.

In presenting the life of St Werburge (who died in about 700) Bradshaw does not focus solely on the saint herself but provides the related histories of the city of Chester, the kingdom of Mercia and the dynastic history of England more widely. Several chapters are devoted to the lives of her saintly relations, such as Ætheldreda of Ely (her great-aunt), Sexburga (her grandmother) and Ermengild (her mother), as well as mentions of Ethelburga (another great-aunt) and Erkengota (her aunt).[61] Bradshaw also tells the story of her two martyr brothers Wulfhad and Ruffin. Book I focuses on Werburge's life, death and first translation and Book II describes her second translation to Chester (during the Viking invasions of the late ninth century), the miracles she performed there and the foundation of the abbey. Thornton argues that Bradshaw's composition 'demonstrated how the history of the privileges of the county, city and especially monastery at Chester could be knitted together to support the abbot in a dispute which ultimately turned on a very specific issue of jurisdiction'.[62]

Bradshaw's sources were in part hagiographic, such as Goscelinus's Latin life written to commemorate the re-foundation of the abbey at Chester in 1095, although this life is a far briefer text containing much less contextual material.[63] Bradshaw also cites a variety of historical works, such as Bede, William of

---

Cardinal Wolsey and the Abbot of Chester', *Bulletin of the John Rylands University Library of Manchester* 81 (1999), pp. 25–47, p. 38.
56 Thornton, 'Opposition Drama', pp. 37–44.
57 Thornton, 'Opposition Drama', pp. 39–40, for a more detailed account.
58 Thornton, 'Opposition Drama', pp. 30, 38.
59 Thornton, 'Opposition Drama', pp. 30–3.
60 Thornton, 'Opposition Drama', p. 44.
61 Through her grandfather, Erconbert of Kent, Werburge was also related to several other saints, Ermenburga and her three daughters Mildred, Milburga and Mildgyth, but they are not mentioned in Bradshaw's life, nor is Withburga, the other saintly sister of Ætheldreda.
62 Thornton, 'Opposition Drama', pp. 43–4.

Malmesbury and the *Polychronicon* (written by another Chester monk, Ranulph Higden) as sources employed to aid in his description:

> Of her fathers kyngedome the realme of Mercyens,
> How longe it endured vnder his tuycyon,
> Vnder how many kynges it had prehemynens;
> Also of her petygre the noble excellence –
> For so many sayntes of one kindred, certayne,
> Is harde to be founde in all the worlde agayne. (121–6)

Bradshaw provides several chapters of background information at the outset, treating English and Mercian history starting with Hengist and Horsa and the establishment of seven kingdoms in England (134–75), and giving particular emphasis to Mercia (176–238) and King Offa (239–59). Citing the evidence of chronicles, Bradshaw describes the three hundred years of Mercia's existence, emphasising the imperial power of its eighteen kings, the magnificence of its towns and the fruitfulness of its fields and rivers. Thus 'In all pleasaunt propurtes no part of all this lande/ May be compared to this foreseyd Merselande' (223–4). Nor could there be any equal to its valiant inhabitants, who are insuperable in battle, and far more manly and brave than others Bradshaw could mention:

> If they [the Mercians] be well ordred vnder a sure capytayne
> And set to suche busynesse theyr honour to auaunce,
> The tryumph they optayne – knowen it is certayne
> In Englande and Scotlande & in the realme of Fraunce;
> Fewe of them haye countred by manhode and valeaunce
> Great nombre of enemyes with knyghthode & polycye,
> We meane them most specyall in the Weest-party. (232–8)

Mercia's superior nature is underlined by the conduct of its greatest king, Offa, who is said to be a confederate of Charlemagne (521) and ever victorious in battle. Bradshaw notes that Offa 'Of Englande first tole the hole monarchie' (523) thus emphasising that Mercia was once the political centre of a united English kingdom. Twice the life states that Offa translated the see of Canterbury to Lichfield (254, line 5), something that Offa never did in fact. This provides an example of Bradshaw's willingness to reshape history in the service of his Mercian/Cheshire agenda. Similarly, when he comes to present the history of Chester itself, Bradshaw does not demur from explicitly dismissing Higden's *Polychronicon* account which claims a Roman foundation for the city, arguing instead that it was a British foundation (379–92). Bradshaw also asserts that Chester was among the first cities to be converted to Christianity under the legendary British king Lucius, second only to London and before York in third place (435–41).[64] Moreover, the origins of Chester's abbey are said to be in this period:

---

[63] *Life of St Werburge*, pp. xix–xxvi for an edition of Goscelin's text.
[64] Tim Thornton has suggested to me that this privileging of Chester over York may have been of particular interest to Birchenshawe as Wolsey was Archbishop of York.

> The perfect begynnyng and first foundacion
> Of the monasterie within the sayd cite
> Was at the same tyme by famus opinion
> That baptym began within this counter (445–9)

This lends the abbey enormous authority, further emphasised by the claim that when the 'Angles Iutes and saxons' (477) invaded and 'with apostasie enfected all Englande' (476), expelling the British in the process:

> The faith of holy churche remained at chestre cite
> In the sayd churche, truly, by singular grace alone,
> Like as the faith of Peter neuer fayled at Rome. (481–3)

Chester's extraordinary religious importance was such that when Augustine arrived to convert the English in 597 he sent to 'a noble monasterie/ xii. myles from Chestre, nominate Bangour' (491–2) in order to obtain assistance from its three thousand exemplary monks, Bradshaw citing Bede as his authority here (497).

Bradshaw's regional partiality also affects his account of later dynastic history because he gives prominence exclusively to those figures who did something for Chester and increased the prestige of its abbey in particular. So, for example, while King Alfred warrants only a passing mention because he happened to be reigning when Werburge was translated to Chester (527–8), his daughter Æthelflæd, Lady of the Mercians ('duchesse of merciens' to Bradshaw (583)) is an important focus. Æthelflæd, having a 'speciall loue and singular affection/ To blessed Werburge' (584–5) was therefore 'mynded with great dilectacion/ To edifie a mynstere ... To this holy virgin' (586–7), persuading her husband and other nobles to make charitable contributions to the enlargement of the church and the institution of secular canons (590–6). Æthelflæd went on to enlarge Chester itself, defending the city from the Welsh and ruling 'the realme of mercelande manfully' (654) after the death of her husband. Another figure on whom Bradshaw focuses is King Edgar, who is presented as an exemplary king, partly for his success against the Vikings, but largely for his interest in monastic reform, Bradshaw noting that during his reign 'Vertue was exalted in all this region' (1144). Moreover, Edgar is worthy of comment because he clearly recognised the importance of Chester, choosing it as the place where he would receive the submission of eight kings at 'his parliament' (1171–7) before proceeding through the town to worship at its parish church and then entering the monastery 'To worschyp saynt Werburge with mynde liberall' and to give 'fredoms and priuileges speciall' (1196) 'Confirmynge the olde grauntes by hye auctorite' (1198). Chester and its abbey are presented as having been central elements in Edgar's kingship and he, in return, confirmed their autonomy. This theme is continued after the Norman Conquest when Hugh Lupus, William the Conqueror's nephew, acquired Cheshire and sent for St Anselm to re-found the monastery in Chester (1241–317). Bradshaw notes:

> Landes rentes libertes and great possession,
> Franches fredoms and priuileges riall
> Were gyuen meekly to that foundacion,

> Maners borowes townes with the people thrall,
> And many faire churches chapels withall,
> Wardes and mariages were gyuen that season
> To god and saynt werburge, cause of deuocion. (1318–24)

William Rufus subsequently confirmed the foundation and honoured it with further freedoms and franchises: 'The place that tyme was mad as fre/ As the sayd erle was in his castell' (1329–30), vestments and jewels were also given of which 'some remayne/ Within the sayd monastery to this day, certayne' (1344–5). Bradshaw's account here links directly to the wider political context within which it was written for he goes on to describe the construction within the monastery of

> Many mighty places conuenient for religion,
> Compased with stronge walles on the west partie
> And on the other syde with Walles of the towne,
> Closed at euery ende with a sure postron,
> In south part the cimiterie inuironed round about,
> For a sure defence enemies to holde out. (1347–52)

As Thornton points out 'It was of course the walled area over which the abbey claimed jurisdiction that was at the heart of the disputes with the city in the early sixteenth century,' and in this way Bradshaw's text established the abbey's position in powerful terms which rested on the authority of its sacred past and holy patron.[65]

St Werburge is presented as the embodiment of abbey, city and region in the life. Her virginal body is seen to be symbolic of the impermeable strength of Chester. After Werburge was made an abbess in Mercia by her uncle King Æthelred, 'a wanton prynce folowyng sensualyte/ And his fragyll appetite in doing amys' (2275–6) decided to rob Werburge of her virginity. Seizing an opportunity when she was alone he attacked her. In order better to facilitate her escape Werburge cast off her veil and the following astonishing event occurred:

> The sonne-beame receyued it whiche hanged that houre
> Whiche miracle sene the prynce fledde away;
> That vyrgyn was preserued by grace that day. (2785–7)

On another occasion when Werburge was in Kent, a similarly wicked and depraved prince also plotted to defile her, 'Consyderynge her persone so fayre and beauteous' (2782). Finding her alone he chased her down and Werburge called to God for help, running to an oak tree in an attempt to find cover.

> By grace the sayd tree opened that same season
> Sufferynge this mayd to haue sure and free entree;
> Wherby she escaped his wicked tyrannye.
> Whiche tree to this day endurynge all the yere
> By myracle is vernaunte fresshe grene and clere. (2804–8)

---

[65] Thornton, 'Opposition Drama', p. 43.

If we take these episodes as deriving from actual events it may be evidence that there was some attempt to take the real Werburge out of the convent for political reasons. According to her life two of her brothers, Wulfhad and Ruffin, were murdered, and the third, Kenred, gave up the crown and retired to a monastery. The throne passed to her father's brother Æthelred, who also abdicated for a monastic life. Werburge would therefore have appeared an attractive prospect to noblemen with kingly ambitions, hence, perhaps, attempts to abduct/rape her and force her into matrimony.

Bradshaw's intention with these episodes, however, is to demonstrate God's protection of Werburge, for this protection is seen to be extended to Chester once she was translated thence. Part of this protection is manifested in the miracles which Werburge performs for the inhabitants of Chester. Book II of the life (chapters 6–14) catalogues a familiar range of miracles performed at the shrine; the lame are healed, a barren woman conceives, a woman who broke the Sabbath and was blinded has her sight restored, an innocent young man who was wrongly hanged is saved and an injured canon is restored. More significant than these miracles however, in terms of the political import of the life, are those instances Bradshaw describes when Werburge protected Chester from external attack. One such miracle was the very first which Werburge performed at Chester. In the time of Edward the Elder (Æthelflaed's brother) a large Welsh host marched on the city and the people cried out to Werburge for help, while the canons set her shrine on the walls (681–712). One of the Welsh was foolish enough to damage the shrine by throwing a stone at it.

> Anone great punysshement vpon them all lyght:
> The [Welsh] kyng and his host were smitten with blyndnesss,
> That of the cite they had no maner of syght;
> And he that smote the holy shrine, doubtles,
> Was greuously vexed with a sprite of darkenes,
> And with hidous payne expired miserably –
> They kynge was sore a-dred and all his company. (716–22)

The Welsh withdrew and Chester was saved. At a later date Chester was assailed by 'innumerable barbaricke nacions' (758) led by Harold, king of the Danes, the king of the Goths, the king of Galway and Malcolm of Scotland (761–2). Once again the canons set up Werburge's shrine in defence, this time at the north gate (772–3). Again one of the enemy threw a stone at it, this time breaking off a corner:

> The sayd malefactour nat passynge the place
> Vexed with the deuill for his greuous offence,
> Roryng and yelling his outrageous trespase,
> Tore his tonge a-sonder in wodely violence,
> Miserable exspired afore them in presence;
> Satan ceased nat to shewe great punysshement
> Vpon his soule and body by signes euident. (786–92)

Unsurprisingly, the enemy beat a hasty retreat, promising Werburge that they would never again attack her city.

On another occasion Werburge prevented enemy horses from destroying Chester's grain supply (989–1030) and Bradshaw notes that:

> From that tyme furth ther dare no nacion,
> Consyderyng the power of this virgin pure,
> Approchyng Chestre cite to make derogacion;
> Denmarke, Goet [Goth], nor Galway-scot, ye may be sure,
> Cruell danes nor walsheman dare nat procure.
> Wherefore the cite3ens haue cause to loue the place
> And thanke this virgin for her helpe and grace. (1031–7)

In fact, the Welsh did make one more attack on Chester despite this, during the rule of Hugh Lupus' son Richard, but Werburge caused sandbanks to rise up in the sea and prevent their approach, much to the relief of the people (1416–85). Later, the same Earl Richard was persuaded by the evil promptings of his wife Matilda (a niece of Henry I) who 'peruerted her husbande by her subtyll counsell' (1511) to ask the abbot to give him the manor of Salton (1512–13). The abbot refused as this property inextricably belonged to the abbey, having been donated by Hugh. The earl and his wife were furious and as a punishment resolved to try to change the foundation of the abbey and give it to another order (1535–41).

The abbot and the monks prayed to Werburge for help:

> Suffre him [Richard] neuer to distroye thy place
> By wyckyd consell, malice and enuy . . .
> Protect defende and saue thy monastery,
> *Thy landes thy libertes and thy seruantes all,*
> As thou afore-tyme hast done continuall.
>   (1556–7, 1560–2; my emphasis)

Werburge heard their prayer and when Richard and Matilda returned to Chester from Normandy a great storm blew up, driving the ship onto rocks and bursting it open (1570–6). All hands were lost and Werburge appeared to the sacristan of the monastery telling him 'ye may be ioyfull in god and mery:/ Erle Richarde is drowned, your mortall enemy' (1589–90). She also appeared to an honest women who was told to pass the news to the abbot and monks who all gave thanks for their deliverance (1591–7). It is pretty clear that those who seek to attack Chester or attempt to compromise the abbey's freedoms do so at great risk, for Werburge will avenge herself on any who threaten or harm her city, her people or her abbey.

The specific miracles described derive from Bradshaw's Latin source and therefore only go up to 1180.[66] However, in chapter 21 Bradshaw gives a further summary of her miraculous interventions on behalf of the people of Chester, citing a now lost 'thrid passionarye' as evidence and stressing that

---

[66] *Life of St Werburge*, p. xviii. This is the date at which the fire described in chapter 20, from which Werburge saved the city, occurred.

> This holy abasse and lady imperiall
> Hath ben president in Chestre monasterie,
> Theyr trust theyr treasure and defence speciall
> In mycle reuerence .vii. hundredth yere, trulie;
> And so shall continue, by grace of god almighty,
> To the worldes ende in hie magnificence. (1746–51)

Werburge's miracles are not just past events, but continue to happen for the benefit of Chester. Moreover, while she is shown to be the protector of the entire city, Bradshaw's chief purpose is to use her on behalf of the abbey against the city. For this reason he devotes one of his final chapters entirely to an exhortation in which he directly addresses his audience: the people of Chester and the surrounding region. He reminds them of what they owe to the abbey, first addressing the local nobility who are instructed to follow the example of their predecessors in honouring the privileges of the abbey and its ancient freedoms, such as the exemption of its tenants from certain tolls (1778–85) and its monopoly on local fairs (1786–93). They owe this to the monastery for the number of times that Werburge has protected their forefathers 'in great perell,/ In ieopardie on see and on londe' (1802–3). Whenever they called on the saint for help she has answered their prayers, so now they must do something for her. Merchants are reminded that Werburge has kept them safe on their travels from land to land (1810–17) and Werburge's many miraculous cures of illness are also mentioned (1818–25). Finally 'honest matrons' are reminded of the many times that Werburge has helped them 'whan ye in trauelyng vpon her do call' (1828) and maidens told to be grateful for all those who have been saved from ravishment (1831–2).

Each stanza in this chapter (there are eighteen in all) ends with the line 'Wherefore to the monasterie be neuer unkynd' just to ram the point home. And if one isn't kind to the monastery, if one attempts 'to infringe their rightes and liberte' (1844) Werburge will send down punishment to avenge her house (1848, 1890–7). Bradshaw then goes on to make some more pointed comments on those who seek to compromise the abbey's rights in terms that relate very explicitly to the contemporary struggles over its autonomy and jurisdiction:

> Other haue ben besy serching day and nyght
> To infringe theyr fraunchis and fridome aunciaent
> By fals recordes, oppugnant to right,
> As hath ben proued by persones indifferent;
> yet they haue procured and sought wronge iugement
> Agaynst their libertes, in conscience blynde;
> Sodayne and euyll deth followed them consequent:
> Wherefore to the monasterye be neuer unkind.
>
> Some other haue be, *parauenture on late*,
> Studious to disquiet the place, the company,
> And diuers libertes haue alienate,
> Als tolled their franchis fraudulently,
> From the sayd place well knowen in memory;
> Suche mysdoers we moue in conscience blynde

> To mende their wronges, lest payne come sodeynly:
> Wherefore to the monasterie be neuer unkynd.
> (1866–81; my emphasis)

In the struggle over the abbey's rights Bradshaw used the life of its patron, St Werburge, as a call to the people of Chester to identify with the monastery and its version both of past and present. Bradshaw combined sacred and secular history within a hagiographic text to present a strong case for the special status of the region, the city and the abbey. Werburge provided the channel for Bradshaw's attempts to unite the people, inculcating a sense of pride in their city as well as feelings of gratitude towards its patron for ensuring their well-being and continued prosperity. In 1521 Werburge also provided Birchenshawe with a weapon in his fight against Cardinal Wolsey and, while the abbot eventually lost, being deposed by Wolsey in 1524, it may be that publication of the life bought him some extra time in charge at least.[67] It is significant that both Bradshaw and Birchenshawe chose this Middle English saint's life as an effective tool in the abbey's dispute, thus demonstrating the ways in which vernacular hagiography could function as a vehicle for propaganda of various kinds, as well as playing a key role in contemporary politics, through an appeal to the sacred past.

---

[67] Thornton, 'Opposition Drama', p. 45.

7

Crossovers and Afterlife

MATTHEW WOODCOCK

Commentators on hagiography have long identified a vocabulary of common narrative themes and motifs deployed in the writing of saints' lives together with an episodic formula or compositional 'grammar' for establishing what has been termed a 'paradigm for the attainment of glory'.[1] Gregory of Tours's observation that 'it is asked by many whether we should say the Life of the saints, or the Lives' testifies to the fact that by the late sixth century models for composing hagiography had become firmly established, be it in the *passio* tradition centring on the martyrdom of early saints in defence of their faith, or in the *vita* tradition recording the lives of more contemplative saints and their daily experience of endurance and asceticism.[2] From the fourth century onwards the structure of hagiography developed from a diametrical model solely representing martyrs' fatal struggles with heathen tyrants towards a more gradational form focusing on the life, not simply the death, of a saint as the basis for emulation.[3] Nowadays the use of a narrative formula in hagiography and attendant repetition (or plagiarism) of motifs between different saints' lives may necessitate an explanatory apology in introductory studies of the field, but for the medieval audiences for whom the lives were initially composed edification might be of more interest than historical accuracy. General characteristics over and above the individual character of a saint were of great utility in providing a timeless model worthy of inspiring emulation on the audience's part. Composition and embellishment of a saint's life drawing upon the common stock of motifs and scenarios not only made up for a paucity of historical 'facts' but related the individual saint's life to the wider saintly community thus reinforcing the essential theme of all hagiography: the wonder of 'divine goodness and mercy'.[4]

However, hagiographic themes and motifs are by no means exclusive to the kinds of narrative found in well-known collections such as the *Golden Legend* and *South English Legendary*, and the morphology of hagiography itself is in turn

---

[1] Michael Swanton, *English Literature Before Chaucer* (London: Longman, 1987), p. 144.
[2] Quoted in Alexandra Hennessey Olsen, ' *"De historiis sanctorum"*: A Generic Study of Hagiography', *Genre* 13 (1980), pp. 407–29, p. 411.
[3] Charles F. Altman, 'Two Types of Opposition and the Structure of Latin Saints' Lives', *Medievalia et Humanistica* n. s. 6 (1975), pp. 1–11, p. 3.
[4] Helen C. White, *Tudor Books of Saints and Martyrs* (Madison: University of Wisconsin Press, 1963), p. 17.

influenced by works from other genres. Perceptions of genre are of course conditioned by historical, social and intellectual contexts. Many of the texts that appear in medieval collections of saints' lives incorporate elements from the types of writing that nowadays constitute separate sub-genres or fields of analysis in themselves, such as horror, sado-masochistic pornography, folklore and the supernatural. Modern generic taxonomies increasingly appear restrictive when examining the initial contexts of production and reception of hagiographies.[5] Saints' lives frequently appear in manuscripts alongside works of chronicle, romance and practical instruction. The *Beowulf* manuscript also includes a prose homily on St Christopher and a poem *Judith*, on the Old Testament heroine, reimagined here as a virgin saint. Likewise, the Auchinleck manuscript (c. 1330) contains a confection of saints' lives, homilies and popular romances such as *Bevis of Hampton* and *Guy of Warwick*. We should also not forget the functional aspect of saints' lives when exploring hagiography's relationship with other literature. For Hippolyte Delehaye the defining characteristic of a hagiographical work is not simply that it must feature a saint, but that it should actively work to edify the reader and stimulate devotion. The increasingly embellished accounts of a saint's martyrdom had their origins in simple calendar entries and readings (*legenda*) commemorating the day of their death in the liturgical calendar, commemoration thus providing the occasion for edification and stimulation of devotion.[6] In order best to achieve this hagiographers readily adapted their works to the needs and tastes of their audiences. The prologues of many medieval hagiographies begin by confronting the evident popularity of secular tales and romance heroes, and stress how the saintly lives that follow offer more worthy, edifying matter.[7] The popular thirteenth-century *South English Legendary* opens by declaring that:

> Men wilneþ [desire] muche to hure [hear] telle · of bataille of kynge
> And of kniȝtes þat hardy were · þat muchedel is lesynge [mostly false]
> Wo [Who] so wilneþ muche to hure · tales of suche þinge
> Hardi batailles he may hure · here þat nis no lesinge
> Of apostles & martirs · þat hardy kniȝtes were
> Þat studeuast [steadfast] were in bataille · & ne fleide noȝt for fere.[8]

Productive analogies that could be drawn between saintly endurance and the heroic virtue demonstrated by secular protagonists of epic and romance are exploited as a didactic strategy from very early on in English hagiographical writing; witness the opening of the early-ninth-century poem on St Andrew,

---

[5] On medieval nomenclature for saints' lives see Paul Strohm, 'Passioun, Lyf, Miracle, Legende: Some Generic Terms in Middle English', *Chaucer Review* 10 (1975–76), pp. 62–75, 154–7.

[6] Hippolyte Delehaye, *The Legends of the Saints*, trans. Donald Attwater (New York: Fordham University Press, 1962), p. 3.

[7] Jocelyn Wogan-Browne, ' "Bet . . . to . . . rede on holy seyntes lyves . . .": Romance and Hagiography Again', *Readings in Medieval English Romance*, ed. Carol M. Meale (Cambridge: Brewer, 1994), pp. 83–97, p. 84.

[8] *SEL*, p. 3, lines 59–65. The text itself appears in one thirteenth-century manuscript (Oxford, Bodleian Library, MS Laud Misc. 108) bound together with versions of the romances *King Horn* and *Havelok the Dane*.

Andreas, which consciously evokes the beginning of *Beowulf*.⁹ As will be shown below, one can identify numerous examples of medieval romances that explore different forms of synthesis between secular and divine virtue.

This essay is little concerned with establishing a rigid definition of what does and does not fall under the heading of 'hagiography' but accepts and explores as an *a priori* concept the ill-defined edges of the genre. What follows is a discursive survey of representative examples of texts and authors that play with the structure, motifs, themes and generic expectations of hagiography, together with a concluding section that briefly explores different forms through which saints' lives were adapted during the English Reformation and beyond.

A convenient distinction may be made between those texts which simply incorporate details and stories relating to saints' lives within their own narrative and those that attempt to adapt and rework hagiographic conventions, actively playing with expectations of genre and audience response. Medieval chronicles offer several examples of the first approach, and of course the organisation of saints' lives into calendars of commemorations read upon relevant feast days also implies an obvious functional similarity between hagiography and chronicle. Many medieval historians from Bede through to John Capgrave wrote examples of both forms. Saints' lives are also incorporated into Geoffrey of Monmouth's *History of the Kings of Britain* (c. 1136), a Latin work which, although a very early example to employ here, is one of the most influential chronicles produced in the British Isles. Geoffrey refers to the Diocletian martyrs, Julius, Aaron and Alban; includes a version of St Ursula and the eleven thousand virgins; and contrives that St David was King Arthur's cousin.¹⁰ At times Geoffrey's incorporation of hagiographical elements has a peculiarly secular bias. Whereas some of his contemporary chroniclers, such as William of Malmesbury or Henry of Huntingdon, incorporate a number of marvellous stories connected with the veneration and exhumation of saintly figures, Geoffrey avoids assigning miracles to saints and shows more interest in marvels used to foreground secular heroes, most famously Arthur.¹¹ In the majority of cases Geoffrey's reasons for mentioning saints are primarily topographical, explaining that a particular event occurred at a particular place, as in the martyrdom of Alban at Verulamium or St Patrick's founding St David's abbey.¹² For Geoffrey the location, more than the narrative, of the martyrdom offers the

---

⁹ *Andreas and The Fates of the Apostles*, ed. Kenneth R. Brooks (Oxford: Clarendon Press, 1961), p. 1, lines 1–6.
¹⁰ Geoffrey of Monmouth, *History of the Kings of Britain*, trans. Lewis Thorpe (Harmondsworth: Penguin, 1966), pp. 130–1, 142–3, 230. See also Lewis in this volume.
¹¹ William of Malmesbury includes, for example, the story of St Patrick's floating altar, St Cuthbert's posthumous appearance to King Alfred, and an angelic voice heard by Dunstan heralding Edgar's birth; see *The Church Historians of England Vol. 3 Part 1: The History of the Kings of England and of his own times by William of Malmesbury*, trans. John Sharpe (London: Seeleys, 1854), pp. 22, 100, 129. See also Henry of Huntingdon, *The Chronicle of Henry of Huntingdon*, trans. Thomas Forester (London: Bohn, 1853), pp. 26–7 (Alban), 108 (Wilfrid), 152 (Edmund). J. S. P. Tatlock, *The Legendary History of Britain: Geoffrey of Monmouth's Historia Regum Britanniae and Its Early Vernacular Versions* (Berkeley: University of California Press, 1950), p. 275.
¹² Geoffrey of Monmouth, *History*, pp. 131, 262.

basis for commemoration and devotion, and when referring to British people martyred during Diocletian's rule he professes that 'even now their tombs and the places where they suffered would kindle an immense glow of divine charity in the minds of all who saw them, had they not been forgotten by their fellow-countrymen'.[13] Local geography provides a means of bridging the temporal gulf separating the martyrs' 'then' and the audience's 'now'.

Geoffrey's allusions to saints in the landscape set a precedent for the incorporation of traces of hagiography within later chronicles. The majority of references to saints focus far less on narratives of their lives or martyrdom but provide details of the translation of the saint's body to the present resting place, their frequent subsequent exhumations and posthumous miracles associated with their tomb or relics. The fourteenth-century prose *Brut*, for example, contains entries on Sts Ursula and Edmund, but the longest reference to a saintly figure is for Thomas of Lancaster, Edward II's rebellious cousin who was beheaded in 1322 at Pontefract, a site which quickly became a popular pilgrimage destination following several miracle cures witnessed there.[14] An exception to the chroniclers' interest purely in saints' relics and miracles are those works produced in the late fourteenth and early fifteenth centuries that begin to treat the persecution of Lollards using language and set pieces from the hagiography, such as Henry Knighton's chronicle or William Thorpe's account of his own heresy trial before Thomas Arundel, Archbishop of Canterbury (c. 1407).[15] This practice would be used again extensively in sixteenth-century writings on proto-Protestant martyrs.

The topographical emphasis observed above naturally leads one on to consider the interaction of hagiography and medieval travel narratives. Fragmentary details of saints' lives and their relics are incorporated into the well-known travel book of 'Sir John Mandeville' (English version c. 1375) amongst the author-figure's accounts of journeys to the Holy Land and beyond. Mandeville refers to how St Anne's body was brought to Constantinople by 'St Elyne'; to how St Luke's bones were conveyed there from Bethany; to the bones of St Mark being transferred to Venice; and to St Katherine's martyrdom in Alexandria.[16] Again the interest is in material objects that bear witness to narrative accounts found in hagiography which can still be visited and seen in the here and now, such as the river where St Eustace lost his children or the chair in which St Jerome studied.[17] Hagiography is part of the implied intellectual backdrop for a work such as Mandeville's *Travels*, as the book builds upon assumptions that its readers are knowledgeable about the lives and deaths of the relevant saints, and thus offers only brief descriptive gestures to direct one towards

---

[13] Geoffrey of Monmouth, *History*, pp. 130–1.
[14] *The Brut, or the Chronicles of England*, ed. Friedrich W. D. Brie, EETS os 131, 136 (Kegan Paul, Trench, Trübner and Co: London, 1906–08), pp. 43–4, 106–7, 228–31.
[15] Antonia Gransden, *Historical Writing in England ii: c. 1307 to the Early Sixteenth Century* (Ithaca NY: Cornell University Press, 1982), p. 170; James Simpson, *The Oxford English Literary History Volume 2. 1350–1547: Reform and Cultural Revolution* (Oxford: Oxford University Press, 2004), pp. 405–6.
[16] *Mandeville's Travels*, ed. M. C. Seymour (Oxford: Clarendon, 1967), pp. 11, 41, 43–4.
[17] *Mandeville's Travels*, pp. 51, 92.

the 'actual' physical evidence that will then compound the veracity and spiritual potency of the saints' legends themselves. Narrative details of commemoration are again supplemented by identification with a physical location. There are also points at which saints' lives themselves read like forms of travel literature, particularly those accounts which present the popular motif concerning the translation of a saint's body. James Simpson gives the example of Osbern Bokenham's *Legendys of Hooly Wummen* (1443–47) in which extensive attention is afforded to how Margaret's body gets from Antioch to Montefiascone near Rome, where the author himself had visited. Bokenham's text, argues Simpson, and specifically the translation of Margaret's story into English, is comparable to the saint's corporal translation. Both processes seek to bring the saint closer both as a physical presence and as a model and intercessor for Bokenham's immediate female lay readership.[18] Studies of hagiography often emphasise how collections like the *Golden Legend* and sermons upon saints' days, such as those in John Mirk's *Festial* (c. 1450), sought to foster a local and personal relationship with the saints through repetition of their stories (combined with repeated exposure to their accompanying images in churches) and direct applicability of saintly intercessors and exemplars to everyday life. In doing so, figures that were both temporally and geographically distant would be made familiar, parochial and thus accessible for emulation.[19] The observations above regarding incorporation of elements from saints' lives into works of chronicle and travel narrative demonstrates how this sense of proximity might be strengthened by locating the saints within a topographical framework, both native and foreign.

In several of the examples given above one sees how quickly incorporation of hagiographical narratives can elide into adaptation. Even as early as Geoffrey of Monmouth's text we witness not only a form of generic hybridity, but a perceptible distinction between representation of the saints and representation of the saint-*like*, that is, those individuals in a work who are described using the narrative motifs and formulae traditionally deployed in hagiographical discourse. Chivalric romance provides plenty of examples of this latter form. At the end of his extensive Arthurian section Geoffrey refers to the British king's final withdrawal to the Isle of Avalon, a topos (both narrative and geographic) that creates an air of uncertainty regarding Arthur's passing, and leaves protruding narrative threads that are taken up and woven into many subsequent works incorporating themes not only of messianic returns and other-worldly sojourns, but also echoes of the posthumous miracles found in saints' legends. The Arthurian example assumes the more familiar pattern of saintly exhumations found in Bede or William of Malmesbury when Arthur's remains are 'discovered' at Glastonbury abbey in 1191. Arthur was never canonised but his relics quickly became a major focus for pilgrims, boosting the abbey's status and revenue, and the story of his connection with Glastonbury evolved into an extensive, institutional form of hagiography.[20] The secular saint's life of Arthur becomes increas-

---

[18] Simpson, *Reform*, pp. 397–9.
[19] White, *Tudor Books*, pp. 27–8; Eamon Duffy, *The Stripping of the Altars: Traditional Religion in England c. 1400–c. 1580* (New Haven: Yale University Press, 1992), pp. 160–3.
[20] See E. M. R. Ditmas, 'The Cult of Arthurian Relics', *Folklore* 75 (1964), pp. 19–33.

ingly Christianised throughout the thirteenth century as a network of associations develops between Glastonbury, its mythical founder Joseph of Arimathea, and the Holy Grail. Originally referred to in the Gospels as a wealthy Judaean who had entombed Christ's body after the Crucifixion, Joseph was said to have brought with him to Britain either a reliquary containing the blood of Christ or simply the blood itself. Building upon Grail romances such as *Perlesvaus* and the *Perceval* continuations, together with Robert de Boron's poem *Joseph d'Arimathie*, the thirteenth-century Vulgate *Estoire del Saint Graal* develops the legend of Joseph and his family removing the Grail to Britain and ultimately combines the trappings of Arthurian romance with the hagiographic narrative motif of reliquary translation.[21] The early portion of *L'Estoire* forms the basis for an English alliterative homiletic romance *Joseph of Arimathea* (c. 1340). A version of Joseph of Arimathea's life appears in the mid-fourteenth-century Latin collection of English saints, *Nova Legenda Angliae*, which was re-edited a century later, used subsequently in several sixteenth-century printed versions of Joseph's legend, and alluded to in Holinshed's *Chronicles* and Spenser's *The Faerie Queene*.[22] Joseph of Arimathea's multi-generic legend demonstrates how an ostensibly secular mythology centred on a British king can engraft itself onto an aspect of popular native hagiography and how in turn the popularity of Arthurian legend maintains and refreshes traditions connected with this peculiarly British saint.[23]

There are many examples in medieval romance where individual hagiographic motifs are played upon during the process of heroic individuation, and there is a shared attention in both genres to the role of divine or providential aid granted to the central heroic figure. The eponymous hero of *Havelok* is marked out from those around by the 'mikel light' that emanates from his mouth whilst he sleeps, a characteristic reminiscent of the angelic light that surrounded St Agnes in the Roman brothel.[24] To prove her honesty, in the romance *Athelstan* the pregnant Dame Edif walks across a fire, nine ploughshares in length. Half-way across she goes into labour and upon reaching the other side, miraculously unharmed, gives birth to St Edmund.[25] The romance deploys motifs from

---

[21] Valerie M. Lagorio, 'The *Joseph of Arimathie*: English Hagiography in Transition', *Medievalia et Humanistica* n.s. 6 (1975), pp. 91–101, pp. 92–3. See also Antonia Gransden, 'The Growth of the Glastonbury Traditions and Legends in the Twelfth Century', *Journal of Ecclesiastical History* 27 (1976), pp. 337–58.

[22] *Holinshed's Chronicles of England, Scotland, and Ireland*, ed. Henry Ellis et al., 6 vols (London, 1807–08), vol. 1, p. 486; Edmund Spenser, *The Faerie Queene*, ed. A. C. Hamilton (London: Longman, 2001), book II, canto x, stanza 53. References in the text are from this edition. Myths concerning Joseph's supposed introduction of Christianity to the Britons were drawn upon during the sixteenth century as reformers sought to contrive a tradition of pre-Roman Christianity free of papal influence; see William Haller, *Foxe's Book of Martyrs and the Elect Nation* (London: Cape, 1963), pp. 145–6, 150.

[23] The myth receives its most recent reworking in Dan Brown's 2003 novel *The Da Vinci Code* (London: Corgi), which identifies the Grail as the remains of Mary Magdalene.

[24] Text in *Middle English Verse Romances*, ed. Donald B. Sands (Exeter: University of Exeter Press, 1986), p. 107, line 2094; *Golden Legend*, trans. Ryan, vol. 1, p. 103.

[25] *Middle English Verse Romances*, pp. 148–9, lines 621–50. This narrative contradicts the canonical (but equally fictive) identification of St Edmund's parents as King Alkmund and Queen Siwara, continental Saxons; Lydgate, *St Edmund Facsimile*, p. 7.

both *passio* and *vita* narratives, combining the kind of physical trials found in martyrs' accounts with the providential birth of a major national saint. In a twist to the orthodox form of a Christian super-being, the fairy king Oberon in *Huon of Burdeux*, like many saints in the *vita* tradition (such as St Martin or St Guthlac) receives advanced warning of his death and is assured of his place in paradise.[26] Helen Cooper also notes a correlation between the lives of virgin saints attempting to avoid marriage and those romances that feature young women (for example Josian in *Bevis of Hampton*) who have to repel successive monstrous suitors who are frequently represented as heathen tyrants.[27] Many of the stories of virgin martyrs in the *Golden Legend* adapt the romance paradigm of having to choose between a bad (in this context, earthly) lover and the good (i.e. heavenly) lover, as in the legend of St Agatha.

Interaction between hagiography and romance goes beyond identification of individual motifs, and one finds that many romances adapt a narrative structure loosely based on the life of specific saints, in particular Sts Alexis and Eustace. Alexis is a Roman nobleman who abandons his worldly lifestyle on his wedding night, urging his bride to maintain her virginity, and travels to Syria to live as a beggar. After seventeen years he returns to Rome and lives in his father's house where, all the while concealing his identity from his family and enduring hardship and scorn from those around, he lives for another seventeen years. Knowing he is soon to die Alexis writes out the story of his life and his family eventually discover his letter together with his dead body, which is later entombed and becomes the site of miraculous cures.[28] As several critics have noted, Alexis's story underlies a number of so-called 'penitential romances', such as *Sir Gowther*, *Bevis of Hampton* and *Roberd of Cisyle*, that see the hero abandoning a worldly chivalric career to go off and serve God.[29] One of the most popular examples of this model is *Guy of Warwick*. In the first half of the romance, seeking to prove himself to his love Felice, Guy quests for worldly glory by aiding noblemen, defeating Saracens and slaying a dragon. In the second part, having married Felice, he realises the limitations of his worldly love and that he has neglected God, and thus sets off to the Holy Land as a pilgrim where he fights for more Christian causes. He returns home where he dies at a hermitage near to his own castle, his soul being carried to heaven by angels; posthumous miracles follow. The key point in the romance is the episode in which Guy realises the error of his earlier life:

> 'Allas', he sayd, 'þat y was born:
> Bodi & soule icham forlorn.

---

[26] *The Boke of Huon of Burdeux, done into English by Lord Berners*, ed. S. L. Lee, EETS es 40, 41, 43, 50 (London: Trübner, 1882–87), p. 605.
[27] Helen Cooper, *The English Romance in Time: Transforming Motifs from Geoffrey of Monmouth to the Death of Shakespeare* (Oxford: Oxford University Press, 2004), pp. 249–50. Paulina similarly fashions Leontes into the role of a tyrant from hagiography in *The Winter's Tale*, 3.2.175–9.
[28] *Golden Legend*, trans. Ryan, vol. 1, p. 371–4.
[29] David N. Klausner, 'Didacticism and Drama in *Guy of Warwick*', *Medievalia et Humanistica* n. s. 6 (1975), pp. 103–19; Andrea Hopkins, *The Sinful Knights: A Study of Middle English Penitential Romance* (Oxford: Clarendon Press, 1990); Cooper, *English Romance*, p. 89.

> Of blis icham al bare.
> For neuer in al mi liif biforn
> For him þat bar þe croun of þorn
> Gode dede dede y nare;
> Bot wer & wo ichaue wrou3t,
> & mani a man to grounde y-brou3t:
> Þat rewes me ful sare.
> To bote min sinnes ichil wende
> Barfot to mi liues ende,
> To bid mi mete wiþ care.'[30]

The rationale for his change of direction is made far more explicit than in Alexis's legend, where the saint's actions are unexplained (though of course such piety should not require any explanation or apology) because this constitutes the text's didactic core, the point at which the reader is encouraged to reassess the concept of virtue and heroism presented up until now and proceed to juxtapose the initial chivalric half of this diptych romance with what Andrew King calls the 'hagiographical' half.[31] Guy does not fully abandon worldly values as Alexis does, and integrates his spiritual commitment with his concern for Felice and their son Reinbroun, in a manner that is somewhat more accessible than the saint's paradoxically selfish asceticism.[32]

The diptych structure also features in the Job-like model of St Eustace's legend. Eustace (initially called Placidus) learns from Christ that he will be tested by the Devil for becoming baptised, and subsequently suffers a series of trials of faith, including losing his wealth and becoming separated from his wife and sons. After living in misery for fifteen years Eustace returns to Rome and reunites with his family, though they are all eventually killed by Hadrian for refusing to forsake their faith.[33] The story has been developed in a series of romances termed the 'Eustace-Constance-Florence-Griselda legends'.[34] To take one example, in *Sir Isumbras* the hero becomes too complacent of his worldly achievements as a knight:

> Into his herte a pryde was browghte
> That of God yafe he ryghte nowghte,
> His mercy ones to nevenne.[35]

As a result, God chastises Isumbras and he not only quickly loses his wealth and status but, closely following events in the Eustace legend, also his wife and chil-

---

[30] *The Romance of Guy of Warwick*, ed. Julius Zupitza, EETS es 42, 49, 59 (London: Trübner: 1883–91), pp. 400–2, Auchinleck MS text, stanza 22.
[31] Andrew King, *The Faerie Queene and Middle English Romance: The Matter of Just Memory* (Oxford: Clarendon Press, 2000), p. 64.
[32] Hopkins, *Sinful Knights*, p. 78.
[33] *Golden Legend*, trans. Ryan, vol. 2, pp. 266–71.
[34] See Lillian Horlands Hornstein, 'Eustace-Constance-Florence-Griselda Legends', *A Manual of the Writings in Middle English 1050–1500*, vol. 1, ed. J. Burke Severs (New Haven: Yale University Press, 1967), pp. 120–32; these include *The King of Tars, Sir Eglamour of Artois, Octavian, Le Bone Florence of Rome, Sir Triamour* and *Sir Torent of Portyngale*.
[35] Text in *Six Middle English Romances*, ed. Maldwyn Mills (London: Dent, 1973), p. 126, lines 37–41.

dren. Like Eustace (and Guy) the turning point comes when Isumbras laments his overwhelming loss and prays to God, specifically requesting guidance to 'som towne'.[36] His prayers seemingly answered, Isumbras finds a nearby blacksmith and there, over many years, works to restore himself to his original state, his rise in fortunes symbolised by the suit of armour that he forges and eventually uses to recover his family and status. The poet closes by telling us that they all finally 'lyved and dyed in gode entente,/ Her sowles I wote to hevenn went'.[37] Unlike the Eustace narrative, the hero is not martyred, instead one sees the working through of a sense of divine justice: a test of faith set and completed, and – as in romance reworkings of Alexis's life – a model of how to combine temporal endeavour with devout commitment ('gode entente').

One also finds variants of the Eustace loss-and-restitution narrative (though again without the martyrdom) centred on a female protagonist in the stories of Constance/ Custance in Gower's *Confessio Amantis* and Chaucer's *Man of Law's Tale*, and in that of Grisilde in the *Clerk's Tale*. The Clerk concludes his tale by admitting that heroines may be as difficult to emulate as saints:

> This storie is seyd nat for that wyves sholde
> Folwen Grisilde as in humylitee,
> For it were inportable, though they wolde,
> But for that every wight, in his degree,
> Sholde be constant in adversitee
> As was Grisilde.[38]

In a similar fashion, in romance recastings of the Alexis and Eustace narratives, there is awareness of the difficulty of living a spiritual life in the material world and a need to apply the lessons offered by some of the more extreme exemplars of virtue and endurance to the abilities of the immediate audience. Guy and Isumbras are not directly represented as saints themselves but display saint-*like* qualities, and in the narratives of each the extremities of the hagiographic model are tempered by recognition of a practical, realistic need to integrate moral didacticism with more secular ideals and modes of living. As Andrea Hopkins identifies, the integration of moral teaching on penance with chivalric narrative would generally offer a more user-friendly model for a popular audience than the 'analytic' approach found in a treatise such as *Handlyng Synne* (1303).[39] This is underpinned by the Augustinian principle resonant throughout medieval literary and exegetical theory that the greatest truth and pleasure is to be gained from a work where one has to labour in uncovering its didactic core.[40]

Chaucer's narratives of calumniated and oppressed women are by no means his only engagements with hagiography and in the *Second Nun's Tale* he offers a

---

[36] *Six Middle English Romances*, p. 135, line 383.
[37] *Six Middle English Romances*, p. 147, lines 790–1.
[38] *The Riverside Chaucer*, gen. ed. Larry D. Benson (Oxford: Oxford University Press, 1987), p. 152, lines 1142–7. In most manuscripts of *The Canterbury Tales* the Host actually refers to Grisilde's story as a 'legende'; p. 153, line 1212d.
[39] Hopkins, *Sinful Knights*, p. 31.
[40] Augustine, *De doctrina Christiana*, ed. and trans. R. P. H. Green (Oxford: Clarendon Press, 1995), pp. 61–3, 207.

polished, aureate rendering of the life of 'mayde and martyr' St Cecilia. Of greater interest to the present essay is Chaucer's manipulation of hagiographical commonplaces in *The Legend of Good Women* (composition began c. 1386), a collection of nine stories centred on famous women, all of whom have been wronged in love. The accompanying prologue contrives Chaucer's reasons for writing the work that follows: as penance for dissuading people from their 'devocioun' to the God of Love through works such as the *Romance of the Rose* and *Troilus and Criseyde*, Cupid commands Chaucer

> Thow shalt, while that thou lyvest, yer by yere,
> The moste partye of thy tyme spende
> In makyng of a glorious legende
> Of goode wymmen, maydenes and wyves,
> That weren trewe in lovnyg al hire lyves.[41]

It might seem entirely appropriate that the author offer a collection of saints' lives as a penitential work in order to avoid his own 'martyrdom' at Cupid's hand. But the 'lovnyg' to be praised here is of a secular nature. Chaucer adapts structures and motifs from hagiography to interrogate the overlap between employment of secular and religious imagery in the discourse of love. Later, in the *Man of Law's Prologue*, he refers to the *Legend* accordingly as 'the Seintes Legende of Cupide'.[42] Chaucer presents a studied parody of hagiography that consciously plays with the principal generic characteristics and expectations but focuses in each story on figures from classical mythology: Cleopatra, Thisbe, Dido, Hypsipyle, Medea, Lucrece, Ariadne, Philomela, Phyllis and Hypermnestra.[43] Chaucer thus inverts the common structural binary of hagiography which sees the non-Christian as a saint's enemy, the 'other' against which the saintly hero is measured. Whilst the details of each woman's life differ, each legend broadly adapts the diametric structure of a *passio* narrative, and depicts the heroine in a situation where she becomes the victim of various male agents who obstruct the path of honest and true love. Manuscript incipits and explicits for the first five legends clearly identify the women as martyrs. Immediately following his initial command in the prologue quoted above, Cupid stipulates that the tyrant–good woman axis should be central to the legends presented:

> And telle of false men that hem bytraien,
> That al hir lyf ne don nat but assayen
> How many women they may doon a shame.[44]

Chaucer thus groups Hypsipyle and Medea together in the same individual

---

[41] *Riverside Chaucer*, p. 601, F version, lines 481–5.
[42] *Riverside Chaucer*, p. 88, line 61.
[43] Boccaccio earlier parodied hagiographic conventions in day four of the *Decameron*, and this (together with Ovid's *Heroides*) was of greater influence upon Chaucer here than Boccaccio's similar-sounding *De claris mulieribus*; see Julia Reinhard Lupton, *Afterlives of the Saints: Hagiography, Typology, and Renaissance Literature* (Stanford: Stanford University Press, 1996), pp. 94–104, and Lisa J. Kiser, *Telling Classical Tales: Chaucer and the* Legend of Good Women (Ithaca NY: Cornell University Press, 1983), pp. 103–4.
[44] *Riverside Chaucer*, p. 601, F version, lines 486–8.

legend as victims of Jason's cruelty. Even Thisbe's story is reworked so as to foreground the tyrannous conditions under which she and Piramus are forced to conduct their relationship; her dying words condemn the constraints of the lovers' 'jelos fadres'.[45] As in a religious martyrology where, despite great variety in the tortures the saints endure, everything is usually brought to a close with the terminal decapitation, so all of Chaucer's heroines meet the same tragic fate even though the individual agent may differ.

Chaucer also makes many teasing verbal allusions to phrases and motifs from hagiography. In addressing Cupid he refers to 'Seynt Venus' and to having written 'many an ympne [hymn] for your halydayes'. Lucrece is similarly called a saint and afforded her own holy day; Procne feigns going on pilgrimage to Bacchus's temple in order to meet her sister Philomela; and whilst Chaucer makes no reference to his heroines' relics or miracles, Phyllis vainly attempts to construct her floating corpse in Athens harbour as a posthumous reminder of Demophon's treachery.[46] One also encounters claims to present a 'storyal soth' similar to those found throughout the *Golden Legend*.[47] Cupid's description of Alceste as a 'kalender . . . To any woman that wol lover bee' also retains a punning allusion to the dual function of saints' lives: as a reference point or model for emulation and as a commemorative temporal guide (i.e. like an almanac).[48] Much has been made of how the *Legend*'s prologue offers oblique insights into Chaucer's conceptions of himself as an author, as the narrator identifies and defends his earlier works. For present purposes, of most interest are the references to an early version of St Cecilia's legend and a (now lost) translation of a homily on Mary Magdalene that reveal traces of Chaucer's previous attempts at writing of 'good women'.[49] However, in the *Legend*, as in his reworking of many other medieval genres in *The Canterbury Tales*, Chaucer adds his own distinct authorial stamp to hagiography and offers a conscious 'over-going' of the form that simultaneously demonstrates his mastery of accepted conventions together with his ability to manipulate the genre and make it his own. Chaucer uses hagiography or 'sacred biography', in which he adopts the pose of writing another's life and narrative, as the basis for presenting his own autobiographical construction and commentary, a practice he would develop further in *The Canterbury Tales*.

Biographical and autobiographical aspects of life-writing also overlap in the *Book of Margery Kempe*, as the text – originally dictated by Margery to a priest many years later than the events described – continually elides between the record of first-hand feelings and experiences and an externalised, third-person representation of 'þis creatur'. Although frequently discussed alongside medieval mystical writings, the book equally displays a complex intertextual relationship with saints' lives. During her travels on pilgrimage around Europe and

---

[45] *Riverside Chaucer*, p. 608, line 900.
[46] *Riverside Chaucer*, p. 620, lines 1870–2; p. 626, lines 2375–6; p. 628, lines 2550–4.
[47] *Riverside Chaucer*, p. 605, line 702.
[48] *Riverside Chaucer*, p. 603, F version, lines 542–3.
[49] See John P. McCall, 'Chaucer and the Pseudo-Origen *De Maria Magdalena*: A Preliminary Study', *Speculum* 46 (1971), pp. 491–509.

the Holy Land, Margery visits the relics of a number of saints, as at Santiago and Aachen. But through her communications with Christ, the saints have a much greater immediacy and she takes comfort from direct communications with Sts Peter, Paul, Katherine, Margaret, Mary Magdalene or 'what seynt in Heuyn þat sche cowde thynke on'.[50] Saintly models also offer authority and validation for Margery's characteristic weeping as her priestly amanuensis instructs her to observe the similar conduct of St Elizabeth of Hungary and the saint-like Mary of Oignies.[51] Like examples shown above of characters struggling to combine a spiritual life with the material world, Margery never completely abandons worldly preoccupations and comparisons in her interaction with the divine as she pictures the Trinity sitting on coloured cushions and imagines Christ physically taking her as a lover.[52]

Margery also demonstrates how the example of a saint's life, such as that of Bridget of Sweden ('Brides boke'), can directly inspire imitation and saintly conduct in another individual. A number of medieval conduct manuals for women recommended looking to hagiography for models of charitable, devout living.[53] But Margery's book goes much further, and although it does not follow the typical chronological hagiographic pattern, one can identify a number of analogies between episodes Margery chooses to focus upon and the kind of scenarios found in saints' lives. Not only does she undertake charitable works and daunting peregrinations but, like the virgin martyrs, she also confronts sexual temptations at several points in her life and on one occasion is troubled by a fantasy of an ecumenical orgy.[54] Although her fourteen children exclude her from joining the ranks of virgin saints such as Sts Agnes or Margaret, the vow of chastity Margery negotiates with her husband in 1413 is a key point in her spiritual awakening and marks her 'emergence into the life-style she so passionately desired'.[55] Like many of the saints in the *Golden Legend* Margery is imprisoned at various points and interrogated by successive ecclesiastical authorities, including in her case Archbishop Arundel. On each occasion she emerges victorious. Margery even imagines – and desires – her own martyrdom: 'to be bowndyn hyr hed & hir fet to a stokke & hir hed to be smet of wyth a scharp ex for Goddys lofe'.[56] Wynkyn de Worde uses this image of would-be martyrdom at the start of his short selection of excerpts from Margery printed in 1501.[57] Christ assures Margery that such sacrifice is unnecessary and later tells her that she will live another fifteen years.[58]

---

[50] *The Book of Margery Kempe*, ed. Sanford Brown Meech and Hope Emily Allen, EETS os 212 (London: Oxford University Press, 1940), p. 215.
[51] *Margery Kempe*, pp. 152–4.
[52] *Margery Kempe*, pp. 210–11, 90.
[53] See, for example, *The Book of the Knight of the Tower*, trans. William Caxton, ed. M. Y. Offord, EETS ss 2 (London: Oxford University Press, 1971), pp. 17, 76.
[54] *Margery Kempe*, p. 145.
[55] *Margery Kempe*, pp. 23–5; Marion Glasscoe, *English Medieval Mystics: Games of Faith* (London: Longman, 1993), p. 289.
[56] *Margery Kempe*, p. 30.
[57] *A shorte treatyse of contemplacyon taught by our lorde Jhesu cryste, or taken out of the boke of Margerie kempe of lynn* (London, 1501), sig. A1r.
[58] *Margery Kempe*, p. 176.

One also finds elements of the miraculous in the incident where Margery survives unscathed after several pounds of stone and timber fall upon her from a church roof in Lynn. God urges her to see this as a miracle and the Carmelite friar Alan of Lynn, hearing of the event and 'desyryng þe werk of God to be magnyfyed', recovers the stone and wood as physical evidence of what occurred, proclaiming widely it was indeed a miracle. Margery records both that 'mych pepyl magnyfied mech God in þis creatur. And also mech pepyl wold not leuyn it, but raþar leuyd it was a token of wreth & veniawns þan þei wold leuyn it was any token of mercy er quemfulnes'.[59] This is one of a number of incidents when her actions become a matter for interpretation and she is subjected to the judgement of the ubiquitous 'pepyl'; she is a signifier open to public construction. At points like this the book comes close to parodying hagiographic conventions by revealing the inner anxieties of the potentially saintly that seldom come through in orthodox saints' lives. It reads in fact like hagiography written in the present tense, hagiography as it happens or *may* be happening. It is full of episodes which have to be correctly interpreted as divinely ordained, and of occasions where Margery stands out from everyone around or is subjected to slanderous scorn (as at Norwich and Rome), and therefore seeks some assurance that she somehow still fits into the saintly mould. Margery's book interrogates the narrative conventions and scenarios employed in hagiography by voicing, and in part addressing, the kind of questions that she and her contemporaries have about the place of the miraculous and divinely inspired in the everyday world. It also shows an individual playing with the generic boundaries of saints' lives as she produces a work which both feeds upon and perpetuates the hagiographic tradition by incorporating some of its principal concerns within an early example of extended life-writing in English.

The sixteenth century initially saw a continued popularity in saints' lives: William Caxton's expanded translation of the *Golden Legend* was frequently reprinted up until 1527 and there were many printed editions of individual lives.[60] But the saints' importance in the liturgy, together with the devotional cults for saints and their relics, were fundamental aspects of the medieval Church against which reformers reacted.[61] The cult of saints repeatedly became the target of extended criticism from preachers such as Thomas Cranmer and Hugh Latimer, and veneration of relics was increasingly identified with idolatry during the monastic visitations beginning in 1535.[62] Successive measures in the mid sixteenth century began to dismantle the cult of saints. In 1536 Henry VIII's Ten Articles decreed that praying to saints should be done 'without any vayne superstition as to thinke, that any saynte is more mercyfull, or wyll here us sooner than Christ, or that any saynt doth serve for one thinge more than an other, or is patron of the same'; a royal injunction enforced the same line.[63] The same year an Act 'for the abrogation of certain holydays' radically reduced the

---

[59] *Margery Kempe*, pp. 21–2.
[60] Simpson, *Reform*, p. 404, n. 50.
[61] White, *Tudor Books*, pp. 68–71.
[62] Duffy, *Stripping of the Altars*, pp. 388–91.
[63] White, *Tudor Books*, pp. 79–80.

number of observed saints' days from the liturgical year. The 1537 *Bishop's Book* instructed preachers to stress to their congregations that saints' images should not be worshipped, and the following year further injunctions reduced the emphasis upon the role of saints in the litany. The *King's Primer* (1545) all but completed the removal of saints from the calendar, and in the first Edwardian Prayer Book (1549) the calendar of readings based on saints' legends was totally supplanted by an annual programme of readings from scripture. Subsequent prayer books in 1552 and 1559 made compliance with the new calendar compulsory by law.

But despite the abolition of the institutional, lectionary function of saints' lives, the practice of adapting motifs and narratives commonly employed in hagiographical writing continued throughout the sixteenth century as overtly Protestant texts began to appropriate genres and iconographic schemes used prior to the Reformation. John Bale, for example, attempts a Protestant recasting of hagiographical drama, once a flourishing tradition between the thirteenth and sixteenth centuries. Based on the evidence of the very few extant examples, saints' plays typically represented a saint's life and/ or martyrdom (as in *Mary Magdalen* and *St Meriasek*), or concentrated on a key episode or miracle (such as the Digby *Conversion of St Paul*). Bale begins by parodying the popular genre of saints' plays about Thomas Becket before reversing the onus of Church–State relations and fashioning the hero of *King Johan* (1538) as a sacrificial proto-Protestant martyr figure.[64] A tradition of Becket plays continued on in Counter-Reformation culture and long after Bale, in a Jesuit play called *St Thomas Cantuar* (1613) performed at the English College, Rome, a figure representing Joseph of Arimathea urges the audience to follow Becket's martyr example.[65]

The centrepiece of early modern appropriations of hagiography is undoubtedly John Foxe's *Acts and Monuments* (first published 1563) as its popular title, *The Book of Martyrs*, cannot help but suggest. Foxe begins by describing how the early-fourth-century ecclesiastical historian Eusebius compiled a collection of martyrs' deeds for daily commemoration, and advocating the need for a similar work recording martyrs killed up until Elizabeth's reign.

> For if then such care was in searching and setting forth the doynges and Actes of Christes faithfull seruauntes, suffering for his name in the primatiue tyme of the Church: why should they now be more neglected of vs in the latter churche, such as geue their bloud in the same cause and like quarell.[66]

For Foxe, the struggles of the English Church to break from Rome provided new opportunities to emulate the early martyrs. Taking in a wide range of figures

---

[64] Benjamin Griffin, *Playing the Past: Approaches to English Historical Drama, 1385–1600* (Cambridge: Brewer, 2001), pp. 37–45. During the 1540s Bale continues to construct a tradition of reformist hagiography, identifying a continuity between those executed for Lollardy and contemporary Protestant martyrs in his accounts of Sir John Oldcastle and Anne Askew; see L. P. Fairfield, 'John Bale and the Development of Protestant Hagiography in England', *Journal of Ecclesiastical History* 24 (1973), pp. 145–60.

[65] Alison Shell, *Catholic Controversy and the English Literary Imagination* (Cambridge: Cambridge University Press, 1999), p. 211.

[66] John Foxe, *Acts and Monuments of these Latter and Perillous Dayes* (London, 1563), sig. B2r.

from fifteenth-century Lollards through to those persecuted under Mary I, Foxe's vast work (over 1800 pages in the 1563 edition) establishes a new tradition of the saint-like, returning time after time to the diametric, binary struggle of good versus evil – and good *over* evil – employed in medieval martyrology in order to justify the eventual victory of English Protestantism. Foxe's descriptive method retains much of the sensationalism found in medieval immolation scenes, featuring often-cited grisly set pieces such as the slow burning of Bishop Hooper or the story of a woman giving birth as she burns at the stake.[67] He incorporates repeated episodes of execution by burning into the hagiographic formula, such repetition serving to glorify the Protestant cause above individual martyrs. Like contemporary primers and prayer books superseding the *Golden Legend*, Foxe includes a new commemorative calendar purged of most of the earlier saints' days but including new commemorations for Lollard and Protestant martyrs and confessors. Counter-Reformation texts of the same period also adapted the hagiographic genre to portray martyrs such as Edmund Campion, with Cardinal William Allen counterpointing Foxe as principal martyrologist for the Catholic faith.[68] The Jesuit Robert Southwell's poem 'Decease Release' similarly fashioned Mary Stuart as a martyr saint following her execution in 1587.

The final example of a Protestant recasting of hagiography that I want to consider is book one of Edmund Spenser's *The Faerie Queene* (1590, 1596). In the Redcrosse knight Spenser continues the tradition identified in *Guy of Warwick* of fashioning a hero combining worldly prowess with spiritual virtue, and the book presents a series of challenges that lead up to revelation of Redcrosse's identity as St George at the House of Holiness.[69] George's life as found in accounts such as the *Golden Legend* is never really used here as a narrative template in the manner of Alexis or Eustace in earlier romance, and there is no reference to his martyrdom. But Spenser plays upon George's established patriotic associations that saw his continued presence in the religious calendar long after most other saints' days were abolished, to construct a champion of specifically English holiness.[70] Just as he did not need to believe in the existence of fairies or King Arthur to realise their mythographic potential, so Spenser did not have to accept the liturgical or intercessionary function of the saints to appreciate the didactic and political expedience of creating a narrative about St George. Whereas the diptych structure of *Guy* divides the hero's pursuit of worldly glory from penitential, Christian adventures, through presenting Redcrosse as an allegorical figure we are provided with a form of plural hero whose tales of 'fierce warres and faithfull loues' may be read through and decoded to discover the formative struggles of the Protestant saint within. For example, we see Redcrosse led astray by Duessa, an enchantress figure not only

---

[67] White, *Tudor Books*, pp. 160–2.
[68] See for example Allen's *A briefe historie of the glorious martyrdom of XII. reuerend priests* (Rheims, 1582).
[69] Spenser, *Faerie Queene*, I.x.61.
[70] On the Tudor cult of St George, see Roy Strong, *The Cult of Elizabeth: Elizabethan Portraiture and Pageantry* (London: Thames and Hudson, 1977), pp. 167–85.

representing a general principle of falsehood but whose description in I.ii.13 clearly evokes the Whore of Babylon from Revelation 17:4, in turn a figure commonly identified in Protestant iconography and exegesis as the Catholic Church itself. In the penultimate canto of book one Spenser takes up the best-known story from legends and folklore on St George as the hero engages in a three-day fight with 'that dreadfull Dragon' that imprisoned Una's parents. Again drawing upon Revelation, the dragon is identified as Satan, imprisoning Adam and Eve, i.e. mankind; George's fight becomes part of a wider eschatological struggle. That is perforce an oversimplification of the dense network of allegorical schemes at work in the poem, but the point to stress is that Spenser signals throughout that we should remain aware of his heroes' polysemic nature. The author defends his employment of allegorical fiction in the prefatory 'Letter to Sir Walter Raleigh' outlining the poem's didactic function arguing that 'so much more profitable and gratious is doctrine by ensample, then by rule'. Such sentiments were no doubt also in the minds of the authors of the medieval penitential romances as they too adapted elements from hagiography.

There are obviously countless further examples that could be drawn upon in exploring the generic boundaries of medieval hagiography and the different ways that it is adapted from the sixteenth century onwards. Critics are often keen to plot the progressive 'secularisation' of saints' lives, and identify the point at which hagiography develops into biography and assumes some of the features considered desirable in modern life-writing: veracity, rationalism, objectivity, originality.[71] But to identify such a transition assumes, firstly, that both hagiographer and biographer share the same conception of their works' function and context of reception, and secondly, that a rigid distinction can always be drawn between sacred and secular representations. As we saw, for example, with Chaucer, Margery Kempe and the penitential romances, there is not only an overlap between religious and secular discourses used to represent the numinous, superlative qualities of a hero/ine, but authors repeatedly play with the professed distinction between sacred and worldly heroism in order to increase the didactic efficacy of their works. The present essay has attempted instead to identify the interplay between those forms of text which represent saints and those which represent the saint-like and suggest how this prepares the way for later, post-medieval reworkings of hagiographic conventions.

---

[71] See Thomas J. Heffernan, *Sacred Biography: Saints and Their Biographers in the Middle Ages* (New York: Oxford University Press, 1988), pp. 38–71; Lupton, *Afterlives*, pp. 94–104.

Bibliography

This is not an exhaustive bibliography: see also John Scahill, *Middle English Saints' Legends*, Annotated Bibliographies of Old and Middle English Literature 8 (Cambridge: Brewer, 2005)

Manuscripts

Brussells, Bibliothèque Royale de Belgique MS 7917
Cambridge
   Corpus Christi College MS 145
   St John's College MS N.17
   University Library Add. MS 4122
   University Library Ee 2 15
   University Library Ff 2 38
   University Library Gg 2 6
Edinburgh, National Library of Scotland MS Advocates 19.2.1
London
   BL MS Add. 21114
   BL MS Add. 22283
   BL MS Add. 36704
   BL MS Add. 36791
   BL MS Add. 36983
   BL MS Arundel 168
   BL MS Arundel 327
   BL MS Arundel 396
   BL MS Cotton Claudius A ii
   BL MS Cotton Faustina B iii
   BL MS Cotton Galba E iv
   BL MS Cotton Tiberius E vii
   BL MS Cotton Titus A xxvi
   BL MS Cotton Titus D xviii
   BL MS Egerton 1993
   BL MS Harley 2247
   BL MS Harley 2250
   BL MS Harley 2253
   BL MS Harley 2278
   BL MS Harley 2382
   BL MS Harley 4012
   BL MS Harley 4196
   BL MS Harley 4755
   BL MS Royal 17 A xxvii
   BL MS Royal 17 C xvii

BL MS Royal 17 D v
BL MS Royal 18 B xxiii
BL MS Royal 18 B xxv
BL MS Sloane 2569
BL MS Stowe 949
Manchester, Chetham's Library MS 6709
New York, Pierpont Morgan Library MS M. 736
Oxford
   Bodleian MS Bodley 34
   Bodleian MS Bodley 779
   Bodleian MS Douce 60
   Bodleian MS Douce 114
   Bodleian MS. Eng. poet. a.1
   Bodleian MS Hatton 96
   Bodleian MS Laud 108
   Bodleian MS Tanner 17
   Corpus Christi College MS 237
   St John's College MS 182
Paris
   Bibliothèque de l'Arsenal MS 596
   Bibliothèque Nationale MS latin 3278
Southwell Minster MS 7

Editions and Translations of Hagiography and Associated Texts

Barclay, Alexander. *The Life of St George*, ed. William Nelson. EETS os 230. London: Oxford University Press, 1955

Barron, W. R. J. and Glyn S. Burgess, eds. *The Voyage of Saint Brendan: Representative Versions of the Legend in English Translation*. Exeter: University of Exeter Press, 2002

Bartlett, Anne Clark and Thomas H. Bestul, eds. *Cultures of Piety: Medieval English Devotional Literature in Translation*. Ithaca NY: Cornell University Press, 1999

Bokenham, Osbern, *Legendys of Hooly Wummen*, ed. Mary J. Serjeantson. EETS os 206. London: Oxford University Press, 1938

———. *A Legend of Holy Women: A Translation of Osbern Bokenham's Legends of Holy Women*, trans. Sheila Delany. Notre Dame: University of Notre Dame Press, 1992

Bradshaw, Henry. *Life of St Radegund*, ed. Fred Brittain. 1925

———. *The Life of St Werburge of Chester*, ed. Carl Horstmann. EETS os 88. London: Trübner, 1887

Buckland, Ralph. *The Lives of Women Saints of our Contrie of England, also Some Other Liues of Holie Women Written by Some of the Auncient Fathers*, ed. Carl Horstmann. EETS os 86. London: Trübner, 1886

Capgrave, John. *John Capgrave's Lives of St Augustine, St Gilbert of Sempringham and a Sermon*, ed. J. J. Munro. EETS os 140. London: Kegan Paul, Trench, Trübner, 1910

———. *The Life of St Katharine of Alexandria*, ed. Carl Horstmann, with a foreword by F. J. Furnivall. EETS os 100. London: Kegan Paul, Trench, Trübner, 1893

———. *Life of St Norbert*, ed. Cyril Lawrence Smetana. Toronto: Pontifical Institute of Medieval Studies, 1977

Christine de Pisan. *The Boke of the Cyte of Ladyes*, trans. Brian Ansley. London: Pepwell, 1521

D'Evelyn, Charlotte and Anna J. Mill, eds. *The South English Legendary, edited from

Corpus Christi College Cambridge MS 145 and British Museum MS Harley 2277, with variants from Bodley MS Ashmole 43 and British Museum MS Cotton Julius D.ix. 3 vols, EETS os 235, 236, 244. London: Oxford University Press, 1956–59
Doyle, A. I., intr. *The Vernon Manuscript: A Facsimile of Bodleian Library, Oxford, MS. Eng. Poet.a.1.* Cambridge: Brewer, 1987
Foreville, Raymonde and Gillian Keir, eds. *The Book of St Gilbert.* Oxford: Clarendon Press, 1987
Görlach, Manfred, ed. *Kalendre of the Newe Legende of Englande, edited from Pynson's Printed Edition, 1516.* Heidelberg: Universitätsverlag C. Winter, 1994
Hamer, Richard and Vida Russell, eds. *Supplementary Lives in Some Manuscripts of the Gilte Legende.* EETS os 315. Oxford: Oxford University Press, 2000
Head, Thomas, ed. *Medieval Hagiography: An Anthology.* New York: Routledge, 2001
Horstmann, Carl, ed. *Altenglische Legenden: Neue Folge.* Heilbronn: Henniger, 1881
―――, ed. *The Early South-English Legendary.* EETS os 87. London: Trübner, 1887
―――, ed. *Nova Legenda Anglie.* Oxford: Clarendon Press, 1901
―――, ed. 'Prosalegenden: Die legenden des ms. Douce 114'. *Anglia* 8 (1885), pp. 103–96
Jacobus de Voragine. *The Golden Legend or Lives of Saints as Englished by William Caxton*, ed. F. S. Ellis. 7 vols. London: Dent, 1900
―――. *The Golden Legend: Readings on the Saints*, trans. William Granger Ryan. 2 vols. Princeton: Princeton University Press, 1993
Kennedy, Ruth, ed. *Three Alliterative Saints' Hymns: Late Middle English Stanzaic Poems.* EETS os 321. London: Oxford University Press, 2003
Lydgate, John. *The Life of Saint Alban and Saint Amphibal*, ed. J. E. van der Westhuizen. Leiden: Brill, 1974
―――. *Saint Albon and Saint Amphibalus*, ed. George F. Reinecke. New York: Garland, 1985
―――. *The Life of St Edmund, King and Martyr: John Lydgate's Illustrated Verse Life Presented to Henry VI: A Facsimile of BL MS Harley 2278*, intr. A. S. G. Edwards. London: British Library, 2004
―――. *The Minor Poems of John Lydgate, Part I*, ed. Henry Noble McCracken. EETS es 107. London: Oxford University Press, 1911
Metcalfe, W. M., ed. *Legends of the Saints in the Scottish Dialect of the Fourteenth Century.* 3 vols. Edinburgh: Blackwood, 1896.
Millett, Bella and Jocelyn Wogan-Browne, eds. *Medieval English Prose for Women: Selections from the Katherine Group and Ancrene Wisse.* Oxford: Clarendon Press, 1992
Mirk, John. *Mirk's Festial: A Collection of Homilies*, ed. Theodor Erbe. EETS es 96. London: Kegan Paul, Trench, Trübner & Co, 1905
Nevanlinna, Saara, ed. *The Northern Homily Cycle: The Expanded Version in MSS Harley 4196 and Cotton Tiberius E vii.* 3 vols. Helsinki: Mémoires de la Société Néophilologique, 1972–84
Peterson, Clifford, ed. *St Erkenwald.* Philadelphia: University of Pennsylvania Press, 1977
Reames, Sherry L., ed., with Martha G. Blalock and Wendy R. Larson. *Middle English Legends of Women Saints.* Kalamazoo: Medieval Institute Publications, 2003
Robertson, James Craigie, ed. *Materials for the History of Thomas Becket, Archbishop of Canterbury.* 7 vols, Rolls Series 67. London: Longman, 1875–85
Savage, Anne and Nicholas Watson, trans., with a preface by Benedicta Ward. *Anchoritic Spirituality:* Ancrene Wisse *and Associated Works.* New York: Paulist Press, 1991

Silvas, Anna, trans. *Jutta and Hildegard: The Biographical Sources*. University Park: Pennsylvania State University Press, 1999

Stouck, Mary-Ann, ed. *Medieval Saints: A Reader*. Ontario: Broadview Press, 1999

Talbot, C. H., ed. and trans. *The Life of Christina of Markyate*. Toronto: University of Toronto Press, 2000

Tracy, Larissa. *Women of the* Gilte Legende*: A Selection of Middle English Saints Lives*. Cambridge: Brewer, 2003

Waters, Claire M., ed. *Virgins and Scholars: A Fifteenth-Century Compilation of the Lives of John the Baptist, John the Evangelist, Jerome, and Katherine of Alexandria*. Turnhout: Brepols, forthcoming

Weatherly, Edward H., ed. *Speculum Sacerdotale*. EETS os 200. London: Oxford University Press, 1936

Winstead, Karen A., ed. and trans. *Chaste Passions: Medieval English Virgin Martyr Legends*. Ithaca NY: Cornell University Press, 2000

Wogan-Browne, Jocelyn and Glyn S. Burgess, ed. and trans. *Virgin Lives and Holy Deaths: Two Exemplary Biographies for Anglo-Norman Women*. London: Dent, 1996

Other Primary Texts

Allen, William. *A briefe historie of the glorious martyrdom of XII. reuerend priests*. Rheims, 1582

Arnold, Thomas, ed. *Memorials of St Edmund's Abbey*. 3 vols, Rerum Britannicarum Medii Aevi Scriptores. London, 1890–96

Augustine of Hippo. *City of God*, trans. Henry Bettenson. Harmondsworth: Penguin, 1984

———. *De doctrina Christiana*, ed. and trans. R. P. H. Green. Oxford: Clarendon Press, 1995

———. *From 'On Marriage and Concupiscence'*. Medieval Sourcebook: http://www.fordham.edu/halsall/source/aug-marr.html

Bede. *The Ecclesiastical History of the English People*, trans. Bertram Colgrave, ed. Judith McClure and Roger Collins. Oxford: Oxford University Press, 1994

Blamires, Alcuin, ed., with Karen Pratt and C. W. Marx. *Woman Defamed and Woman Defended: An Anthology of Medieval Texts*. Oxford: Clarendon Press, 1992

Brie, Friedrich W. D., ed. *The Brut, or the Chronicles of England*. EETS os 131, 136. London: Kegan Paul, Trench, Trübner and Co, 1906–08

Brooks, Kenneth R., ed. *Andreas and The Fates of the Apostles*. Oxford: Clarendon Press, 1961

Bruce, John, ed. *Historie of the Arrivall of Edward IV*. Camden Society, 1st ser. 1. London: Camden Society, 1838

Capgrave, John. *The Chronicle of England*, ed. F. C. Hingeston. New York: Kraus Reprint, 1964

Chaucer, Geoffrey. *The Riverside Chaucer*, gen. ed. Larry D. Benson. Boston: Houghton Mifflin, 1987

Clark, Andrew, ed. *The English Register of Godstow Nunnery, Part 1*. EETS os 129. London: Kegan Paul, Trench, Trübner and Co, 1905

Davis, Norman, ed. *Paston Letters and Papers of the Fifteenth Century*. 2 vols. Oxford: Clarendon Press, 1971–76

Foxe, John. *Acts and Monuments of these Latter and Perillous Dayes*. London, 1563

Geoffrey of Monmouth. *History of the Kings of Britain*, trans. Lewis Thorpe. Harmondsworth: Penguin, 1966

Geoffroy de la Tour Landry. *The Book of the Knight of the Tower*, trans. William Caxton, ed. M. Y. Offord. EETS ss 2. London: Oxford University Press, 1971

Gerald of Wales. *The Journey Through Wales and The Description of Wales*, trans. Lewis Thorpe. Harmondsworth: Penguin, 1978

Grace, Mary, ed. *Records of the Gild of St George in Norwich, 1389–1547*. Norfolk Record Society, 9. Norwich, 1937

Henry of Huntingdon. *The Chronicle of Henry of Huntingdon*, trans. Thomas Forester. London: Bohn, 1853

Holinshed, Raphael. *Holinshed's Chronicles of England, Scotland, and Ireland*, ed. Henry Ellis et al. 6 vols. London, 1807–08

Hudson, Anne, ed. *Selections from English Wycliffite Writings*. Toronto: University of Toronto Press, 1997

Julian of Norwich. *A Book of Showings to the Anchoress Julian of Norwich*, ed. Edmund Colledge and James Walsh. Toronto: Pontifical Institute of Medieval Studies, 1978

Kempe, Margery. *The Book of Margery Kempe*, ed. Sanford Brown Meech and Hope Emily Allen. EETS os 212. London: Oxford University Press, 1940

———. *A shorte treatyse of contemplacyon taught by our lorde Jhesu cryste, or taken out of the boke of Margerie kempe of lynn*. London, 1501.

Kipling, Gordon, ed. *The Receyt of the Ladie Kateryne*. EETS os 296. Oxford: Oxford University Press, 1990

Lancashire, Ian. *Dramatic Texts and Records of Britain: A Chronological Topography to 1558*. Cambridge: Cambridge University Press, 1984

Lee, S. L., ed. *The Boke of Huon of Burdeux, done into English by Lord Berners*. EETS es 40, 41, 43, 50. London: Trübner, 1882–87

Legg, J. Wickham and W. H. St John Hope, eds. *Inventories of Christchurch Canterbury*. Westminster: Constable and Co., 1902

Lydgate, John. *A Critical Edition of John Lydgate's* Life of Our Lady, ed. Joseph A. Lauritis, Ralph A. Klinefelter and Vernon F. Gallagher. Pittsburgh: Duquesne University Press, 1961

———. *Minor Poems of John Lydgate, Part II*, ed. Henry Noble McCracken. EETS os 192. London: Oxford University Press, 1934

———. *Troy Book*, ed. Robert R. Edwards. Kalamazoo: Medieval Institute Publications, 1998

'Mandeville, John'. *Mandeville's Travels*, ed. M. C. Seymour. Oxford: Clarendon, 1967

Sands, Donald B., ed. *Middle English Verse Romances*. Exeter: University of Exeter Press, 1986

Salisbury, Eve, ed. *The Trials and Joys of Marriage*. Kalamazoo: Medieval Institute Publications, 2002

Spenser, Edmund. *The Faerie Queene*, ed. A. C. Hamilton. London: Longman, 2001

Suso, Henry. 'Orologium Sapientiae or The Seven Poyntes of Trewe Wisdom, Aus MS. Douce 114', ed. Carl Horstmann. *Anglia* 10 (1887), pp. 323–89

William of Malmesbury. *The Church Historians of England Vol. 3 Part 1: The History of the Kings of England and of his own times by William of Malmesbury*, trans. John Sharpe. London: Seeleys, 1854

Worcestre, William. *Itineraries*, ed. John H. Harvey. Oxford: Clarendon Press, 1969

Zupitza, Julius, ed. *The Romance of Guy of Warwick*. EETS es 42, 49, 59. London: Trübner, 1883–91

Critical Works

Abou-el-Haj, Barbara. *The Medieval Cult of Saints: Formations and Transformations.* Cambridge: Cambridge University Press, 1994

Acker, Paul. 'Saint Mildred in the *South English Legendary*'. *The South English Legendary: A Critical Assessment*, ed. Klaus P. Jankofsky. Tübingen: Francke Verlag, 1992, pp. 140–53

Aers, David. 'Faith, Ethics, and Community: Reflections on Reading Late Medieval English Writing'. *Journal of Medieval and Early Modern Studies* 28.2 (1998), pp. 341–69

———. *Faith, Ethics and Church: Writing in England, 1360–1409.* Cambridge: Brewer, 2000

——— and Lynn Staley. *The Powers of the Holy: Religion, Politics, and Gender in Late Medieval English Culture.* University Park: Pennsylvania State University Press, 1996

Allmand, Christopher. *Henry V.* London: Methuen, 1992

Altman, Charles F. 'Two Types of Opposition and the Structure of Latin Saints' Lives'. *Medievalia et Humanistica* n. s. 6 (1975), pp. 1–11

Amassian, Margaret. 'A Verse Life of John of Bridlington'. *Neuphilologische Mitteilungen* 71 (1970), pp. 136–45

Anderson, Benedict. *Imagined Communities: Reflections on the Origin and Spread of Nationalism*, rev. edn. London: Verso, 1991

Anson, John. 'The Female Transvestite in Early Monasticism: The Development of a Motif'. *Viator* 5 (1974), pp. 1–32

Arnold, John H. 'The Labour of Continence: Masculinity and Clerical Virginity'. *Medieval Virginities*, ed. Anke Bernau, Ruth Evans and Sarah Salih. Cardiff: University of Wales Press, 2003, pp. 102–18

Ashley, Kathleen and Pamela Sheingorn. 'Introduction'. *Interpreting Cultural Symbols: St Anne in Late Medieval Society*, ed. Ashley and Sheingorn. Athens GA: University of Georgia Press, 1990, pp. 1–68

——— and Pamela Sheingorn. *Writing Faith: Text, Sign and History in the Miracles of Sainte Foy.* Chicago: University of Chicago Press, 1999

Ashton, Gail. *The Generation of Identity in Late Medieval Hagiography: Speaking the Saint.* London: Routledge, 2000

Astell, Ann. 'Chaucer's "St Anne Trinity": Devotion, Dynasty, Dogma, and Debate'. *Studies in Philology* 94.4 (1997), pp. 395–416

Aurner, Nellie Slayton. *Caxton, Mirror of Fifteenth-Century Letters: A Study of the Literature of the First English Press.* New York: Russell and Russell, 1965

Bale, Anthony P. ' "House Devil, Town Saint": Anti-Semitism and Hagiography in Medieval Suffolk'. *Chaucer and the Jews: Sources, Contexts, Meanings*, ed. Sheila Delany. New York: Routledge, 2002, pp. 185–209

———, ed. *St Edmund, King and Martyr: Contexts and Interpretations.* Medieval Institute Publications, forthcoming

Beadle, Richard. 'Prolegomena to a Literary Geography of Later Medieval Norfolk'. *Regionalism in Late Medieval Manuscripts and Texts*, ed. Felicity Riddy. Cambridge: Brewer, 1991, pp. 89–108

Beckett, Neil. 'St Bridget, Henry V, and Syon Abbey'. *Studies in St Bridget and the Brigittine Order* 2, ed. James Hogg. Analecta Cartusiana 35.19. Salzburg: Institut für Anglistik und Amerikanistik Universität Salzburg, 1993, pp. 125–50

Beckwith, Sarah. *Christ's Body: Identity, Culture, and Society in Late Medieval Writings*. London: Routledge, 1993
———. 'Passionate Regulation: Enclosure, Ascesis, and the Feminist Imaginary'. *South Atlantic Quarterly* 93.4 (1994), pp. 803–24
Bernau, Anke. 'Virginal Effects: Text and Identity in *Ancrene Wisse*'. *Gender and Holiness: Men, Women and Saints in Late Medieval Europe*, ed. Samantha J. E. Riches and Sarah Salih. London: Routledge, 2002, pp. 36–48
———. 'A Christian *Corpus*: Virginity, Violence, and Knowledge in the Life of St Katherine of Alexandria'. *St Katherine of Alexandria: Texts and Contexts in Western Medieval Europe*, ed. Jacqueline Jenkins and Katherine J. Lewis. Turnhout: Brepols, 2003, pp. 109–30
———. 'The Translation of Purity in the Lives of St Eugenia and St Euphrosyne'. *Studies in Anglo-Saxon England*, ed. Kathryn Powell and Donald Scragg. Special issue of *the Bulletin of the John Rylands University Library of Manchester* 86 (forthcoming), pp. 11–37
Biller, Peter and A. J. Minnis, eds. *Medieval Theology and the Natural Body*. York: York Medieval Press, 1997
Blamires, Alcuin. *The Case for Women in Medieval Culture*. Oxford: Clarendon Press, 1997
Boffey, Julia. 'Middle English Lives'. *The Cambridge History of Medieval English Literature*, ed. David Wallace. Cambridge: Cambridge University Press, 1999, pp. 610–34
Boureau, Alain. 'Franciscan Piety and Voracity: Uses and Strategies in the Hagiographic Pamphlet'. *The Culture of Print: Power and the Uses of Print in Early Modern Europe*, ed. Roger Chartier, trans. Lydia G. Cochrane. Princeton: Princeton University Press, 1989, pp. 15–58
Brasington, Bruce C. 'Non imitanda set veneranda: The Dilemma of Sacred Precedent in Twelfth-Century Canon Law'. *Viator* 23 (1992), pp. 135–52
Braswell, Laura. 'Chaucer and the Art of Hagiography'. *Chaucer in the Eighties*, ed. Julian N. Wasserman and Robert J. Blanch. Syracuse: Syracuse University Press, 1986, pp. 209–21
Brown, Dan. *The Da Vinci Code*. London: Corgi, 2003
Brown, Jennifer. 'A Critical Edition of and Commentary on MS Douce 114: The Middle English Vitae of Elizabeth of Spalbeek, Christina Mirabilis, and Marie D'Oignies'. CUNY Ph.D. thesis, 2003
Brown, Peter. 'The Rise and Function of the Holy Man in Late Antiquity'. *Journal of Roman Studies* 61 (1971), pp. 80–101
———. *The Cult of the Saints: Its Rise and Function in Latin Christianity*. Chicago: University of Chicago Press, 1981
Brundage, James A. *Law, Sex, and Christian Society in Medieval Europe*. Chicago: University of Chicago Press, 1987
Bullough, Vern. *Sexual Variance in Society and History*. Chicago: University of Chicago Press, 1976
Butler, Judith. *Gender Trouble: Feminism and the Subversion of Identity*. New York: Routledge, 1990
———. *Bodies That Matter: On the Discursive Limits of 'Sex'*. New York: Routledge, 1993
Bynum, Caroline Walker. *Holy Feast and Holy Fast: The Religious Significance of Food to Medieval Women*. Berkeley: University of California Press, 1987
———. *Fragmentation and Redemption: Essays on Gender and the Human Body in Medieval Religion*. New York: Zone Books, 1991

Cadden, Joan. *Meanings of Sex Difference in the Middle Ages: Medicine, Science, and Culture*. Cambridge: Cambridge University Press, 1993
Cartwright, Jane, ed. *Celtic Hagiography and Saints' Cults*. Cardiff: University of Wales Press, 2003
Churchwell, Sarah. *The Many Lives of Marilyn Monroe*. London: Granta Books, 2004
Clanchy, Michael. *From Memory to Written Record: England 1066–1307*. London: Arnold, 1979
Cohen, Jeffrey Jerome, ed. *The Postcolonial Middle Ages*. New York: Palgrave, 2001
——— and Bonnie Wheeler, eds. *Becoming Male in the Middle Ages*. New York: Garland, 1997
Coletti, Theresa. *Mary Magdalene and the Drama of Saints: Theater, Gender and Religion in Late Medieval England*. Philadelphia: University of Pennsylvania Press, 2004
Connolly, Margaret. 'Books for the "helpe of every persoone þat þenkiþ to be saved": Six Devotional Anthologies from Fifteenth-Century London'. *The Yearbook of English Studies* 33.1 (2003), pp. 170–81
Coon, Lynda L. *Sacred Fictions: Holy Women and Hagiography in Late Antiquity*. Philadelphia: University of Pennsylvania Press, 1997
Cooper, Helen. *The English Romance in Time: Transforming Motifs from Geoffrey of Monmouth to the Death of Shakespeare*. Oxford: Oxford University Press, 2004
Cullum, P. H. 'Gendering Charity in Medieval Hagiography'. *Gender and Holiness: Men, Women and Saints in Late Medieval Europe*, ed. Samantha J. E. Riches and Sarah Salih. London: Routledge, 2002, pp. 135–51
Cummings, James. 'Contextual Studies of the Dramatic Records in the Area around The Wash, c. 1350–1550'. University of Leeds Ph.D. thesis, 2001
Cunningham, Lawrence S. *A Brief History of Saints*. Oxford: Blackwell, 2005
Damon, John Edward. *Soldier Saints and Holy Warriors: Warfare and Sanctity in the Literature of Early England*. Aldershot: Ashgate, 2003
Davidson, Clifford. 'The Middle English Saint Play and its Iconography'. *The Saint Play in Medieval Europe*, ed. Davidson. Kalamazoo: Medieval Institute Publications, 1986, pp. 31–122
Deacon, Richard and Phillip Lindley. *Image and Idol: Medieval Sculpture*. London: Tate Publishing, 2002
Delany, Sheila. *Impolitic Bodies: Poetry, Saints and Society in Fifteenth-Century England: The Work of Osbern Bokenham*. New York: Oxford University Press, 1998
Delehaye, Hippolyte. *The Legends of the Saints*, trans. Donald Attwater. New York: Fordham University Press, 1962
Delooz, Pierre. 'Towards a Sociological Study of Canonized Sainthood in the Catholic Church', trans. Jane Hodgkin. *Saints and their Cults: Studies in Religious Sociology, Folklore and History*, ed. Stephen Wilson. Cambridge: Cambridge University Press, 1983, pp. 189–216
D'Evelyn, Charlotte and Frances A. Foster. 'Saints' Legends'. *A Manual of the Writings in Middle English 1050–1500*, vol. 2, ed. J. Burke Severs. New Haven: Connecticut Academy of Arts and Sciences, 1970, pp. 410–39, 553–635
Ditmas, E. M. R. 'The Cult of Arthurian Relics'. *Folklore* 75 (1964), pp. 19–33
Dobson, E. J. *The Origins of Ancrene Wisse*. Oxford: Oxford University Press, 1976
Doyle, A. I. 'Books Connected with the Vere Family and Barking Abbey'. *Transactions of the Essex Archaeological Society* n. s. 25.11 (1958), pp. 222–43
———. 'Publication by Members of the Religious Orders'. *Book Production and Publishing in Britain, 1375–1475*, ed. Jeremy Griffiths and Derek Pearsall. Cambridge: Cambridge University Press, 1989, pp. 109–23
——— and M. B. Parkes. 'The Production of Copies of the *Canterbury Tales* and the

Confessio Amantis in the Early Fifteenth Century'. *Medieval Scribes, Manuscripts and Libraries: Essays Presented to N. R. Ker*, ed. Parkes and Andrew G. Watson. London: Scolar Press, 1978, pp. 163–210

Duffy, Eamon. *The Stripping of the Altars: Traditional Religion in England c. 1400–c. 1580*. New Haven: Yale University Press, 1992

———. 'The Dynamics of Pilgrimage in Late Medieval England'. *Pilgrimage: The English Experience from Becket to Bunyan*, ed. Colin Morris and Peter Roberts. Cambridge: Cambridge University Press, 2002, pp. 164–77

Dutton, Anne. 'Piety, Politics, and Persona: MS Harley 4012 and Anne Harling'. *Prestige, Authority and Power in Late Medieval Manuscripts and Texts*, ed. Felicity Riddy. York: York Medieval Press, 2000, pp. 133–46

Easton, Martha. 'Saint Agatha and the Sanctification of Sexual Violence'. *Studies in Iconography* 16 (1994), pp. 83–119

Edwards, A. S. G. 'The Transmission and Audience of Osbern Bokenham's *Legendys of Hooly Wummen*'. *Late-Medieval Religious Texts and Their Transmission: Essays in Honour of A. I. Doyle*, ed. A. J. Minnis. Cambridge: Brewer, 1994, pp. 157–67

———. 'Fifteenth Century English Collections of Women Saints' Lives'. *The Yearbook of English Studies* 33.1 (2003), pp. 131–41

——— and Carol M. Meale. 'The Marketing of Printed Books in Late Medieval England'. *The Library* 6th ser., 15 (1993), pp. 95–124

Elliott, Dyan. *Spiritual Marriage: Sexual Abstinence in Medieval Wedlock*. Princeton: Princeton University Press, 1993

Erler, Mary C. *Women, Reading, and Piety in Late Medieval England*. Cambridge University Press, 2002

Evans, Ruth. 'The Jew, the Host and the Virgin Martyr'. *Medieval Virginities*, ed. Anke Bernau, Evans and Sarah Salih. Cardiff: University of Wales Press, 2003, pp. 167–86

Fairfield, L. P. 'John Bale and the Development of Protestant Hagiography in England'. *Journal of Ecclesiastical History* 24 (1973), pp. 145–60

Farmer, David Hugh. *Oxford Dictionary of Saints*. Oxford: Oxford University Press, 1987

Finnegan, Mary Jeremy. 'An Involved Narrator: The Redactor of the *Gilte Legende* MS BM Add. 35298'. *Studies in Medieval Culture* 4.3 (1974), pp. 467–71

Finucane, Ronald C. *Miracles and Pilgrims: Popular Beliefs in Medieval England*. London: Dent, 1977

Ford, Boris, ed. *New Pelican Guide to English Literature: Medieval Literature 1*, rev. edn. Harmondsworth: Penguin, 1982

Forde, Simon, Lesley Johnson and Alan V. Murray, eds. *Concepts of National Identity in the Middle Ages*. Leeds: Leeds Studies in English, 1995

Foster, Frances A. 'Legends of Jesus and Mary'. *Manual of the Writings in Middle English 1050–1500*, vol. 2, ed. J. Burke Severs. New Haven: Connecticut Academy of Arts and Sciences, 1970, pp. 447–57, 639–44.

Frederick, Jill. 'The *South English Legendary*: Anglo-Saxon Saints' Lives and National Identity'. *Literary Appropriations of the Anglo-Saxons*, ed. Donald Scragg and Carole Weinburg. Cambridge: Cambridge University Press, 2000, pp. 57–73

Freedman, Paul and Gabrielle Spiegel. 'Medievalisms Old and New: The Rediscovery of Alterity in North American Medieval Studies'. *The American Historical Review* 103 (1998), pp. 677–704.

French, Katherine L. 'Women in the Late Medieval English Parish'. *Gendering the Master Narrative: Women and Power in the Middle Ages*, ed. Mary C. Erler and Maryanne Kowaleski. Ithaca NY: Cornell University Press, 2003, pp. 156–73

Fournée, Jean. 'Le Culte de Saint Georges en Normandie'. *Annuaire des Cinq Départements de la Normandie*. Association Normande et les Assises de Caumont, Congres de Louviers, 1986, pp. 105–27.
Gaunt, Simon. *Gender and Genre in Medieval French Literature*. Cambridge: Cambridge University Press, 1995
Geary, Patrick J. *Furta sacra: Thefts of Relics in the Central Middle Ages*. Princeton: Princeton University Press, 1978
Genet, J. P. 'English Nationalism: Thomas Polton at the Council of Constance'. *Nottingham Medieval Studies* 38 (1984), pp. 60–78
Gibson, Gail McMurray. *The Theater of Devotion: East Anglian Drama and Society in the Late Middle Ages*. Chicago: University of Chicago Press, 1989
———. 'The Religion of Childbed: Some East Anglian Texts and Talismans'. *Interpreting Cultural Symbols: Saint Anne in Late Medieval Society*, ed. Kathleen Ashley and Pamela Sheingorn. Athens GA: University of Georgia Press, 1990, pp. 95–110
Giffin, Mary. *Studies on Chaucer and His Audience*. Québec: Éditions 'L'Éclair', 1956
Gill, Miriam. 'The Saint with a Scythe: A Previously Unidentified Wall Painting in the Church of St Andrew, Cavenham'. *Journal of the Suffolk Institute of Archaeology and History* 38.3 (1995), pp. 245–54.
Given-Wilson, Chris. *Chronicles: The Writing of History in Medieval England*. London: Hambledon and London, 2004
Glasscoe, Marion. *English Medieval Mystics: Games of Faith*. London: Longman, 1993
Goodich, Michael. 'Biography 1000–1350'. *Historiography in the Middle Ages*, ed. Deborah Mauskopf Deliyannis. Leiden: Brill, 2003, pp. 353–85
Goodman, Anthony. *Margery Kempe and her World*. London: Longman, 2002
Görlach, Manfred. *The* South English Legendary, Gilte Legende *and* Golden Legend. Braunschweig: Technische Universität Carolo-Wilhelmina zu Brauschweig Institut für Anglistik und Amerikanistik, 1972
———. *The Textual Tradition of the South English Legendary*. Leeds: School of English, University of Leeds, 1974
———. 'Middle English Legends, 1220–1530'. *Hagiographies: Histoire internationale de la littérature hagiographique latine et vernaculaire en Occident, des Origines à 1550*, vol. 1, ed. Guy Philippart. Turnhout: Brepols, 1994, pp. 429–85
———. *Studies in Middle English Saints' Legends*. Heidelberg: Universitätsverlag C. Winter, 1998
Gransden, Antonia. 'The Growth of the Glastonbury Traditions and Legends in the Twelfth Century'. *Journal of Ecclesiastical History* 27 (1976), pp. 337–58
———. *Historical Writing in England 2: c. 1307 to the Early Sixteenth Century*. London: Routledge and Kegan Paul, 1982
Grantley, Darryl. 'Saints' Plays'. *Cambridge Companion to Medieval English Theatre*, ed. Richard Beadle. Cambridge: Cambridge University Press, 1994, pp. 265–89
Gravdal, Kathryn. *Ravishing Maidens: Writing Rape in Medieval French Literature and Law*. Philadelphia: University of Pennsylvania Press, 1991
Green, Miranda. *Celtic Goddesses: Warriors, Virgins and Mothers*. London: British Museum Press, 1995
Green, Richard Leighton. *The Early English Carols*. Oxford: Clarendon Press, 1977
Griffin, Benjamin. *Playing the Past: Approaches to English Historical Drama, 1385–1600*. Cambridge: Brewer, 2001
Hahn, Cynthia. *Portrayed on the Heart: Narrative Effect in Pictorial Lives of Saints from the Tenth through the Thirteenth Century*. Berkeley: University of California Press, 2001
Haller, William. *Foxe's Book of Martyrs and the Elect Nation*. London: Cape, 1963

Halperin, David M. *Saint Foucault: Towards a Gay Hagiography*. New York: Oxford University Press, 1995

Hamelinck, Renee. 'St Kenelm and the Legends of the English Saints in the *South English Legendary*'. *Companion to Early Middle English Literature*, ed. N. H. G. E. Veldhoen and H. Aertsen. Amsterdam: Free University Press, 1988, pp. 21–30

Hanna, Ralph. *Pursuing History: Middle English Manuscripts and Their Texts*. Stanford: Stanford University Press, 1996

Harris, Kate. 'Patrons, Buyers and Owners: The Evidence for Ownership and the Rôle of Book Owners in the Book Production and the Book Trade'. *Book Production and Publishing in Britain 1375–1475*, ed. Jeremy Griffiths and Derek Pearsall. Cambridge: Cambridge University Press, 1989, pp. 163–99

Heffernan, Thomas J. 'Dangerous Sympathies: Political Commentary in the *South English Legendary*'. *The South English Legendary: A Critical Assessment*, ed. Klaus P. Jankofsky. Tübingen: Francke Verlag, 1992, pp. 1–17

———. *Sacred Biography: Saints and their Biographers in the Middle Ages*. New York: Oxford University Press, 1992

———. 'Christian Biography: Foundation to Maturity'. *Historiography in the Middle Ages*, ed. Deborah Mauskopf Deliyannis. Leiden: Brill, 2003, pp. 115–54

Higgins, Ann. 'The Mark of the Hero: Language, Identity and the Middle English Romance'. University of Massachusetts Amherst Ph.D. thesis, forthcoming

Hilles, Carroll. 'Gender and Politics in Osbern Bokenham's Legendary'. *New Medieval Literatures 4*, ed. Wendy Scase, Rita Copeland and David Lawton. Oxford: Oxford University Press, 2001, pp. 189–212

Hopkins, Andrea. *The Sinful Knights: A Study of Middle English Penitential Romance*. Oxford: Clarendon Press, 1990

Hornstein, Lillian Horlands. 'Eustace-Constance-Florence-Griselda Legends'. *A Manual of the Writings in Middle English 1050–1500*, vol. 1, ed. J. Burke Severs. New Haven: Yale University Press, 1967, pp. 120–32

Hotchkiss, Valerie R. *Clothes Make the Man: Female Cross-Dressing in Medieval Europe*. New York: Garland, 1996

Hughes, Jonathan. *Pastors and Visionaries: Religion and Secular Life in Late Medieval Yorkshire*. Woodbridge: Boydell, 1988

Huntington, Joanna. 'Edward the Celibate, Edward the Saint: Virginity in the Construction of Edward the Confessor'. *Medieval Virginities*, ed. Anke Bernau, Ruth Evans and Sarah Salih. Cardiff: University of Wales Press, 2003, pp. 119–39

Hurley, Margaret. 'Saints' Legends and Romance Again: Secularization of Structure and Motif'. *Genre* 8.1 (1975), pp. 60–73

Ingham, Patricia Clare. *Sovereign Fantasies: Arthurian Romances and the Making of Britain*. Philadelphia: University of Pennsylvania Press, 2001

Innes-Parker, Catherine. 'Sexual Violence and the Female Reader: Symbolic "Rape" in the Saints' Lives of the Katherine Group'. *Women's Studies* 24 (1995), pp. 205–17

Jambeck, Karen K. 'Patterns of Women's Literary Patronage: England, 1200–c. 1475'. *The Cultural Patronage of Medieval Women*, ed. June Hall McCash. Athens GA: University of Georgia Press, 1996, pp. 228–65

James, M. R. 'Lives of St Walstan'. *Norfolk Archaeology* 19 (1917), pp. 238–67

James, Sarah. 'Debating Heresy: Fifteenth-Century Vernacular Theology and Arundel's Constitutions'. University of Cambridge PhD thesis, 2004

Jankofsky, Klaus. 'National Characteristics in the Portrayal of English Saints in the *South English Legendary*'. *Images of Sainthood in Medieval Europe*, ed. Renate Blumenfeld-Kosinski and Timea Szell. Ithaca NY: Cornell University Press, 1991, pp. 81–93

Jenkins, Jacqueline. 'St Katherine and Laywomen's Piety: The Middle English Prose Life in London, British Library, Harley MS 4012'. *St Katherine of Alexandria: Texts and Contexts in Late Medieval Europe*, ed. Jenkins and Katherine J. Lewis. Turnhout: Brepols, 2003, pp. 153–70

———. 'Reading Women Reading: Feminism, Culture and Memory'. *Maistresse of My Wit: Medieval Women, Modern Scholars*, ed. Louise D'Arcens and Juanita Feros Ruys. Turnhout: Brepols, 2004, pp. 317–34

——— and Katherine J. Lewis. 'Introduction'. *St Katherine of Alexandria: Texts and Contexts in Western Medieval Europe*, ed. Jenkins and Lewis. Turnhout: Brepols, 2003, pp. 1–18

Jones, Graham, ed. *Saints of Europe: Studies towards a Survey of Cults and Culture*. Donington: Tyas, 2003

Jones, Kathleen. *Who are the Celtic Saints?* Norwich: Canterbury Press, 2002

Jordan, Mark D. *The Invention of Sodomy in Christian Theology*. Chicago: University of Chicago Press, 1997

Karras, Ruth Mazo. *From Boys to Men: Formations of Masculinity in Late Medieval Europe*. Philadelphia: University of Pennsylvania Press, 2003

Kay, Sarah. 'The Sublime Body of the Martyr: Violence in Early Romance Saints' Lives'. *Violence in Medieval Society*, ed. Richard W. Kaeuper. Woodbridge: Boydell, 2000, pp. 3–20

———. *Courtly Contradictions: The Emergence of the Literary Object in the Twelfth Century*. Stanford: Stanford University Press, 2001

Keiser, George R. 'Patronage and Piety in Fifteenth-Century England: Margaret, Duchess of Clarence, Symon Wynter and Beinecke MS 317'. *Yale University Library Gazette* 60 (1985), pp. 32–46

Kelly, Kathleen Coyne. *Performing Virginity and Testing Chastity in the Middle Ages*. London: Routledge, 2000

Kennedy, Ruth. 'Spalding's *Alliterative Katherine Hymn*: A Guild Connection from the South-East Midlands?' *Viator* 35 (2004)

Kieckhefer, Richard. *Unquiet Souls: Fourteenth Century Saints and their Religious Milieu*. Chicago: University of Chicago Press, 1984

———. 'The Holy and the Unholy: Sainthood, Witchcraft and Magic in Late Medieval Europe'. *Journal of Medieval and Renaissance Studies* 24.3 (1994), pp. 355–86.

——— and George D. Bond, eds. *Sainthood: Its Manifestations in World Religions*. Berkeley: University of California Press, 1988

King, Andrew. *The Faerie Queene and Middle English Romance: The Matter of Just Memory*. Oxford: Clarendon Press, 2000

Kiser, Lisa J. *Telling Classical Tales: Chaucer and the Legend of Good Women*. Ithaca NY: Cornell University Press, 1983

Klaniczay, Gábor. *Holy Rulers and Blessed Princesses: Dynastic Cults in Medieval Central Europe*, trans. Eva Pálmai. Cambridge: Cambridge University Press, 2002.

Klausner, David N. 'Didacticism and Drama in *Guy of Warwick*'. *Medievalia et Humanistica* n. s. 6 (1975), pp. 103–19

Kleinberg, Aviad M. *Prophets in their own Country: Living Saints and the Making of Sainthood in the Later Middle Ages*. Chicago: University of Chicago Press, 1992

Krautheimer, Richard. 'Towards an Iconography of Medieval Architecture'. *Journal of the Warburg and Courtauld Institutes* 5 (1942), pp. 1–33

Krug, Rebecca. *Reading Families: Women's Literate Practices in Late Medieval England*. Ithaca NY: Cornell University Press, 2002

Kurtz, Patricia Deery. 'Mary of Oignies, Christine the Marvelous, and Medieval Heresy'. *Mystics Quarterly* 14.4 (1988), pp. 186–96

Lagorio, Valerie M. 'The *Joseph of Arimathie*: English Hagiography in Transition'. *Medievalia et Humanistica* n. s. 6 (1975), pp. 91–101

Lapidge, Michael. 'The Saintly Life in Anglo-Saxon England'. *Cambridge Companion to Old English Literature*, ed. Malcolm Godden and Lapidge. Cambridge: Cambridge University Press, 1991, pp. 243–62

Laqueur, Thomas. *Making Sex: Body and Gender from the Greeks to Freud*. Cambridge MA: Harvard University Press, 1992

Larson, Wendy R. 'The Role of Patronage and Audience in the Cults of Sts Margaret and Marina of Antioch'. *Gender and Holiness: Men, Women and Saints in Late Medieval Europe*, ed. Samantha J. E. Riches and Sarah Salih. London: Routledge, 2002, pp. 23–35

———. 'Who Is the Master of This Narrative? Maternal Patronage of the Cult of St Margaret'. *Gendering the Master Narrative: Women and Power in the Middle Ages*, ed. Mary C. Erler and Maryanne Kowaleski. Ithaca NY: Cornell University Press, 2003, pp. 94–104

Lavezzo, Kathy, ed. *Imagining a Medieval English Nation*. Minneapolis: University of Minnesota Press, 2003

Leech-Wilkinson, Daniel. 'Il libro di appunti di un suonatore di tromba del quindicesimo secolo (London, British Library, Cotton Titus A.xxvi)'. *Rivista italiana di Musicologia* 16 (1981), pp. 16–39

Lewis, Katherine J. 'Model Girls? Virgin-Martyrs and the Training of Young Women in Late Medieval England'. *Young Medieval Women*, ed. Lewis, Kim M. Phillips and Noel James Menuge. Stroud: Sutton, 1999, pp. 25–46

———. 'Pilgrimage and the Cult of St Katherine of Alexandria in the Later Middle Ages'. *Pilgrimage Explored*, ed. J. Stopford. York: York Medieval Press, 1999, pp. 145–60

———. *The Cult of St Katherine of Alexandria in Later Medieval England*. Woodbridge: Boydell, 2000

———. ' "Let me suffre": Reading the Torture of St Margaret of Antioch in Late Medieval England'. *Medieval Women: Texts and Contexts in Late Medieval Britain: Essays for Felicity Riddy*, ed. Jocelyn Wogan-Browne, Rosalynn Voaden, Arlyn Diamond, Ann Hutchison, Carol Meale and Lesley Johnson. Turnhout: Brepols, 2000, pp. 69–82

———. 'Becoming a Virgin King: Richard II and Edward the Confessor', *Gender and Holiness: Men, Women and Saints in Late Medieval Europe*, ed. Samantha J. E. Riches and Sarah Salih. London: Routledge, 2002, pp. 86–100

———. 'Anglo-Saxon Saints' Lives, History and National Identity in Late Medieval England'. *History, Nationhood and the Question of National Identity*, ed. Helen Brocklehurst and Robert Phillips. Basingstoke: Palgrave, 2004, pp. 160–70

———. 'Edmund of East Anglia, Henry VI and Ideals of Kingly Masculinity'. *Holiness and Masculinity in the Middle Ages*, ed. P. H. Cullum and Lewis. Cardiff: University of Wales Press, 2004, pp. 158–73

———. 'Margery Kempe and Saint Making in Later Medieval England'. *A Companion to The Book of Margery Kempe*, ed. John H. Arnold and Lewis. Cambridge: Brewer, 2004, pp. 195–215

Lifshitz, Felice. 'Beyond Positivism and Genre: Hagiographical Texts as Historical Narrative'. *Viator* 25 (1994), pp. 95–113

Liszka, Thomas R. 'The *South English Legendaries*'. *The North Sea World in the Middle Ages: Studies in the Cultural History of North-Western Europe*, ed. Liszka and Lorna E. M. Walker. Dublin: Four Courts Press, 2001, pp. 243–80

Lochrie, Karma, Peggy McCracken and James A. Schultz, eds. *Constructing Medieval Sexuality*. Minneapolis: University of Minnesota Press, 1997

Long, Mary Beth. 'Reading Female Sanctity: English Legendaries of Women, c. 1200–1650', University of Massachusetts Amherst Ph.D. thesis, 2004

Lupton, Julia Reinhard. *Afterlives of the Saints: Hagiography, Typology, and Renaissance Literature*. Stanford: Stanford University Press, 1996

Margherita, Gayle. *The Romance of Origins: Language and Sexual Difference in Middle English Literature*. Philadelphia: University of Pennsylvania Press, 1994

Marks, Richard. *Image and Devotion in Late Medieval England*. Stroud: Sutton, 2004

Marston, Thomas E. 'An Early English Bestseller'. *Yale University Library Gazette* 46.1 (1971), pp. 86–8

McCall, John P. 'Chaucer and the Pseudo-Origen *De Maria Magdalena*: A Preliminary Study'. *Speculum* 46 (1971), pp. 491–509

McInerney, Maud Burnett. 'Rhetoric, Power, and Integrity in the Passion of the Virgin Martyr'. *Menacing Virgins: Representing Virginity in the Middle Ages and Renaissance*, ed. Kathleen Coyne Kelly and Marina Leslie. London: Associated University Presses, 1999, pp. 50–70

———. *Eloquent Virgins: From Thecla to Joan of Arc*. New York: Palgrave Macmillan, 2003

McLaren, Mary-Rose. *The London Chronicles of the Fifteenth Century: A Revolution in English Writing*. Cambridge: Brewer, 2002

Meale, Carol M. ' ". . . alle the bokes that I haue of latyn, englisch, and frensch": Laywomen and Their Books in Late Medieval England'. *Women and Literature in Britain, 1150–1500*, ed. Meale. Cambridge: Cambridge University Press, 1993, pp. 128–58

Millett, Bella. *Ancrene Wisse, the Katherine Group, and the Wooing Group*. Annotated Bibliographies of Old and Middle English Literature 2. Cambridge: Brewer, 1996

Mills, Robert. '"Whatever You Do is a Delight to Me!": Masculinity, Masochism and Queer Play in Representations of Male Martyrdom'. *Exemplaria* 13 (2001), pp. 1–37

———. 'Can the Virgin Martyr Speak?' *Medieval Virginities*, ed. Anke Bernau, Ruth Evans and Sarah Salih. Cardiff: University of Wales Press, 2003, pp. 187–213

Mitchell, Shelagh. 'Richard II: Kingship and the Cult of Saints'. *The Regal Image of Richard II and the Wilton Diptych*, ed. Dillian Gordon, Lisa Monnas and Caroline Elam. London: Harvey Miller, 1997, pp. 115–24

Mooney, Catherine M. *Gendered Voices: Medieval Saints and Their Interpreters*. Philadelphia: University of Pennsylvania Press, 1999

Moore, R. I. *The Formation of a Persecuting Society: Power and Deviance in Western Europe, 950–1250*. Oxford: Blackwell, 1987

Morris, Bridget. *Saint Birgitta of Sweden*. Woodbridge: Boydell, 1999

Mulder-Bakker, Anneke B. 'The Invention of Saintliness: Texts and Contexts'. *The Invention of Saintliness*, ed. Mulder-Bakker. London: Routledge, 2002, pp. 3–23

———. 'Saints without a Past: Sacred Places and Intercessionary Power in Saints' Lives from the Low Countries'. *The Invention of Saintliness*, ed. Mulder-Bakker. London: Routledge, 2002, pp. 38–57

Nixon, Virginia. *Mary's Mother: Saint Anne in Late Medieval Europe*. University Park: Pennsylvania State University Press, 2005

Oliver, Judith H. *Gothic Manuscript Illumination in the Diocese of Liège (c. 1250–c. 1330)*. 2 vols. Leuven: Uitgeverij Peeters, 1988

Olsen, Alexandra Hennessey. '"*De historiis sanctorum*": A Generic Study of Hagiography'. *Genre* 13 (1980), pp. 407–29

Oppel, John. 'Saint Jerome and the History of Sex'. *Viator* 24 (1993), pp. 1–22

Pearsall, Derek, ed. *Studies in the Vernon Manuscript*. Cambridge: Brewer, 1990
Petroff, Elizabeth. 'Medieval Women Visionaries: Seven Stages to Power'. *Frontiers* 3.1 (1978), pp. 34–45
Phillips, Kim M. 'Desiring Virgins: Maidens, Martyrs and Femininity in Late Medieval England'. *Youth in the Middle Ages*, ed. P. J. P. Goldberg and Felicity Riddy. York: York Medieval Press, 2004, pp. 45–59
Pickering, O. S. 'The "Defence of Women" from the *Southern Passion*: A New Edition'. *The South English Legendary: A Critical Assessment*, ed. Klaus P. Jankofsky. Tübingen: Francke Verlag, 1992, pp. 154–76.
———. 'The Outspoken *South English Legendary* Poet'. *Late-Medieval Religious Texts and Their Transmission: Essays in Honour of A. I. Doyle*, ed. A. J. Minnis. Cambridge: Brewer, 1994, pp. 21–37
———. 'Saints' Lives'. *A Companion to Middle English Prose*, ed. A. S. G. Edwards. Cambridge: Brewer, 2004, pp. 249–70
Price, Jocelyn. 'The Virgin and the Dragon: The Demonology of *Seinte Margarete*'. *Leeds Studies in English* 16 (1984), pp. 337–57
Pridgeon, Eleanor. 'Saint Christopher in English Medieval Wall Painting, c. 1250–1500'. University of Leicester Ph.D. thesis, forthcoming
Radway, Janice A. *Reading the Romance: Women, Patriarchy and Popular Literature*. Chapel Hill: University of North Carolina Press, 1984
Rawcliffe, Carole. 'Curing Bodies and Healing Souls: Pilgrimage and the Sick in Medieval East Anglia'. *Pilgrimage: The English Experience from Becket to Bunyan*, ed. Colin Morris and Peter Roberts. Cambridge: Cambridge University Press, 2002, pp. 108–40
Reames, Sherry L. 'The Sources of Chaucer's "Second Nun's Tale"'. *Modern Philology* 76 (1978), pp. 111–35
———. 'The Cecilia Legend as Chaucer Inherited It and Retold It: The Disappearance of an Augustinian Ideal'. *Speculum* 55.1 (1980), pp. 38–57
———. *The Legenda aurea: A Reexamination of its Paradoxical History*. Madison: University of Wisconsin Press, 1985
———. 'A Recent Discovery concerning the Sources of Chaucer's "Second Nun's Tale"'. *Modern Philology* 87.4 (1990), pp. 337–61
———. 'Artistry, Decorum and Purpose in Three Middle English Retellings of the Cecilia Legend'. *The Endless Knot: Essays in Honor of Marie Boroff*, ed. M. Teresa Tavormina and R. F. Yeager. Cambridge: Brewer, 1995, pp. 177–99
———. 'The Second Nun's Prologue and Tale'. *Sources and Analogues of* The Canterbury Tales, vol. 1, ed. Robert M. Correale and Mary Hamel. Cambridge: Brewer, 2002
Riches, Samantha. *St George: Hero, Martyr and Myth*. Stroud: Sutton, 2000
———. 'St George as a Male Virgin Martyr'. *Gender and Holiness: Men, Women and Saints in Late Medieval Europe*, ed. Riches and Sarah Salih. London: Routledge, 2002, pp. 65–85
———. 'St George and the Dragon'. *Gothic: Art for England 1400–1547*, ed. Richard Marks and Paul Williamson. London: V&A Publications, 2003, p. 137
Riddy, Felicity. 'Contextualizing *Le Morte Darthur*: Empire and Civil War'. *A Companion to Malory*, ed. Elizabeth Archibald and A. S. G. Edwards. Cambridge: Brewer, 1996, pp. 55–74
Robertson, Elizabeth. *Early English Devotional Prose and the Female Audience*. Knoxville: University of Tennessee Press, 1990
———. 'The Corporeality of Female Sanctity in *The Life of St Margaret*'. *Images of*

Sainthood in Medieval Europe, ed. Renate Blumenfeld-Kosinski and Timea Szell. Ithaca NY: Cornell University Press, 1991, pp. 268–87

Robinson, Pamela R. 'A Study of Some Aspects of the Transmission of English Verse Texts in Late Medieval Manuscripts'. Oxford University Ph.D. thesis, 1972

———. 'The "Booklet": A Self-contained Unit in Composite Manuscripts'. *Codicologica* 3 (1980), pp. 46–69

Rubin, Miri. *Corpus Christi: The Eucharist in Late Medieval Culture*. Cambridge: Cambridge University Press, 1991

———. *Gentile Tales: The Narrative Assault on Late Medieval Jews*. New Haven: Yale University Press, 1999

——— and Sarah Kay, eds. *Framing Medieval Bodies*. Manchester: Manchester University Press, 1994

Salih, Sarah. *Versions of Virginity in Late Medieval England*. Cambridge: Brewer, 2001

Salmon, J. C. 'Saint Christopher in Medieval Art and Life'. *Journal of the British Archaeological Association* 61 (1936), pp. 76–115

Sanok, Catherine. 'Performing Feminine Sanctity in Late Medieval England: Parish Guilds, Saints' Plays, and the *Second Nun's Tale*'. *Journal of Medieval and Early Modern Studies* 32.2 (2002), pp. 269–303

Saul, Nigel. 'Richard II's Ideas of Kingship'. *The Regal Image of Richard II and the Wilton Diptych*, ed. Dillian Gordon, Lisa Monnas and Caroline Elam. London: Harvey Miller, 1997, pp. 27–32

Saunders, Corinne. *Rape and Ravishment in the Literature of Medieval England*. Cambridge: Brewer, 2001

Scarry, Elaine. *The Body in Pain: The Making and Unmaking of the World*. Oxford: Oxford University Press, 1985

Scase, Wendy. 'Writing and the "Poetics of Spectacle": Political Epiphanies in the *Arrivall of Edward IV* and Some Contemporary Lancastrian and Yorkist Texts'. *Images, Idolatry and Iconoclasm in Late Medieval England*, ed. Jeremy Dimmick, James Simpson and Nicolette Zeeman. Oxford: Oxford University Press, 2002, pp. 172–84

Schibanoff, Susan. 'Worlds Apart: Orientalism, Antifeminism and Heresy in Chaucer's *Man of Law's Tale*'. *Exemplaria* 8 (1996), pp. 59–96

Schmitt, Jean-Claude. *The Holy Greyhound: Guinefort, Healer of Children since the Thirteenth Century*, trans. Martin Thom. Cambridge: Cambridge University Press, 1983

Schulenburg, Jane Tibbetts. 'Strict Active Enclosure and its Effects on the Female Monastic Experience (ca. 500–1100)'. *Medieval Religious Women I: Distant Echoes*, ed. John A. Nichols and Lillian Thomas Shank. Kalamazoo: Cistercian Publications, 1984, pp. 51–86

———. 'Saints and Sex, ca. 500–1100: Striding down the Nettled Path of Life'. *Sex in the Middle Ages: A Book of Essays*, ed. Joyce E. Salisbury. New York: Garland, 1991, pp. 203–31

Sekules, Veronica. *Medieval Art* (Oxford: Oxford University Press, 2001)

Sheingorn, Pamela. 'Appropriating the Holy Kinship: Gender and Family History'. *Interpreting Cultural Symbols: St Anne in Late Medieval Society*, ed. Kathleen Ashley and Sheingorn. Athens GA: University of Georgia Press, 1990, pp. 169–98

———. ' "The Wise Mother": The Image of St Anne Teaching the Virgin Mary'. *Gesta* 32 (1993), pp. 69–80

———. ' "The Wise Mother": The Image of St Anne Teaching the Virgin Mary'. *Gendering the Master Narrative: Women and Power in the Middle Ages*, ed. Mary C. Erler and Maryanne Kowaleski. Ithaca NY: Cornell University Press, 2003, pp. 105–34

Shell, Alison. *Catholic Controversy and the English Literary Imagination*. Cambridge: Cambridge University Press, 1999
Simpson, James. *The Oxford English Literary History Volume 2. 1350–1547: Reform and Cultural Revolution*. Oxford: Oxford University Press, 2004
Southern, R. W. 'Aspects of the European Tradition of Historical Writing: 4. The Sense of the Past'. *Transactions of the Royal Historical Society* 5th ser. 23 (1973), pp. 242–63
Spearing, A. C. 'Margery Kempe'. *A Companion to Middle English Prose*, ed. A. S. G. Edwards. Cambridge: Brewer, 2004, pp. 83–97
Stanbury, Sarah. 'The Vivacity of Images: St Katherine, Knighton's Lollards, and the Breaking of Idols'. *Images, Idolatry and Iconoclasm in Late Medieval England*, ed. Jeremy Dimmick, James Simpson and Nicolette Zeeman. Oxford: Oxford University Press, 2002, pp. 131–50
Stiller, Nikki. *Eve's Orphans: Mothers and Daughters in Medieval English Literature*. London: Greenwood, 1980
Stouck, Mary-Ann. 'Saints and Rebels: Hagiography and Opposition to the King in Late Fourteenth-Century England'. *Medievalia et Humanistica* n. s. 24 (1997), pp. 75–94
Strohm, Paul. 'Passioun, Lyf, Miracle, Legende: Some Generic Terms in Middle English'. *Chaucer Review* 10 (1975–6), pp. 62–75, 154–7
Strong, Roy. *The Cult of Elizabeth: Elizabethan Portraiture and Pageantry*. London: Thames and Hudson, 1977
Summit, Jennifer. *Lost Property: The Woman Writer and English Literary History, 1380–1589*. Chicago: University of Chicago Press, 2000
Swanton, Michael. *English Literature Before Chaucer*. London: Longman, 1987
Szarmach, Paul, ed. *Holy Men and Holy Women: Old English Prose Saints' Lives and their Contexts*. Albany: State University of New York Press, 1996
Tatlock, J. S. P. *The Legendary History of Britain: Geoffrey of Monmouth's Historia Regum Britanniae and Its Early Vernacular Versions*. Berkeley: University of California Press, 1950
Taylor, Andrew. 'Manual to Miscellany: Stages in the Commercial Copying of Vernacular Literature in England'. *The Yearbook of English Studies* 33.1 (2003), pp. 1–17
Thompson, Anne B. *Everyday Saints and the Art of Narrative in the South English Legendary*. Aldershot: Ashgate, 2003
Thornton, Tim 'Opposition Drama and the Resolution of Disputes in Early Tudor England: Cardinal Wolsey and the Abbot of Chester'. *Bulletin of the John Rylands University Library of Manchester* 81 (1999), pp. 25–47
Tilley, Maureen A. 'The Ascetic Body and the (Un)Making of the World of the Martyr'. *Journal of the American Academy of Religion* 59.3 (1991), pp. 467–79
Turville-Petre, Thorlac. *England the Nation: Language, Literature and National Identity, 1290–1340*. Oxford: Clarendon, 1996
Ullmann, Walter. *The Growth of Papal Government in the Middle Ages: A Study in the Ideological Relation of Clerical to Lay Power*, 3rd edn. London: Methuen, 1970
Vauchez, André. *Sainthood in the Later Middle Ages*, trans. Jean Birrell. Cambridge: Cambridge University Press, 1997
Vitz, Evelyn Birge. 'From the Oral to the Written in Medieval and Renaissance Saints' Lives'. *Images of Sainthood in Medieval Europe*, ed. Renate Blumenfeld-Kosinski and Timea Szell. Ithaca NY: Cornell University Press, 1991, pp. 97–114
Wakelin, Martyn. 'The Manuscripts of John Mirk's Festial'. *Leeds Studies in English* s. s. 1 (1967), pp. 93–118

Walker, Simon. 'Political Saints in Later Medieval England'. *The MacFarlane Legacy: Studies in Late Medieval Politics and Society*, ed. R. H. Britnell and A. J. Pollard. Stroud: Sutton, 1995, pp. 77–106

Wall, J. Charles. *Shrines of British Saints*. London: Methuen, 1905

Warren, Nancy Bradley. 'Kings, Saints, and Nuns: Gender, Religion, and Authority in the Reign of Henry V'. *Viator* 30 (1999), pp. 307–22

Waters, Claire M. *Angels and Earthly Creatures: Preaching, Performance, and Gender in the Later Middle Ages*. Philadelphia: University of Pennsylvania Press, 2003

Watson, Nicholas. 'Censorship and Cultural Change in Late-Medieval England: Vernacular Theology, the Oxford Translation Debate, and Arundel's Constitutions of 1409'. *Speculum* 70 (1995), pp. 822–64

———. 'The Politics of Middle English Writing'. *The Idea of the Vernacular: An Anthology of Middle English Literary Theory, 1280–1520*, ed. Jocelyn Wogan-Browne, Watson, Andrew Taylor and Ruth Evans. University Park: Pennsylvania State University Press, 1999, pp. 331–52

Webb, Diana. *Pilgrimage in Medieval England*. London: Hambledon Press, 2000

Weisl, Angela Jane. *The Persistence of Medievalism: Narrative Adventures in Contemporary Culture*. New York: Palgrave, 2002

White, Helen C. *Tudor Books of Saints and Martyrs*. Madison: University of Wisconsin Press, 1963

Whitelock, Dorothy. 'Fact and Fiction in the Legend of St Edmund'. *Proceedings of the Suffolk Institute of Archaeology* 31 (for 1969), pp. 217–33

Weinstein, Donald and Rudolph M. Bell. *Saints and Society: The Two Worlds of Latin Christendom, 1000–1700*. Chicago: University of Chicago Press, 1982

Wiesner, Merry E. 'Women's Defense of Their Public Role'. *Women in the Middle Ages and the Renaissance*, ed. Mary Beth Rose. New York: Syracuse University Press, 1986, pp. 1–27

Winstead, Karen A. 'Piety, Politics, and Social Commitment in Capgrave's *Life of St Katherine*'. *Medievalia et Humanistica* 17 (1991), pp. 59–80

———. 'Capgrave's Saint Katherine and the Perils of Gynecocracy'. *Viator* 25 (1994), pp. 361–76

———. 'Lydgate's Lives of Saints Edmund and Alban: Martyrdom and Prudent Pollicie'. *Mediaevalia* 17 (1994), pp. 361–76

———. *Virgin Martyrs: Legends of Sainthood in Late Medieval England*. Ithaca NY: Cornell University Press, 1997

Wogan-Browne, Jocelyn. ' "Clerc u lai, muïne u dame": Women and Anglo-Norman Hagiography in the Twelfth and Thirteenth Centuries'. *Women and Literature in Britain 1150–1500*, ed. Carol M. Meale. Cambridge: Cambridge University Press, 1993, pp. 61–85

———. 'The Apple's Message: Some Post-Conquest Hagiographic Accounts of Textual Transmission'. *Late Medieval Religious Texts and their Transmission: Essays in Honour of A. I. Doyle*, ed. A. J. Minnis. Cambridge: Brewer, 1994, pp. 39–53

———. ' "Bet . . . to . . . rede on holy seyntes lyves . . .": Romance and Hagiography Again'. *Readings in Medieval English Romance*, ed. Carol M. Meale. Cambridge: Brewer, 1994, pp. 83–97

———. 'The Virgin's Tale'. *Feminist Readings in Middle English Literature: The Wife of Bath and All Her Sect*, ed. Ruth Evans and Lesley Johnson. London: Routledge, 1994, pp. 165–94

———. 'Wreaths of Thyme: The Female Translator in Anglo-Norman Hagiography'. *The Medieval Translator 4*, ed. Roger Ellis and Ruth Evans. Binghampton: State University of New York Press, 1994, pp. 46–65

———. 'Outdoing the Daughters of Syon? Edith of Wilton and the Representation of Female Community in Fifteenth-Century England'. *Medieval Women: Texts and Contexts in Late Medieval Britain: Essays for Felicity Riddy*, ed. Wogan-Browne, Rosalynn Voaden, Arlyn Diamond, Ann Hutchison, Carol Meale and Lesley Johnson. Turnhout: Brepols, 2000, pp. 393–409

———. *Saints' Lives and Women's Literary Culture c. 1150–1300: Virginity and its Authorizations*. Oxford: Oxford University Press, 2001

Woodward, Kenneth. *Making Saints: Inside the Vatican: Who Become Saints, Who Do Not, and Why*. London: Chatto and Windus, 1991.

Yalom, Marilyn. *A History of the Breast*. London: Pandora, 1998

Žižek, Slavoj. *The Sublime Object of Ideology*. London: Verso, 1989

Websites

Catholic Encyclopaedia: http://www.newadvent.org/cathen/
Christian Classics Ethereal Library: http://www.ccel.org/
Early English Books Online: http://eebo.chadwyck.com/home
Electronic Text Centre: http://etext.lib.virginia.edu/
Hagiography Society: http://mendota.english.wisc.edu/~hagio/
Medieval Sourcebook: http://www.fordham.edu/halsall/sbook3.html
Patron Saints Index: http://www.catholic-forum.com/saints/indexsnt.htm
Société des Bollandistes: http://www.kbr.be/~socboll/
TEAMS Middle English Texts: http://www.lib.rochester.edu/camelot/teams/
Virtual Norfolk: http://virtualnorfolk.uea.ac.uk/

Index

Abbo of Fleury, 36–7
Adam, 52, 53, 156
Ælfric of Eynsham, 13, 36
Aers, David, 16
Æthelflæd, lady of the Mercians, 135
Æthelred, King, 136–7
Æthelstan, King, 36, 131
Agincourt, battle of, 130
Alcock, John, bishop of Ely, 132
Alexandria, 144
Alexis Master, **39, 40,** 41
Alfred, King, 135, 143
Allen, William, 155
Allmand, Christopher, 129
anchoresses, 55–6
Ancrene Wisse, 53, 55–6
Anderson, Benedict, 132
Andreas, 13, 142–3
Anglo Saxon Chronicle, 36, 38
Anglo-Norman, 11, 12, 50, 55, 72, 92, 100
Ansley, Brian, 10
apostles, 2, 18, 58, 60, 84, 142
Arnold, John H., 118–19
Arthur, King, 127, 143, 145, 155
Arundel, Thomas, archbishop of Canterbury, 72, 144, 152
asceticism, 79–82, 113, 148
Askew, Anne, 154
Asser, *Life of Alfred*, 36, 38
Athelstan, 146
authority, 16, 70–86, 110–11, 113, 120, 133, 135–6, 152

Babington, Katherine, 68
badges, 28, **29,** 45
Bale, Anthony, 5, 22, 154
Bale, John, 2, 68, 154
baptism, 105
Barclay, Alexander, 13, 18, 33, 35, 63, 68–9
Bede, 125–6, 133, 135, 143, 145
Bell, Rudolph M., 122, 125
Beowulf, 142–3
Bernau, Anke, 70
Bevis of Hampton, 142, 147
Bible, 2, 57, 60
biography, 15, 19, 20, 22, 151, 156
Birchenshawe, John, abbot of Chester, 133, 140
Boccaccio, Giovanni, 150
Bokenham, Osbern, 8, 11, 12, 14–15, 16, 19, 25–6, 51, 58, 63, 65–7, 68, 69, 75, 81, 83–5, 88, 107, 109–10, 111–12, 116–17, 125, 127, 131–2, 145

Bourchier, Isabel, countess of Eu, 12, 67
Boureau, Alain, 49
Bradshaw, Henry, 13, 63, 69, 130, 132–40
Brigitte, Princess, 59
Brown, Dan, 146
Brown, Jennifer, 61
Brut, 144
Buckland, Ralph, 62
Burgh, Beatrice, 66
Burgh, Benedict, 53
Burgh, Thomas, 19, 66–7
Bury St Edmunds, abbey of, 11, 16, 27, 28, 35–6, 39, 41–4, 64–5

Cadden, Joan, 106
calendar, 32, 62, 142, 155
canonisation, 4, 12, 22, 45, 61, 83, 124
Canterbury, 8, 32, 134
Capgrave, John, 14, 15, 16, 18, 19, 48, 50, 62, 63, 65, 67–8, 110, 116–17, 125, 143
castration, 102
Cato, 53, 58
Caxton, William, 13, 53, 59, 62, 63, 83, 107–20, 123, 126–9, 132, 153
Cerdic, 131
charity, 75, 78, 81
Charlemagne, 134
chastity, 37, 105–10, 114
Chaucer, Geoffrey, 11, 51, 65, 67, 72, 83, 149–50, 156
  Second Nun's Tale, 5, 16, 63–4, 73–4, 78–9, 83, 124, 149–50
  Legend of Good Women, 63, 67, 150–1
Chester, 7, 69, 132–40
childbirth, 7, 10, 52
Christ, 1, 2, 6, 14, 30, 37–9, 60, 78, 80, 90, 91, 96, 97–8, 99, 105, 107, 109, 110, 116–17, 146, 148, 152, 153
Christine de Pisan, 11
Christmas, 12, 32, 52
chronicles, 125–7, 143–4
Churchwell, Sarah, 20
Clensynge of Man's Sowle, 53
Cloud of Unknowing, 11
Cnut, King, 41
Cologne, 5
communion, 95, 97
confession, 95
Constantinople, 144
conversion, 14, 80, 85, 97–8
Conversion of St Paul, 154
Cooper, Helen, 147
coronation, 7

Corpus Christi, 32
Cotton, Robert, 50
Coventry, 30
Cranmer, Thomas, 153
Cursor Mundi, 53
Cynewulf, 13

Danish invasions, 36–41, 96, 131, 133, 135, 137
decapitation, 89, 144, 151
Delany, Sheila, 16, 58, 65, 67, 127
Delehaye, Hippolyte, 142
Delooz, Pierre, 3
Denston, John, 25–6, 67, 84–5
Denston, Katherine, 11, 25–6, 67, 84–5
de Vere, Elizabeth, countess of Oxford, 12, 67
devils, 17, 30, 91, 102, 115, 148
de Worde, Wynkyn 53, 62, 152
Dismas, 44
Dobson, E. J., 55
Dolan, Fran, 70
Doyle, A. I., 60, 67–8
dragons, 7, 17, 30–4, 147, 156
drama, 9, 27, 33, 35, 45, 56, 154
Duffy, Eamon, 6

Early English Texts Society, 20
Easton, Adam, 63
Edward II, 71, 79, 124, 144
Edward IV, 6, 65, 68
Edwards, A. S. G., 63–4, 65, 67
Elene, 13
Ely, 7, 35
Enlightenment, 123
epic, 142
Erbe, Theodor, 59
Erconbert, king of Kent, 133
Erler, Mary, 67
Estoire del Saint Graal, 146
Estorie del Euangelie, 53
etymology, 56
eucharist, 90, 97–8, 110
eunuchs, 114
Eusebius, 154
Eve, 52, 53, 156

fasting, 3
Fates of the Apostles, 13
fatherhood, 109
feasting, 1, 9, 33–4
fertility, 85
Flegg, Agatha, 67
Foxe, John, 154–5

Gast of Gy, 58
Gaunt, Simon, 105–7, 111
Gawain, 11
Geoffrey of Monmouth, 143–5
Gerald of Wales, 7
Gesta Romanorum, 60
Gibbon, Edward, 123
Gibson, Gail McMurray, 6, 122
Giffin, Mary, 63

Gilte Legende (1438), 58–9, 65, 75–7, 81–5, 128–32
Given-Wilson, Chris, 127
Glastonbury Abbey, 145
Godwin, earl of Wessex, 76–7
Golden Legend (all versions), 13, 54, 56–60, 62, 65, 68, 83–4, 107–116, 119–21, 125–6, 128–32, 141, 145, 146–7, 151, 152, 153, 155
Görlach, Manfred, 54, 57, 62
Goscelin, 133
Gospel of Nicodemus, 58
Gower, John, 149
Grail romances, 146
Guild of St George, Norwich, 30–4
Guy of Warwick, 142, 147–9, 155

Halperin, David, 19
Harold Godwinson, 77
Havelok the Dane, 142
Heffernan, Thomas J., 14, 16, 123
Hengist, 131
Henry I, 77
Henry II, 77–9, 113
Henry III, 101
Henry V, 34, 82, 129–30
Henry VI, 4, 7, 11, 16, 18, 65, 68, 124, 130
Henry VIII, 34, 55, 153
Henry of Huntingdon, 143
heretics, 96
 see also Lollards
Higden, Ralph, 126, 134
Higgins, Ann, 47, 48
Hilton, Walter, 53, 62
historical writing, 15, 20–2, 122–40, 143–4
Hoccleve, Thomas, 11
Holford, Matthew, 124
Holinshed, Raphael, 146
Holy Grail, 146
Holy Helpers, 2, 17
Holy Kinship, 83, 85
Holy Maidenhood, 115–16
homilies, 57–60
Hopkins, Andrea, 149
Horsa, 131
Horstmann, Carl, 20
Howard, Katherine, 67
Humphrey, duke of Gloucester, 68
Hundred Years War, 71, 129
Hunt, Isabel, 67
Huon of Burdeux, 147

idolatry, 4–5, 72, 153
images, 1, 4–6, 8, 9, 10, 16, 27–31, 35, 36, 38–41, 45–6, 49, 69, 85, 96–7, 145
imitation, 18, 72, 82, 152
incest, 109
incorruption, 37, 41–2
infertility, 84
Ingham, Patricia Clare, 128
intercession, 4, 17, 26, 35, 45, 71–2, 130
Invocation to St Anne, 65
Islam, 95

INDEX

Jacobus de Voragine
  see Golden Legend
Jenkins, Jacqueline, 19
Jews, 95–9
John of Tynemouth, 62
Joscelin of Brakelond, 41
Judith, 142
Julian of Norwich, 18

Kalendre of the Newe Legende of Englande, 13, 17, 62, 124, 129
Katherine of Aragon, 17
Katherine Group, 13, 51, 54–6, 69, 88, 100
Kay, Sarah, 92
Kelly, Kathleen Coyne, 93, 118
Kempe, Margery, 3, 18, 125, 151–3, 156
King Horn, 142
King, Andrew, 148
kingship, 37, 71, 76, 82, 135
kinship, 84–5, 110
knighthood, 78, 92
Knighton, Henry, 144
Kurtz, Patricia Deery, 61

Lanfranc, archbishop of Canterbury, 100
Larson, Wendy R., 17
Lateran IV, 51, 54, 95, 102
Latimer, Hugh, 153
Legenda aurea, 53, 56–60, 64, 65, 84, 125
Légende dorée, 58
legendaries, 54–62
Lent, 60
Lewis, Katherine J., 18, 37, 82
Lichfield, 134
Lifshitz, Felice, 15, 123
Lincoln, 96
liturgy, 22, 25, 45, 153
Lollards, 4, 16, 60, 144, 154–5
London, 17, 41, 65, 96, 130, 134
Lupus, Hugh, 135, 138
Lydgate, John, 10, 11, 16, 17, 48, 50, 53, 63, 64–5, 125, 129, 130

Malory, Thomas, 127
Mandeville's Travels, 144
Maner of Offering in the Cyte of London, 53
Mannyng, Robert, 62, 100, 149
manuscripts, 10–11, 28, 47–68, 87, 91, 101, 125, 142
  Brussells, Bibliothèque Royale de Belgique MS 7917, 61
  Cambridge, Corpus Christi College MS 145, 91, 93
  Cambridge, University Library Add. MS 4122, 53
  Cambridge, University Library Ee 2 15, 60
  Cambridge, University Library Ff 2 38, 60
  Cambridge, University Library Gg 2 6, 58
  Edinburgh, National Library of Scotland MS Advocates 19.2.1 (Auchinleck MS), 50, 53, 142
  London, BL MS Add. 21114, 61
  London, BL MS Add. 22283 (Simeon MS), 57–8
  London, BL MS Add. 36704, 68
  London, BL MS Add. 36791, 60
  London, BL MS Arundel 168, 48–50, 53, 68
  London, BL MS Arundel 327, 51, 65–7
  London, BL MS Arundel 396, 68
  London, BL MS Cotton Claudius A ii, 60
  London, BL MS Cotton Faustina B iii, 53
  London, BL MS Cotton Galba E iv, 32
  London, BL MS Cotton Tiberius E vii, 57–8
  London, BL MS Cotton Titus A xxvi, 50
  London, BL MS Cotton Titus D xviii, 52
  London, BL MS Egerton 1993, 98
  London, BL MS Harley 2247, 60
  London, BL MS Harley 2250, 60
  London, BL MS Harley 2253, 51, 62
  London, BL MS Harley 2278, 11, 65
  London, BL MS Harley 4012, 47–50, 53
  London, BL MS Harley 4196, 57–8
  London, BL MS Royal 17 A xxvii, 55
  London, BL MS Royal 17 C xvii, 52
  London, BL MS Royal 17 D v, 53
  London, BL MS Royal 18 B xxiii, 60
  London, BL MS Royal 18 B xxv, 60
  London, BL MS Sloane 2569, 52
  London, BL MS Stowe 949, 57
  London, Lambeth Palace 223, 59
  New York, Pierpoint Morgan Library MS M 736, **39–40**, 41
  Oxford, Bodleian MS Bodley 34, 55
  Oxford, Bodleian MS Bodley 779, 57
  Oxford, Bodleian MS Douce 60, 60
  Oxford, Bodleian MS Douce 114, 50–2, 61, 69
  Oxford, Bodleian MS. Eng. poet. a.1 (Vernon MS), 53, 57, 58, 62
  Oxford, Bodleian MS Hatton 96, 60
  Oxford, Bodleian MS Laud 108, 57, 101, 142
  Oxford, Bodleian MS Tanner 17, 57
  Oxford, Corpus Christi College MS 237, 52
  Oxford, St. John's College MS 182, 61
  Paris, Bibliothèque de l'Arsenal MS 596, 64
  Paris, Bibliothèque Nationale MS latin 3278, 64
Margaret, duchess of Clarence, 68
Marks, Richard, 8
marriage, 19, 53, 74, 82, 93, 106–12, 114, 115, 147
marriage, mystic, 107, 117, 126, 147
martyrdom, 27, 31, 37–9, 78–80, 86, 87–94, 96, 99–100, 102, 105, 108–10, 113, 120, 141–4, 150, 152, 154–5
Mary I, 155
Mary queen of Scots, 155
Maude, Queen, 77
Meale, Carol M., 52
Mechtild of Hackeborn, 53, 59
Mercia, 69, 99, 133–6
Millett, Bella, 55
miracles, 4–8, 14, 26, 36, 37, 41–5, 60, 70, 72, 76, 79, 91, 96–7, 118, 132–3, 136–9, 143–7, 153

Mirk, John, 3, 20, 52, 59, 60, 145
Mirror of Sins, 53
monarchy, 27, 30, 101
Monroe, Marilyn, 20
motherhood, 19, 81, 83–5, 109
Mulder-Bakker, Anneke B., 7
Muslims, 95–6, 100

nakedness, 8, 37–9, 94, 102
Neville, Cecily, duchess of York, 59
Norman Conquest, 71, 76–7, 100–1, 131, 135
Northern Homily Cycle, 51–3, 56–8, 62
Norton Priory, 1
Norwich, 9, 27, 30–5, 63
Norwich Cathedral, 30–4
Nova Legenda Angliae, 62, 129, 146

obedience, 18, 75, 110–11, 117
Oberon, 147
Offa, 134
Oldcastle, John, 154
ordeal, 146
Oxford University, 65

pagans, 73–4, 95–6, 110–11, 120, 150
Paris, William, 48, 63, 64
parish, 7, 9, 28, 50, 135
Paston, John, II, 35
Paston, John, III, 35
Paston, Margaret, 1, 9
patronage, 4, 6–7, 12, 15, 25, 29, 35, 40, 44, 52, 53, 65, 68, 69, 84, 129, 133, 136, 140
penance, 50, 60, 75, 79, 95, 102, 111–13, 149, 150
Penda, 131
penitential romances, 147–9
Perceval, 146
Perlesvaus, 146
Piers Plowman, 53
pilgrimage, 4, 26, 28, 41, 43, 49, 129, 144, 151
Pontefract, 144
Poor Caitiff, 53
power 6–8, 15–17, 28, 32, 42–5, 49, 59, 70–86, 90–1, 100–2, 110, 117, 122, 129, 134, 138
Prick of Conscience, 53, 58
printing, 13, 53, 59, 62, 68, 69, 123, 153
processions, 9, 30–4, 41, 45, 130
prophecy, 75–7
prostitution, 112
psalters, 50, 61
Pynson, Richard, 62, 68, 69

Radway, Janice A., 21
rape, 74, 88, 93–4, 109, 117–18, 136–7
Rawcliffe, Carole, 6
Raymond of Capua, 53
Reading Abbey, 8
Reames, Sherry L., 15, 21, 63, 64
Reformation, 5, 13, 20, 23, 34, 55, 62, 68, 123, 143, 153–5
relics, 1, 5, 8–9, 10, 14–15, 21, 27, 30–2, 34–5, 36, **40**–2, 44, 45, 144–6, 152, 153
Richard I, 41, 96

Richard II, 71, 82
Riches, Samantha J. E., 119
Riddy, Felicity, 127
Roberd of Cisyle, 147
Robert de Boron, 146
Robertson, Elizabeth, 56, 91
Robin Hood, 35
romance, 2, 19, 21–2, 53, 60, 92, 100, 104, 109, 142–9
Romance of the Rose, 58, 150

Saints
  Aaron (martyr), 143
  Achilleus (legendary eunuch martyr), 114
  Aelred of Rievaulx (abbot and writer), 53
  Ætheldreda (queen and abbess), 7, 9, 41, 53, 68, 129, 131, 133
  Agatha (legendary virgin martyr), 66, 89–91, 93, 147
  Agnes (legendary virgin martyr), 66, 93, 116–17, 146, 152
  Alban (British protomartyr), 8, 64–5, 129, 130, 143
  Aldhelm (abbot and bishop), 58
  Alexis (legendary pilgrim), 50, 63, 107–9, 118, 147–9, 155
  Alphege (archbishop and martyr), 58, 96
  Ambrose (theologian), 2
  Anastasia (legendary virgin martyr), 93, 101
  Andrew (apostle), 58, 109, 142
  Anne (apocryphal mother of Virgin Mary), 2, 5, 6, 22, 25–6, 48, 66, 83–6, 107, 116, 122, 144
  Anselm (archbishop), 135
  Anthony (hermit), 52, 118
  Athanasius (bishop), 13, 53
  Augustine of Canterbury (archbishop and missionary), 58, 64, 135
  Augustine of Hippo (theologian), 2, 67–8, 85, 107, 149
  Barbara (legendary virgin martyr), 7, 44, 68
  Barnabas (apostle), 96
  Becket, Thomas (archbishop and martyr), 2, 6, 8, 77–81, 85, 96, 101, 113–14, 124, 129, 154
  Benedict (abbot), 2, 102, 114–15, 118, 120
  Bernard of Clairvaux (abbot), 58, 107
  Brendan (abbot), 12, 58, 131
  Bridget of Ireland (abbess), 2, 58, 131
  Bridget of Sweden (visionary), 3, 22, 62, 68, 152
  Campion, Edmund (martyr), 155
  Catherine of Siena (visionary), 53, 59, 61, 125
  Cedd (bishop), 131
  Chad (bishop), 58, 130
  Cecilia (virgin martyr), 5, 16, 18, 63–4, 66, 73–4, 78–9, 85, 107–8, 117, 124, 149–51
  Christina of Markyate (prioress), 56
  Christina *mirabilis* (ascetic), 61
  Christine (legendary virgin martyr), 48, 64, 66, 89, 90, 94, 109–10, 115

INDEX

Christopher (legendary giant and martyr), 1, 28, 44, 89, 142
Columba (abbot), 58
Cuthbert (bishop), 2, 58, 129, 143
David (bishop), 143
Denis (bishop), 90
Dominic (founder), 4, 52, 101
Dorothy (legendary virgin martyr), 48, 53, 66, 68
Dunstan (archbishop), 36, 58, 129, 130, 143
Edgar (king), 62, 130, 135, 143
Edith (nun), 53, 130
Edmund (king and martyr), 2, 4, 9–10, 11, 16, 18, 22, 27–8, **29**, 35–45, **38–40**, 58, 64, 65, 82, 89, 96, 129, 130, 131, 144, 146
Edward the Confessor (king), 7, 8, 41, 71, 75–8, 81–2, 85, 101, 129, 130
Edward the Elder (king and martyr), 58, 99, 131, 137
Elizabeth of Hungary (queen), 12, 19, 66, 74–5, 81, 111, 116, 152
Elizabeth of Spalbeek (ascetic beguine), 61
Erkengota (nun), 133
Erkenwald (bishop), 63
Ermenburga (abbess), 133
Ermengild (queen and abbess), 69, 133
Ethelburga (abbess), 133
Eugenia (legendary transvestite), 5, 120
Eustace (legendary martyr), 144, 147–9, 155
Faith (legendary virgin martyr), 44, 66, 116
Felicitas (martyr), 2
Felix of Dunwich (missionary bishop), 131
Finan of Kinnity (abbot), 2
Francis of Assisi (founder), 4
Frideswide (abbess), 58
George (dragon-slayer and martyr), 2, 13, 18, 27–36, 44–5, 64, 68–9, 89–90, 94, 97, 113, 129, 155–6
Gervase (martyr), 8
Gilbert of Sempringham (founder), 67–8, 124
Giles (legendary hermit), 64
Gregory the Great (pope), 13, 53
Gregory of Tours (bishop, historian, hagiographer), 13, 14, 127, 141
Guinefort (dog), 21
Guthlac (hermit), 13, 147
Helena (mother of emperor Constantine), 13, 144
Hilary (bishop), 95
Hildegard of Bingen (abbess, visionary, writer), 56
James the Great (apostle), 102
James the Less (apostle), 84
Jerome (theologian), 52, 62, 68, 106, 119, 144
Joachim (apocryphal father of Virgin Mary), 84, 107
John the Almoner, 109
John the Baptist, 9, 68, 84
John of Beverley (bishop), 130
John of Bridlington (prior), 124, 130
John the Evangelist, 19, 68, 84
John Schorne (priest), 124
Josaphat (king and hermit), 118
Joseph (husband of Virgin Mary), 84
Joseph of Arimathea, 146, 154
Jude (apostle), 84
Julian the Hospitaller, 50, 99
Juliana (legendary virgin martyr), 13, 55, 89, 90, 93, 100
Julius (martyr), 143
Katherine of Alexandria (legendary virgin martyr), 2, 6–7, 8, 10–11, 17, 22, 48, 50, 52, 53, 55, 66, 67, 68, 74, 80–1, 85, 89, 110, 116–17, 123, 125, 128, 144, 152
Kenelm (martyred prince), 58, 99, 131–2
Lawrence (martyr), 90, 94
Leger (bishop and martyr), 58
Louis (king of France), 7, 130
Lucy (legendary virgin martyr), 44, 66, 93
Luke (evangelist), 144
Machor (monk), 58
Marcellian (martyr), 8
Margaret of Antioch (legendary virgin martyr), 1, 3, 7, 8, 10, 14–15, 17, 19, 32, 48, 52, 53, 55, 63–5, 66, 68–9, 91, 93, 96–7, 123, 145, 152
Margaret/Pelagien (legendary transvestite), 5, 119–20
Marina/us (legendary transvestite), 5, 108, 120
Mark (evangelist), 144
Mark (martyr), 8
Martin of Tours (bishop), 13, 147
Mary of Egypt (penitent), 52, 62, 112, 115
Mary Magdalene, 12, 50, 52, 53, 66, 111–12, 116, 146, 151, 152, 154
Mary of Oignies (beguine), 61, 152
Mary, Virgin, 5, 33, 37, 48, 53, 58, 60, 83–5, 97, 102, 107, 116
Matthias (apostle), 9, 113
Meriasek (bishop), 154
Michael (archangel), 7
Milburga (abbess), 133
Mildgyth (nun), 133
Mildred (abbess), 2, 133, 98–100
Nereus (legendary eunuch martyr), 114
Nicholas (bishop), 4, 44, 96–7, 107
Norbert (founder), 14, 18, 67
Osana (obscure princess), 8
Oswald (bishop), 58, 129
 Oswald (king), 96, 131
Patrick of Ireland, 48, 143
Paul the Apostle, 14, 105, 107, 152, 154
Paul the Hermit, 115
Paula (widow), 109
Pelagia (legendary penitent), 62
Perpetua (martyr), 2
Peter the Apostle, 75, 108, 152
Peter the Dominican, 96
Petronilla (legendary daughter of Apostle Peter), 64, 108
Prothase (martyr), 8
Quentin (martyr), 90, 94

Quiriac (martyr), 89–90
Quirine (child martyr), 108
Radegund (queen and founder), 132
Remigius (bishop), 108
Rich, Edmund (archbishop), 53, 58, 124, 129
Robert of Bury (dubious child martyr), 5
Robert of Knaresborough (hermit), 124
Roch (hermit), 44
Rolle, Richard (hermit and writer), 53, 58, 67
Ruffin (martyr), 133, 137
Scrope, Richard (archbishop and 'martyr'), 4
Sebastian (martyr), 37–9, 89–93, 109, 120
Seven Sleepers, 50
Sexburga (abbess), 69, 133
Silvester (pope), 113
Simon (apostle), 84
Simon de Montfort ('martyr'), 79, 101
Swithun (bishop), 58, 129
Thaïs (legendary penitent), 112, 115
Theodora (legendary penitent transvestite), 5
Theophilus (bishop), 97
Thomas the Apostle, 110, 114
Thomas of Lancaster ('martyr'), 4, 124, 144
Ursula (legendary virgin martyr), 5–6, 17, 66, 93, 116, 143–4
Valentine (martyr), 8, 116
Vincent (martyr), 89–90, 92
Walstan of Bawburgh (legendary prince-ploughman), 2, 7, 10
Werburge (abbess), 4, 7, 13, 69, 130, 132–40
Winifred (nun), 131
Withburga (recluse), 133
Wulfhad (martyr), 133, 137
Wulfstan (bishop), 100–1
Zita of Lucca (servant), 10
St Paul's Cathedral, 41
St Thomas Cantuar, 154
Salo, Anne, 70
Samson, abbot of Bury, 42
Sanok, Catherine, 130
Scarry, Elaine, 93
Scottish Legendary, 58, 62
sculpture, 1, 4, 10, 28, 29, 30, **31**
Serjeantson, Mary, 65
sermons, 45, 57, 59–60, 113, 123, 126, 129, 145
sexuality, 104–21
shipwreck, 43–4
shrines, 5–8, 14, 28, 35, 41–5, 124, 129, 132, 133, 137
Simpson, James, 145
Sir Gowther, 147
Sir Isumbras, 148–9
South English Legendary, 17, 51, 53, 56–7, 62, 74, 77–81, 83, 87–103, 128, 131, 141–2
Southern Passion, 99
Southern, R. W., 128
Southwell, Robert, 155

Speculum Ecclesie, 53
Speculum Sacerdotale, 50, 52, 59, 60, 126
Speculum Vitae, 58
Spenser, Edmund, 146, 155–6
Spoto, Donald, 20
Stafford, Anne Neville, duchess of Buckingham, 59
Stafford, Anne, countess of March, 65
Staley, Lynn, 16
Sulpicius Severus, 13
Suso, Henry, 61
Syon Abbey, 62, 68

Taylor, Andrew, 51
temptation, 115, 118
Thetford, 36–7
Thomas, Duke of Norfolk, 35
Thornton, Tim, 132, 133, 136
Thorpe, William, 144
tombs, 7, 27, 35–6, 41–2, 45, 79, 101, 144
torture, 7, 74, 79, 87–94, 96–100, 109, 115–18, 151
Tractatus de Legenda Sanctorum, 57
translation, 12, 25, 53–62, 64–5, 68, 83, 85, 91, 124, 145
transvestism, 5, 108, 119–120
Trevisa, John, 126
Tuddenham, Thomas, 68

Venice, 144
violence, 87–103, 111, 137, 155
virginity, 7, 18–19, 73–4, 81–2, 87–8, 90–1, 93–4, 98, 105–9, 111, 114–19, 136–7, 147, 152
Vitas Patrum, 62
Vitz, Evelyn Birge, 124

wall paintings, 28–9, 36, **38**–40
Walsingham, Thomas, 127
Waters, Claire M., 68
Watson, Nicholas, 17
Weatherly, Edward, 60
Weinstein, Donald, 122, 125
Weisl, Angela Jane, 20
West, Nicholas, bishop of Ely, 35
Whethamstede, John, abbot of St Albans, 65
William of Malmesbury, 37, 134, 143, 145
William I, 77, 100–1, 135
William II, 77, 136
Wilton Abbey, 130
Wingfield, Anne Harling, 47, 50
Winstead, Karen A., 16, 21, 64, 65, 67, 72, 90–1, 123
Wogan-Browne, Jocelyn, 21, 55, 82, 124, 130
Wolsey, Thomas, 133, 140
Woodstock, Anne, countess of Stafford, 65
Worcestre, William, 7
Wynter, Symon, 63, 68

York, 57, 96, 134

www.ingramcontent.com/pod-product-compliance
Lightning Source LLC
Chambersburg PA
CBHW060954230426
43665CB00015B/2198